Alma Mater

Other books by P. F. Kluge

NOVELS

The Day That I Die
Eddie and the Cruisers
Season for War
MacArthur's Ghost

NONFICTION

The Edge of Paradise: America in Micronesia

Alma Mater

—— *A College Homecoming* ——

P. F. Kluge

▲▲ ADDISON-WESLEY PUBLISHING COMPANY

Reading, Massachusetts · Menlo Park, California · New York
Don Mills, Ontario · Wokingham, England · Amsterdam · Bonn
Sydney · Singapore · Tokyo · Madrid · San Juan
Paris · Seoul · Milan · Mexico City · Taipei

The lines from Robert Frost's poem "On the Sale of My Farm," which appear on page 213, is reprinted by permission of The Huntington Library, San Marino, California, manuscript number HM 7237. Permission has also kindly been granted by the Estate of Robert Lee Frost.

The epigraph on page ix is from *Fiske Guide to Colleges 1993,* by Edward B. Fiske, reprinted by permission of Times Books, a division of Random House, Inc. Copyright 1992 by Fiske Futures, Inc.

Many of the designations used by manufacturers and sellers to distinguish their products are claimed as trademarks. Where those designations appear in this book and Addison-Wesley was aware of a trademark claim, the designations have been printed in initial capital letters (i.e., Kleenex).

Library of Congress Cataloging-in-Publication Data
Kluge, P. F. (Paul Frederick), 1942–
  Alma mater : a college homecoming / P.F. Kluge.
    p. cm.
  ISBN 0-201-56793-8
  1. Kenyon College—History. 2. Kenyon College—Description. 3. Kluge, P. F. (Paul Frederick), 1942– . I. Title.
LD2791.K42K58 1993
378.771'52—dc20
                93-19823
#28113832   CIP

Jacket design by Jean Seal
Text design by Diane Levy
Set in 10½-point Sabon by .eps Electronic Publishing Services,
  Woburn, MA

1 2 3 4 5 6 7 8 9 -MA-96959493
First Printing, October 1993

KENYON COLLEGE

Gambier, OH 43022-9623

M any would say that "the middle of no-where" is at worst a fair description of Kenyon's location. Indeed, located in the rural town of Gambier, Ohio, we're not exactly talking New York here. Heck, we're not even talking Cleveland. But that doesn't really matter, because this little school makes up for what it might lack in location by the strength of its academics, now rivaling Oberlin for the reputation as Ohio's best.

Once students actually arrive at Kenyon's 800-acre campus, they're usually hooked. Set on a wooded hillside with grand Gothic architecture and "a few gargoyles thrown in for effect," Kenyon's campus is as beautiful as they come. "Fall in Gambier is like fall in heaven, I'm sure," marvels one student. Another proclaims, "A Rockwell picture image is an appropriate comparison." The college's oldest building, Old Kenyon, dates from 1836 and is one of the oldest collegiate buildings in the nation.

Along with the physical beauty, Kenyon's tight sense of community sets the tone for a learning experience that one student describes as "liberal arts education in a pure form." The strongest programs are the social sciences and humanities. This is the home of *The Kenyon Review,* a prestigious literary quarterly, and not coincidentally, the English department is exceptionally strong. . . .

—FISKE GUIDE TO COLLEGES, 1993

Location: Rural
Total Enrollment: 1,490
Undergraduates: 1,490
Male/Female: 48/52
SAT Ranges: V 530–610
M 550–650
ACT Range: 26–29
Financial Aid: 33%
Expense Pr $ $ $ $
Phi Beta Kappa: Yes
Applicants: 2,220
Accepted 68%
Enrolled: 27%
Grad in 5 years: 82%
Returning Freshmen: 93%
Academics: ★ ★ ★ ★
Social: ☎ ☎ ☎
Q of L: ● ● ●
Admissions: (614)427-5776
(800)848-2468

CONTENTS

❧ *Admissions*   1

❧ *Orientation*   17

❧ *September*   35

❧ *October*   59

❧ *November*   87

❧ *December*   107

❧ *January*   133

❧ *February*   159

❧ *March*   179

❧ *April*   207

❧ *May*   225

❧ *Commencement*   245

Alma Mater

🌿 *Admissions*

EVERY TIME I TRAVEL this way, driving north from Columbus, coming in off the interstate highway, I feel that I'm entering another country and that somewhere along these winding roadkill roads, somewhere among these small farms with Mail Pouch chewing tobacco signs splashed on rickety barns, somewhere near a sleepy, white-clapboard Ohio town like Homer or Brandon, there should be a guardhouse and a gate across the road, customs and immigration agents checking passport and visa, shots and tickets, before waving me on toward Kenyon College, a dozen miles away.

"Where you headed?" I imagine one guard asking, while his partner walks around the back, peering at boxes of books, suitcases, food, and spices I won't be able to find at Kroger or Big Bear. Both men have the tired, spavined walk of a failed farmer kicking through a field of stubble. Everyone who works around here looks like a farmer doing something else on the side, delivering mail, cutting hair, whatever.

"Up the road to Gambier," I say. "Kenyon College."

"Uh huh . . . you a professor?"

"Part-time, sort of," I say, glancing over at my wife. "I write and I teach."

"A writer. You written anything I might have . . ."

"Herm," the second guard interrupts, pointing into the back of our jeep. "Got something here you should maybe look at it."

He reaches in and lifts up a jar filled with decaying vegetables swimming in orange-flecked fluid that might be formaldehyde.

"It's kim chee," I protest. "Cabbage that's aged . . . and soaked in peppers and . . . Koreans eat it."

"You in the Korean Department at Kenyon?" He sounds suspicious.

Word is out, I guess. There are all kinds of departments at Kenyon these days.

"English," I say. That calms them both, it seems. They've heard of the Kenyon English Department, by God.

"Hope you know what you're getting into," Herm says, waving me through.

"I hope so, too," I answer, pulling away, but not so rapidly that I fail to hear one of them saying to the other: "It's okay. He's not tenure-track."

The miles of garden apartments and shopping malls, ranchettes and golf courses around Columbus have finally dropped away, though every year it takes longer to lose them. Now we move through a downbeat, abandoned-feeling country where weeds grow in railroad tracks that lead to rusted trestle bridges left behind from an America that used to be. It's as though all these towns were once connected to something larger but they got unplugged fifty years ago. Trains connect. Roads bypass. Or obliterate.

If it is not another country that I am coming into, it is a particular place. Sometimes I think of it as an island, with all the island qualities: a sense that everything is connected, nothing is ever over, and everything that happens ought to be taken personally. The kind of place that, on its good days, can feel like the heart of the universe, the perfect center of a well-spent life. On other days it's simply nowhere, it's nowhere squared: not just a small college but a small rural college, a small rural college in the Midwest, a lightly endowed, wrist-slicingly isolated college with English roots and eastern airs, national and international aspirations, some wishful, some warranted, a college poor but proud, less conservative than old-fashioned, less elitist than peculiar, not a pushy, voguish college, not this one, but a college that stands at the edge of the party and waits and waits politely, sometimes it seems like forever, to be recognized and remembered and appropriately introduced: Kenyon College, Gambier, Ohio. A place I sometimes love, with a history that rolls like the seasons, down through the years, and moods that change like the weather.

It's not your typical college. With fewer than 1,500 students, it's smaller, far smaller, than most. It's also far more expensive: Kenyon costs around $20,000 per year. Eighty percent of American college students attend public institutions; Kenyon is private. Still, chances are that when you picture a college, you see a place like Kenyon. For here in Gambier, Ohio, is the very image of a college—the college of memory and dream, out of Hollywood movies and Plato's cave, a college that is a confluence of people and place, of character and fate, architecture and landscape, college as a personal style, a way of life, college as a place where history matters and people remember, an island in space and time. Also, my alma mater.

✿

> I SHOULD BEGIN *by telling you something about my parents. They are both naturalized citizens, having been born in Germany and come here in the 1920's. My father is a machinist and his father was a tinsmith. . . . I have lived in "Suburbia" all my life.*

My application to Kenyon College, dated November 20, 1959, shows a snapshot of someone I have trouble acknowledging; bad haircut, big ears, black knit tie, solemn but inexperienced face. Spaces are filled, "in ink" as instructed, in a handwriting that barely resembles what I write this morning. I see the New Jersey address I called home till Kenyon came along, and I see a phone number that I haven't dialed for years, except in memory. I listed Pop as a machinist foreman. They didn't ask what Mom did. Reading on, I discover the awkward, unformed kid I was, earnest and sweet and clueless, proud of being a newspaper editor, a Key Club member, a National Honor Society inductee, who listed "foreign service work or foreign correspondence" as his life's goals. Early failure faces me when I note that I was a Boy Scout, a junior assistant scoutmaster, a member of the Order of the Arrow, and yet just a Life Scout, never an Eagle. I went for soft, nerdy merit badges, things like World Citizenship, Soil and Water Conservation. Physical Fitness daunted me: those impossible, non-negotiable chin-ups.

> *My minor interests, which may or may not interest you, are taking walks, looking at sunsets, and humming to myself. I don't suppose any of my "ideas" would strike you as particularly original or profound. I've done a lot of watching, listening, and reading, and am beginning to get an idea of what "beauty" and "good" and "truth" are like. My thoughts still remain vague, but are generally becoming clearer. I hope that with the benefits and encouragement of a college education they will become clearer still.*

I smile and wince at all this, at the odd blend of high seriousness and utter naïveté, blended shyness and arrogance I can still find in myself. No doubt about it, I was a child of the fifties, a scholarship kid and, any way you looked at it, a virgin. When it came to college, we all were virgins, the whole family, that whole generation of immigrant parents who wanted their kids to have the chances they'd never had, not that they knew where that might lead.

I won't pretend that I come from an extremely poor family—I don't. I have always had enough to eat and wear. But my parents, already in their mid-fifties, are approaching old age and have never been rich. I will not impoverish my parents and risk their well being in old age in order to go to college. Bluntly, I cannot attend Kenyon or any college of a similar caliber without substantial scholarship aid.

True believers, my parents operated on faith about the value of an education, never imagining what it was like to have a son who was an English major. Who knew from colleges? Colleges were an unknown America, something about success and happiness, however they combined. I was "college material," school counselors had warned them. And someone told us that a *small* college was a good place to be. That must have appealed to our immigrant caution: *Sure, a small college, that sounds about right for Freddy.* Start small. Kenyon, Wesleyan, Hamilton, and, for insurance, Rutgers. Free-agent style, we would let the money decide, the scholarship money, and, when it turned out they all offered the same amount, I chose the last place I'd visited. I'd seen the others in winter when they were bleak and daunting. I made my first trip to Kenyon in April when the quads were green, when arching maples turned Middle Path into an arcade, when ancient classrooms exhaled dark-wood wisdom and there were violets coming up in the grass outside the chapel. It was beautiful then. And with forty faculty, five hundred students, all male, it was small. It was plenty small, all right, a small and improbable place: an English campus surrounding a rickety Appalachian village, perched on a hill in the middle of Ohio. Almost the last hill. Ahead, west, lay thousands of miles of cornbelt plains. The East was a day's ride behind, that whole twinkling, magic coast I soon learned to miss, high school girlfriends, daily newspapers, bread with a crust, all gone. The nights were dark in Gambier, the stars bright. Did Pascal say he worried about the distance between the stars? I was concerned about the hundreds of turnpike miles that divided me from home. I pondered the distance between radio stations, those horrifying, staticky silences, broken only by hog belly and Bible quotes.

I was isolated, shipwrecked, stranded. I was on an island. And that, it turned out, had been the point, back in 1825, when the college's founder, Episcopal Bishop Philander Chase, selected this hill as the permanent home for the college-seminary-grammar school he'd founded near Columbus the year before. A mural on the Gambier post office wall depicts the founder's first visit: two men on horseback pausing in a wooded clearing, one carrying a map and the other, Philander Chase, pointing toward a rolling green horizon, a river, a valley, distant undulating hills. "Well, this will do," Philander Chase said that morning the college was born here. Chase was a passionate, imperious man, larger than life. Opposed by rival prelates in his plans for an Ohio college, Chase journeyed to England to raise money from aristocrats. The town, the college, its streets and buildings carry their names, and something of their style. And something of his style, too: heroic beginning, heartfelt commitment. And bitter ending. In 1831 he left the college he'd built, the place he'd called "the Star of the West," ousted by an alliance of faculty and trustees. "Bishop Chase never could believe that any way was so good as his way, or that those who opposed him did so from motives entirely pure," writes a college historian. Leaving Kenyon, Chase wintered in a run-down cabin in a neighboring county. From his exile, he headed to Illinois, where he founded another college near Peoria, Jubilee College. It didn't survive. Its grounds, a state park, include Philander Chase's grave.

After Chase's departure, through the rest of the nineteenth century, the college's growth was anything but steady. Power struggles, intramural Episcopalian disputes, chronic money shortages, and up-and-down enrollments brought Kenyon to the edge of bankruptcy. The college entered the twentieth century with just thirty-three students. There was vitality in the place, there was quality. There was also chronic poverty and frustration. And a dismaying series of accidents.

In 1905 a vigorous young president, William Foster Peirce, had just been installed. With the support of Mark Hanna and other Midwest industrialists, the college was poised to grow into a heartlands Princeton. But on Saturday evening, October 28 of that year, Stuart L. Pierson, a Kenyon freshman about to be initiated into Delta Kappa Epsilon fraternity, was placed on a railroad trestle and run over by an unscheduled train. Did he fall asleep on the tracks? Did he awaken, disoriented, and lurch toward his death? Or was he tied, unable to move off the tracks? The college's history, otherwise lucid, gets vague and speculative on this point, finally concluding that the sleep-deprived Pierson ran, staggered, fell into the train's path. The tabloid press surmised otherwise, concocting "Perils of Pauline" illustrations that showed a bound victim about to go under the wheels. "Newspapers in America and in foreign lands continued for months to speak of it," the college history reports. "Some eminent preachers told of it in their sermons; parents declared that never should their sons be sent to a college where it was the custom to tie freshmen to the railroad track. The enrollment at Kenyon immediately fell off, and not until ten years had gone by did it fully recover."

In 1949 Kenyon made the papers again, the only time a Gambier, Ohio, dateline has appeared on the front page of the *New York Times*. Old Kenyon, the massive pile of stone and timber that was the heart of the college, was destroyed in a fire that took the lives of nine students. The lightly endowed college diverted funds, scrambled for donations, and managed to rebuild Old Kenyon, stone for stone, but the fire remains "by far the greatest tragedy ever to strike Kenyon College."

The death on the railroad tracks was ancient history when I arrived in 1960. So was the Kenyon fire. They were the stuff of ghost stories, local color. But on May 8, 1956, there had been another sudden death, that of Kenyon's fifty-two-year-old president, Gordon Keith Chalmers, from which Kenyon had still not recovered. An intense, beetle-browed authoritarian, Chalmers arrived at Kenyon in 1937 and set about turning a likable, genteel college—a place where students played polo and faculty played bridge—into a first-rate institution. Indifferent to balanced budgets, inept at fund-raising, frequently at war with the faculty he hired and fired, or attempted to fire, Chalmers built Kenyon's reputation with star recruitments, with an advanced placement plan that became a national model, and with a flurry of activity in Gambier, speeches, symposia, conferences. Above all, he hired the poet-critic John Crowe Ransom to teach at Kenyon and to become founding editor of a new literary quarterly, the *Kenyon Review*.

There's nothing like a writer—the right sort of writer—to spruce up a neighborhood. Robert Lowell came to study under Ransom, Peter Taylor to teach, Randall Jarrell to teach and coach tennis. Other poets and writers followed: James Wright, Robert Mezey, William Gass, E. L. Doctorow. And then there were those summer conferences, the foundation-funded Kenyon School of English, which brought together murderers' rows of literary critics, Barzun, Bentley, Burke, Brooks, Empson, Kazin, Mizener, Rahv, Schorer, Tate, Warren, and Winters.

It's tempting to make too much of this. The *Kenyon Review*'s circulation never exceeded 3,000, and it had little contact with students. The rigorous, text-oriented "New Criticism" associated with the *Review* was soon supplemented, if not superseded, by other approaches to literature. Ransom abandoned it himself by the mid-1940s. Those glittering summer conclaves lasted only three years. The whole literary-critical culture was in fact a subculture, temporary and fortuitous, a college within a college. Later, E. L. Doctorow described himself and his cohorts as "the exotics," a tiny cabal in a student body characterized by "the drinkers and the jocks and the proud C-average second or third generation Kenyon men who wore grey flannels and white bucks and school sweaters in the monarchial colors of purple and white."

Granted, Kenyon under Chalmers was no Camelot. The president was opinionated, headstrong, obstinate. He spurned psychology, a pseudo-science, inappropriate for Kenyon. Ditto sociology. His abrupt firings galvanized the faculty, some of whom were obsessed by hate for him. And there were always money problems. Visiting Kenyon in the forties, the University of Chicago president, Robert Maynard Hutchens, praised Chalmers. "Don't ever let him balance the budget," he advised. Alas, Chalmers kept the promise. His last years were fiscally grim.

Still, Chalmers had succeeded in his drive to make an obscure place important. People still speak of him in Gambier: Chalmers making a point to spend at least half an hour, one on one, with every Kenyon student; Chalmers saving money by taking the upper berth on night trains to New York; Chalmers inviting a college janitor who wrote poetry to have dinner with Robert Frost. Chalmers serving hot mulled wine to the college faculty on Christmas Eve.

When I arrived in 1960, the place had a feeling of—what to call it?—aftermath, as though I'd gone to Paris, searching for the Lost Generation, in 1935. Chalmers's successor, the gentle, ineffectual F. Edward "Buck" Lund, had come to Kenyon, he later confessed, "looking for a place to put my feet up." On arrival in 1957, at a welcoming dinner, he'd sat through a speech that old-timers still talk about, a long, lethal performance by John Crowe Ransom. The poet-critic warned the new president that Chalmers's style of arbitrary leadership wouldn't work anymore: the faculty ran Kenyon. It was the sort of testing speech that demands a retort. It never came. Instead, people recall, Lund gave a speech in which he mentioned William Butler Yeats. Only he pronounced *Yeats* as though it rhymed with *Keats,* or *beets.* "It was all downhill from there," someone tells me.

Kenyon's years of congenial adequacy, of being a pretty good place, comfortable and clubby, had been interrupted by a quality-driven president who thought of Kenyon as first-rate, "an eastern college misplaced." The place had enjoyed a few seasons of glory, and, though much of that was over now, the reputation persisted, like a nickname you can't shake. And what you do with reputations is a tricky business, a thin line between living off of them and living up to them. That was Kenyon's predicament, and mine.

❧

WE'VE HAD A LONG DAY of driving in August heat, but now conversation perks up again. My wife senses my excitement, and my dog Max does, too. Comatose on interstates, he awoke the first time I flipped the turn signal, and now he stirs and sniffs. I imagine the scents that will be coming to him: fallen pears and apples, dormitory smells and dining commons smells and classroom funks. Though my wife will come and go—her job is in Chicago—Max will stay with me in the year ahead, while I teach where I once learned.

I remember my Kenyon professors, not my courses. Who keeps college notebooks, all those years of stenography, context fading, handwriting indecipherable, memories and morals turning into mulch? Likewise, those big-ticket textbooks gather dust, those pages of underlining, exclamation marks, and marginal notes that remind you of an earlier self, some too confident hunter roaming through print with a ballpoint pen, marking, gotcha, gotcha, gotcha. You remember the professors.

I remember Denham Sutcliffe, an English professor. He knew me before I knew him, knew me before I knew myself. I can picture him now, a round, florid man, who limped as he walked—a hunting accident had lamed him. I can even smell him, a not unpleasant combination of sweat and books I detected whenever I cruised by his office, hoping he'd throw me a word, a compliment. And I can hear him, sardonic and ironic, skewering a student who'd used *wise* as an all-purpose suffix— "how are you doing, *sex-wise?*"—or reciting long chunks of Pope's "Essay on Man" from memory, or addressing us at the college's opening banquet our freshman year. He talked about the college's founders, dead Episcopalians whose portraits lined the walls. He advised us on study habits: "Do not have *her* photograph in view." He told us it was sin to crack a book's spine or deface its pages. Then he told us how Kenyon College was beginning its 136th year, a long time as time was measured in Knox County, Ohio, and Harvard was beginning its, say, 300th year, which was certainly a long time in America, and Oxford was beginning—I'm guessing now—its 1,200th year, and *that* was a long time anywhere. Suddenly this small hick college was part of a great, timeless enterprise. Sutcliffe was like that: he put *here* into *there*. Your coming, and your staying, made sense.

A lot of the time, of course, I was miserable. Being miserable was an art form in isolated, all-male colleges, a theatrical melancholy spawned in dormitories that stank of unwashed clothing, spilled beer, masturbation, in hangdog February classrooms, all tracked with mud, at fraternity parties where the chance of romance was extinguished like a lit cigarette plunged into a handy bowl of cheese dip. At the end of my sophomore year, I'd had enough. Part of it was about women. If you had a scholarship, you couldn't have a car, because that meant you shouldn't have a scholarship. And if you didn't have a car, you needed to be able to borrow a car, to pick up your woman at the Columbus airport, or the Mansfield bus station, or a neighboring college: neighboring, as in forty, fifty, eighty miles away. Fraternity boys had the cars and the connections. So on those big dance weekends, fall and spring, I wandered from party to party, casting myself as an observer, sardonic and—you'd better believe it—unattached, moving from one fraternity lounge to another, three lounges per building in three buildings, the nine circles of hell and I was Dante. Sure: if Dante were a virgin from New Jersey.

Women were only part of it. Tolerated, liked, even spoiled, I still sensed I was an outsider, a New Jersey boy in Ohio, an agnostic in Episcopalia, a working-class kid among the upper class, a first-generation German-American among long-settled WASPS, an independent at a place where 90 percent of the student body joined fraternities. I felt like a foreign student, sometimes. I could sense it the way some of the old-timers checked me out; I could guess what they were thinking. "Scholarship . . . New Jersey . . . is that a vowel at the end of his name? . . . not our type exactly. . . . You say he's doing well?"

I was doing too well, acing courses, flirting with a four-point. Much was made of that, much was made of me, and that bothered me too. Life was a series of increasing challenges, I'd been told. In grammar school, I was warned about high school, a regional high school that drew from five communities, some of them with lots of Jews. What a killer arena that was going to be! I'd be lucky if I passed wood shop! And then in high school, when they'd sorted us into college prep and vocational ed types, sorted us like apples, some mashed into cider and applesauce, others polished, wrapped in tissue paper, crated and marked for export, I was cautioned about life-and-death combat in college. In college, they'd take me down a notch or two, all right, and high time!

Now, at Kenyon, I discovered the first truth about college. It was easy. It was easy if you worked, and it was negotiable even if you didn't work. That was the meaning of the gentleman's C: minimal effort, moderate attendance, in exchange for a middling grade. I worked. I worked because my parents worked, because my machinist father got up while it was still dark to drive to a factory he hated and my mother earned tuition money as a cashier at a high school cafeteria. But those other students amazed me, the ones who bagged lectures—lectures that their parents were paying for, you could figure it out, so many dollars per slept-through class! They weren't upset, they didn't feel guilty, they weren't even worried. No, they walked the campus with a certain air of entitlement, relaxed, controlled, proprietary. They seemed content at Kenyon, and Kenyon seemed content with them.

Now I was getting cocky. Throwing immigrant caution aside, I applied to Yale, applied for admission and aid, and got both. Then the agony began. Four letters, four envelopes, four stamps: to Yale, yes and no, to Kenyon, I'm leaving, I'm returning. My bewildered, heartsick parents couldn't advise me. They just wanted me to be happy. Was that so much to ask? In the end, I mailed the letters that told Kenyon I was returning, told Yale they'd have to get by without me. I wasn't out of the post office parking lot before I'd convinced myself I'd made the wrong decision, the cowardly, minor league, big fish–small pond, play-it-safe, bird-in-hand, chickenshit German-American decision, but I could not imagine the look on Denham Sutcliffe's face when he learned of my desertion. The next two years of my life were his.

If I could cast him as Mr. Chips and leave it at that, I would remember him less well. But I learned there was more to him: streaks of bitterness and anger, working-class anger, something that savaged piety and hated wealth and chafed at the life of the local hero, his life. I recall a lecture he gave and the person who introduced him lingered on his accomplishments, which, though not insubstantial, fell short of major book-length scholarship. "Thank you," Sutcliffe said when he arose to speak. "At one time I would have said that the person you describe sounds like a promising young man."

Sutcliffe taught everyone who came to him, but he lived for exceptional students. They redeemed him. They atoned for rage. A Rhodes scholar, Sutcliffe had ambitions for me and for another English major, Perry Lentz. It was hard to see how he could miss hitting the jackpot with one of us, maybe both. A reserved, diligent Alabaman whose shyness was often mistaken for hauteur, Lentz was a solid, thoughtful, conservative, Episcopalian DKE. He was writing a novel for his honors thesis, and, what's more, he played soccer. I was the scholarship boy, the campus critic, churning out two hundred pages on Edmund Wilson and John Dos Passos for my honors thesis. One establishment student, one anti. The Rhodes people could take their choice, Sutcliffe must have thought. I hoped that we would both succeed. Or . . . *both* . . . God, please! . . . fail.

My senior year, I pulled all-nighters, every night, reading while the dormitory slept, reading not just books but whole careers, Orwell, Lawrence, Dos Passos, Edmund Wilson, orgies of reading, night-long roller coaster trips. Maybe, later, I got wiser, but I was never faster, smarter, more receptive. I watched dawn roll in from Pennsylvania, lighting up barns, birds starting to sing, and there'd still be an hour before breakfast, and I'd walk around, exhilarated, all full of what I'd been reading, greeting the night watchman on his last round, watching the flag-raising in front of the post office, that flagpole that was the epicenter of this small island, the point from which distance was measured: faculty weren't supposed to live more than ten miles away from that pole, that was as far as anybody was supposed to go, and then I'd head into Peirce Hall, the first customer for their breakfast, which was my supper, and then one morning, it all fell short, fell apart, because Dean of Students Tom Edwards walked in and quietly announced that Sutcliffe had died the night before.

Lentz and I were pallbearers. We'd both missed the Rhodes, after all. Sutcliffe died before I could bring myself to ask for help on this multiple-choice question I was having trouble with: whether I had failed Kenyon, or whether Kenyon had failed me, or whether something else was wrong. There was a lesson in all this, and with Sutcliffe dead, it was something I had to work out myself. The lesson was about Kenyon: that success in a small place doesn't lead to triumph elsewhere, doesn't transplant, doesn't compound. There were limits to being a local hero. Sutcliffe was my professor and my guide, and I thought he had it all figured out for me, my life's design and purpose. But toward the end, I'd started wondering if he hadn't just wanted company inside this small trap of a place. I was beginning to have doubts, beginning to sense what Sutcliffe must have known, all along, the way pride and despair accompany each other in a small place, the way love and anger, trust and treason, come together on a college island. Returning now, middle-aged, I detect a surge of nostalgia and—is it coming from inside the jeep?—a whiff of doubt.

✣

A FEW YEARS AGO, while I was on magazine assignment in South Africa, my wife got a call from Kenyon. There'd been some bloodletting in the Kenyon English Department, a sudden opening created, a stopgap replacement required. My old classmate, Perry Lentz, had remembered me. Would I like to come for one semester, teach two courses, both in fiction writing, for $15,000? She wasn't calling to talk it over: she'd already said yes.

I ended up teaching at Kenyon for chunks of the next three years. It was all ad hoc: I never knew, when I left, if I'd be returning. And closed-ended: no thoughts of tenure-track employment. And part-time: two courses per semester instead of the usual three. This is my fourth return trip. I'm staying all year this time, teaching one course of fiction writing, fall semester, one course of something called "American Literature since 1945" in the spring. And I am going to write about Kenyon, which, it occurs to me, is a lot like writing about your parents while they are still alive and tinkering with their will.

Kenyon's president, Phil Jordan, was equivocal when I first described this project to him: "a year in the life of a liberal arts college, a lively, knowledgeable, pungent, top-to-bottom examination of the dynamics, the character, the traditions, tensions and pretensions, predicaments and prospects of one of America's least examined, least understood institutions." And so forth. He wasn't wowed. He wondered what good could come of it at a time when higher education is under heightening criticism. He also worried that my poking around might cause local discomfiture. Kenyon, like all colleges, is dedicated to critical inquiry, free speech, open dialogue, the play of ideas. It is also, like other colleges, thin-skinned and image-conscious, a jealous guardian of its own self-esteem. Never mind, there's no resisting an idea whose time has come. Even a dangerous idea. And in the months since we talked, the news about higher education has gotten worse. Costs are rising, salaries lagging, enrollments declining, test scores dropping. Admissions departments are in turmoil, professors are mud-wrestling over what to teach, and college presidents are fending off federal price-fixing charges. Add multiculturalism and political correctness to the list. "Nothing feels settled anymore," an article in the *New York Times* declared a few weeks ago. The headline: "Higher Education Feels the Heat." I can't blame Phil Jordan for having his doubts; I've got some doubts myself.

The choice of college is the most extraordinarily uninformed decision otherwise bright people make. If they bought a house for the same money—$100,000, say, though education's going up faster than real estate—they'd check out title search, termite inspection, public schools, property taxes, roof, cellar. With colleges, it's a glossy brochure, a walk around campus in good weather, and a hearsay reputation that's thirty years out of date. That's my first audience, I told Jordan, the parents you see touring the liberal arts gulag with their kids, prospective students, all nods and grins, shopping colleges with little more information than you can get about the average kennel: "This is the cage, this is the run, we walk them twice a day, our pets are happy here." There's another group I'll be writing for, more elusive, but I know they're out there. I've seen that distant smile that appears on the face of the $300,000-a-year executive when he hears I teach at a small private college in the country. I've seen that killer polish recede, if only for a moment, and yield to something much older, or younger: "I've always thought about going back and teaching." I hear what they are hearing, choral songs and courtly voices, chapel bells. I can see what they are seeing, classrooms lined with dark wood, white houses with friendly porches, cordial campus paths, years passing in a lively, lovely, resonant place, a place like Kenyon, small but fine, pink and white dogwoods in the springtime, leaf raking and fresh cider in the fall, and I know that, for a moment anyway, I'm envied.

None of this talk of audiences, ripe and ready, persuaded Kenyon's president to cooperate so much as that bellwether argument that, one way or another, with or without, there was going to be a book. I couldn't blame him. I told him, later on, to try not to worry much: I was better than anyone who was more loyal, more loyal than anyone who was better. He laughed at that, his hearty, locally famous laugh—hearty if not necessarily convinced—and promised cooperation. How much cooperation remains to be seen.

The way a traveler learns a village, I want to know this college. Who runs Kenyon College? How are decisions made? What is the dialectic between the president, the provost, the board of trustees? What about the faculty? Are they scholars? Dedicated teachers? Can they manage being both? Can they get away with being neither? Are they happy campers? Whining mercenaries? How should I picture this island I'm coming to? As a feudal structure, a benign fiefdom? A business? A scholarly kibbutz? A summer camp, a country club, a finishing school?

What are the customers getting for their money? What about grades, standards, intellectual rigor? Is the customer always right? How hard is it to succeed at Kenyon? How hard is it to fail?

I want to know what it's like to be a college professor. Amazingly, every academic novel I've read—*Pictures from an Institution, The Groves of Academe, A New Life*—has been about personal crisis or marital politics. There's never a classroom scene, a student dropping by to manipulate a grade, a lecture that went from good to bad to good again, a seminar that was a three-hour march through a mountain range of ups and downs. And where's the one scene that goes right to the heart of college life, its bane, its cross, its mainstay: the mind-numbing, migraine-making reading and grading of one, two, three *War and Peace*-size piles of student prose?

The students. I want to know what it's like for them, to get as close as I can to answering the ultimate question: What does it feel like to be you? I've no kids of my own, and I'm not complaining. The $20,000 I've gotten for my most recent book, years of work, just matched what it would cost to send an offspring to Kenyon. For one year. Still, I wonder about the Kenyon students who occupy my old premises, the people who will be in their prime when I am old. What do they know? What do they care about? What is funny to them? Do they crave excellence? Fear mediocrity? Do all-nighters? Do any of the things that matter to me matter to them?

Maybe it'll be a quiet year in Gambier, but I doubt it. As sure as shit and feathers on a chicken coop floor, there's always something. There are underlying dramas in admissions and money-raising, there's deep-dish Kremlinology about the plans and ambitions of the president and provost. There are student uproars: date rape, fraternities, and all. There's the melodrama of hiring searches. Add all this to the real work of the college, the teaching and the learning, and if you don't have the makings of a movie you're certainly assured of a long-running television show, something between "Night Court" and "Northern Exposure."

🌿

NOW WE COME into Mount Vernon, seat of Knox County, Ohio, the town to Kenyon's gown. Just a few miles more. With its cobbled brick street, Civil War monument town square, block after block of handsome turn-of-the-century housing, Mount Vernon would be a chic place if it were in reach of a major city. It would be Williamstown, Massachusetts, and Kenyon might be Williams, Williams with a lusty $333 million endowment, compared to Kenyon's piddling $35 million. Kenyon would be Williams, sure, and every go-go girl would be a ballerina. Never mind: we try harder, maybe, sometimes. Meanwhile, Mount Vernon is another town where growth and decline seem tenuously balanced, its downtown Main Street subverted by an ugly, edge-of-town gamut of supermarkets, discount stores, fast-food franchises. Hometown of Paul Lynde, boasts Mount Vernon, another American city that defines itself by the ones who leave. And yet, there is something congenial about the place: stately houses, modest bungalows, backyard gardens, quiet streets, a sense of late summer torpor, terminal and full. Better this than prosperity, which would spell video dishes outside of mobile homes, subdivisions in cornfields, and a new, newer, newest shopping center on the outskirts of town.

Outside of Mount Vernon, Route 229 goes uphill, past a few showy mansions, old money and new, past a retirement home for Masonic women, past bungalows and cornfields, the same landscape we've been driving through for hours, but I am so close now I couldn't be more stirred if, time warping, I were somehow crunching over the gravel in my parents' driveway and it was thirty years ago and they were outside on a late summer weekend, my mother in the garden weeding. Days after rain were good days for weeding, she said. And he'd be on the stoop, relaxing after spading the garden, a short, barrel-chested man with a Ballantine Ale in his hand, wearing a pair of shorts with boxer-style underwear beneath, and the underwear always was an inch longer than the shorts. That neighborhood is gone now. Coming to Kenyon is as close as I can get to coming home. Like salmon to spawning stream, like eagle to nest, like dog to vomit, I return.

Now I've come to the crest of a hill, and, across a valley where cornfields curve along the Kokosing River and an old railroad trestle hides in trees, I see the college hill and race toward it. At the entrance, a sizable marker, donated by a trustee, names the college and displays its coat of arms. "The tomb of the unknown college," students call it. We turn up the hill, turn left at the top, arrive in the parking lot outside the freshman dormitory, Lewis Hall, the same dorm I lived in thirty-two years ago. My wife steps out of the jeep. Max jumps gingerly onto the ground. Suddenly, as we head toward the dormitory door, vintage fears assert themselves.

"Got a guy here sneaking a woman into the dorm," I imagine someone saying. It's the same off-duty farmer I pictured down the road, right across the county line, or his brother. Only now he wears the uniform of campus security. His arrival is SWAT-like, with flashing lights and crackling intercoms. "What's your name?"

"P. F. Kluge . . . class of '64."

"Her name?"

"Pamela Hollie." The security guard's pause stretches into an embarrassing silence. A Knox County sheriff's vehicle pulls in beside the security guard's jeep. And lights snap on in the faculty house across the way. Who lives there, I ask myself. Joan Slonczewski, Biology Department. Writes feminist science fiction. Great!

"Look, we're married," I hear myself saying. I glare at my wife, as an old irritation revives. "Legally married. She kept her name." God, I don't mind women getting a fair shake, honest, only why did I have to be in the first generation to live through it?!

"No women in the dorms," my nemesis repeats. Down the road—it's hard to be sure—I see a couple people walking a pair of dogs. Untrained dogs, straining at the leash, spotting Max and pulling Kenyon's president and his wife toward the scene of the crime.

But no. I open the door, and the long corridor, freshly waxed, awaits me. My wife and my dog and I walk down the hall, and the building swallows us.

❧ *Orientation*

S UMMER STILL BLANKETS GAMBIER. The worst drought in years fills the air with dust, bakes the ground adobe, turns grass into thin, sad strands an old man might comb over a bald spot. Papery corn, dead on its feet, riffles in a wind that brings no rain, small streams, called "runs," have gone dry, and the Kokosing is less a river than a drainage ditch, green and stagnant. Up on the hill, Kenyon just begins to stir, sluggishly, the way you rouse yourself after a night when you've gotten too much sleep or too little.

I never feel that I'm back at Kenyon until I've walked the campus from end to end. Unpacking will wait, calls and visits, a dog-food run to Big Bear. First we need to walk the place. This isn't about people—hi, hello, you're back, what are you working on? is it a novel? no? nonfiction? with real names?—this is memory lane stuff, tying up past and present, right here where they meet under a mopey August moon. In a few days this place will fill up with all ranks and types: it belongs as much to them as to me. But this first walk makes another point: the place belongs as much to me as to anybody.

Max dawdles behind Pamela and me, not greeting the campus with the enthusiasm I'd hoped for. He sniffs like a prospective student forced by parents to go through the paces at a third-choice college. He senses the emptiness too, maybe. At the south end of campus, the three older dorms, Hanna, Leonard, and Old Kenyon, are ominously dark; the only lights, running straight up and down, are in the stairwells. Doors are locked, lawns are clear, and the absence of noise is unsettling. These buildings are most alive when suffering. Now they've gone mute: a zoo with empty cages. The library, too, is dark, like a patient gone brain-dead. That's what it comes to when there aren't students: no vital signs.

We walk the village of Gambier, that one block of businesses and offices that separates the south end of campus from the newer north end. This is the place people picture when they think about returning, this college village. The picture varies with the amount of time they've been away. In my time, the place was run-down, like a New England hamlet hijacked to the Ozarks: wooden sidewalks, creaking floors, false-fronted shops. The Peoples Bank was the solidest place in town, and it—we boasted—had been robbed, back in the thirties, by an offshoot of John Dillinger's gang. That was Gambier: the sort of place robbers might knock over on a whim, and not the starting team, either, not the ten most wanted, but some felons way down the list, wanna-be wanteds. The post office sat next to the bank. Next door, the bookstore, mostly textbooks, then a couple faculty houses, then the alumni house, where visitors stayed. Across the street, a gas station, a couple grocery stores, a couple barbers, and a one-pump gas station.

Endearing and decrepit in my memory, Gambier has been spruced up now, Williamsburged into a state of postcard prettiness, so that it makes that all-important nice first impression, like a roughneck, climb-under-the-hood garage grease monkey converted into a beaming, crisply uniformed, clipboard-carrying Mr. Goodwrench. Things have been pruned, planted, painted, and red-brick buildings stand where the ricketiest of the old structures used to be. Moved across the street, the Kenyon Bookstore dominates the village, a likable, late-night, seven-days-a-week place doubling and tripling as a candy store, snack shop, and sweatshirt emporium. Faculty don't live on Main Street anymore. The sole residential holdout is Jim Hayes, a longtime grocer, who lives in a red-brick house next to the Village Inn restaurant. In his seventies now, Hayes spends half the year in Florida. When in Gambier, he misses the old all-male days, the fraternities singing up and down Middle Path at night. He also misses that black ceramic stable boy he had in front of his house: some students offed it during the seventies, making Jim Hayes Gambier's first victim of political correctness.

Gambier looks outward more than it used to, counting on company, and the outside presses in more than it used to. But tonight it's still Philander Chase's small college on a hill in the middle of nowhere, a place that 1,500 students are heading for this minute. A few are already present, soccer and football players, residence hall advisers. Tonight will be the last quiet night. You can almost hear them coming, packing compact discs and fake IDs, piling into cars, first the freshmen, then the upper-class students, bundles of talent and dyslexia, procrastination and possibility. Sutcliffe used to say that every student who came to Kenyon, every one, would leave a mark. I wonder if that's true. Tonight, though, Gambier doesn't belong to this year's paying customers, the ones who raise their hands when roll is called. It belongs to the past. At Kenyon, the past isn't over. It sticks around.

❧

"I STILL REMEMBER going out into absolute darkness," Bruce Haywood recalls, "glimpses of trees, a road that dipped and twisted, and, my God, I wondered, is there a college at the end of this?" I spent a lot of time foraging in Kenyon's past last summer, talking with trustees, alumni, and—for the first time in fifteen years—with Bruce Haywood, a professor of German at Kenyon when I was a student. Later, he served as college provost, before leaving in 1980 to become president of Monmouth College in Illinois. It's remarkable how people remember their first sight of this god-blessed, god-forsaken college, their tales of driving through town and missing the place entirely, asking a befuddled farmer the whereabouts of "downtown Gambier," getting off a train and walking through dark woods, up the hill. Right then, I suspect, a basic choice is made: some begrudge every mile they have to travel, others love arriving in a far-off, small place. Two groups: the passers-through and the stayers-on, the ones who say, "Oh, my," and the others who pronounce "Oh, shit!"

Haywood was in the "Oh, my!" group. Born in Yorkshire, working-class, Bruce Haywood served in World War II, came to the United States in 1951, did graduate work at Harvard, which he disliked. Early in 1953, his Ph.D. still incomplete, he traveled to New York to interview for a job at Kenyon. He went to a hotel. Gordon Keith Chalmers, Kenyon's president, sat on the edge of a bed, Haywood in the room's only chair, and they talked about Thomas Mann. Soon afterwards, he was asked to visit Kenyon.

"The first sense I had about the senior faculty," Haywood continues, "was that, with a few exceptions, they were men who had been hand-picked by Gordon Chalmers because they embraced his ideas about liberal arts and the identity of the college. That was the word I heard again and again. The *college*. 'The college would have it . . .' 'The interests of the college . . .' One never heard about the department. The department didn't count for much. Our offices were all together in Ascension Hall, economics and math professors across from each other. If ever a place deserved the rubric 'community of scholars,' the little

Kenyon of that time did. Everybody knew everybody. Looking back, it seems every Friday afternoon you were at somebody's house, visiting, talking."

How good a place was it? I wondered aloud. If I asked that question today at Kenyon, I would be asking for trouble. The short answers are suspect, and the long answers go from here to the airport, breaking into divisions, ranks, categories, into lists of the schools you compete with for students, for money, for prestige, the schools you compete with in fact and in fancy. A simple question—*how good is this wine?*—backfires till your curiosity seems vulgar and you wonder why you ever bothered asking.

"I suppose if Amherst, Haverford, Williams were the best, if you thought of them as an A, then Kenyon was not, Kenyon was a B," Haywood replies. "Damn good. The best students had the opportunity to spend time with the best teachers. Sometime in the midfifties, the *Chicago Tribune* published a list of the ten best men's colleges. And Kenyon was the third-best, behind Amherst and Haverford. That was the kind of quality Kenyon aspired to. That was the controlling sense. Kenyon wasn't encouraged to relate to Ohio Wesleyan or Ohio State but to Williams, Amherst, Haverford. Everyone walked about four feet off the ground, until Sutcliffe told them what the *Chicago Tribune* called itself: the world's greatest newspaper. That ended it."

This was Haywood's Kenyon, the Kenyon of the Magic Mountain. A professor of German, he took Thomas Mann's huge metaphor and imprinted it on an Ohio hillside, persuading generations of Kenyon students that four years of clean, clear thought, of dialogue and discovery in isolation was something that they should esteem, not resent, because they would be better for it, and the world better for them. By teaching skill and force of personality, Haywood became a prevailing figure, especially after Sutcliffe's death. Then things changed, and the first change was one that Haywood had himself endorsed: coeducation.

"Everything we saw told us that young men were not lining up to enter all-male institutions," he says. "The really prestigious ones could go on for a while, but they changed, too." Then he reminds me of one of my own lines, something from an editorial I wrote in the student newspaper, one of those lines that goes off and gets quoted and takes on a life of its own. "'Going to Kenyon is like traveling cabin class on a sinking ship,'" Haywood quotes. "Kenyon was going under if not for radical change. There was simply no choice."

By 1965 plans were in place to bring women to Kenyon, plans made without the participation or support of the college president, F. Edward Lund, Haywood says. "I think he was confident that the trustees would shut it down." In 1967 the trustees approved the plan; President Lund was not enthusiastic. "He came in one morning at 9:00 A.M.," Haywood says, "at a time of day I'd never seen Buck Lund in Ascension Hall. He plunked himself in a chair, while I was still catching my breath at seeing Buck Lund at that time of day. 'I've got to tell you,' he said, 'I'm not going to allow it to happen.'"

Within a week, with the intervention of a powerful trustee, Lund was on his way out. Haywood was offered the presidency, which he didn't feel ready for. He suggested the job be offered to William Caples, a Kenyon alumnus who was a vice president at Inland Steel. The idea was that Caples would be a Mr. Outside, Haywood a Mr. Inside. Their relations were marked, however, by what Haywood saw as "an increasing antagonism" toward a faculty the president criticized as lazy. Then, when Phil Jordan followed Caples in 1975, Haywood was troubled by the new president's way of looking at the college. Haywood saw the college as a centered, conservative place, a "community of scholars." Jordan, it seemed to him, saw the college as a confluence of elements and factions, "a body politic." Quick to acknowledge Jordan's intelligence, Haywood felt that Jordan "always seemed to be quoting someone else." But Haywood's deepest discontent had less to do with presidents than with the way Kenyon itself was changing.

"My arguments for a larger, coeducational Kenyon had brought it to a state I wasn't happy with," Haywood says. Part of it, surely, was growth: the college almost doubled in a four-year period. Another part was *how* it grew. Kenyon shunned doing what it in any case could only rarely afford: hiring senior, tenured professors away from other institutions. Its new hires tended to be young, mobile, ambitious, and they were divided—by youth, mobility, ambition—from Kenyon's older faculty. The old-timers, mostly, were content to repose in Gambier forever, to live and teach. Some did scholarship, i.e., published work. For others, scholarship was reading, at least they said it was. Still others didn't read: gentility faded, unmarked, into senility. The newcomers were different. They wanted to do research. They wanted recognition outside of Gambier. They wanted employment for their spouses. They wanted whatever the college could provide and some things it couldn't, and their whole lives didn't necessarily point toward the churchyard in back of Rosse Hall. They were free agents.

The first fault lines that developed between generations were followed by fissures between departments, now grown large enough to be segregated, self-serving, combative. The congenial *gemütlichkeit* of Ascension Hall, Classics hobnobbing with English, Math drinking coffee with Economics, all that disappeared as the larger departments, English, History, Political Science, were moved into separate houses on the edge of campus, a Balkanization that led to war.

As a result of a number of decisions, many of them correct, some unavoidable, a small college had turned into a larger place, a place that despite its size and health was somewhere Haywood felt less at home. Philander Chase's isolated college on a hill, Chalmers's eastern college misplaced, Haywood's Magic Mountain was now more like other colleges, like a quirky country town annexed, subdivided, and suburbanized. Grow or die: that had been the word, back in the sixties. But growth didn't only enlarge, it transformed; it enriched and it diluted. Make that, grow *and* die.

"By 1980 the only thing that was left to celebrate at Kenyon College was toleration," Haywood says. He had reservations about the sports center, the swimming pool. He was tired of refereeing departments. He didn't want to have to fight off gender studies, which was headed Kenyon's way. By the time he left, even his famous comparison of Gambier to the Magic Mountain had fallen out of favor: it was dated, it was literary, snobby, elitist. ("Bruce had an image of the college that, when he articulated it, had great justificatory and explanatory power," Phil Jordan tells me later. "That Magic Mountain gave you a glimpse of eternity. What troubled the faculty was, they weren't always sure that was the facility they were at. It was inspiring, but it was not the college they wanted to attend.")

Just before leaving, Haywood spoke at Kenyon's precommencement baccalaureate ceremony, delivering the Magic Mountain speech, as it had come to be called, for the last time: "Go now, your college says to you, go to the flatland in Kenyon's name, and let your years here sustain you in the fight." One faculty member who attended, no friend of Haywood's, thought it was the wrong speech at the wrong time: "It was wrong. Not untrue, but it felt wrong. There were no black students, no interest in minorities, just a narrow spectrum of upper-class whites. A typical Kenyon ceremony, heavy PR for parents, names in Latin, a great deal of pomp and circumstance. Even the metaphor appealed to the privileged, the intelligent. A lot of people wouldn't know what the Magic Mountain was."

People still talk of Haywood in Gambier, I discover later. When word gets out that we've spent a day together, people approach me. I learn to be careful about this, to answer with an uninflected nod, because there's no way of knowing how people remember him. When Haywood left, one professor tells me, it felt like Marcos's flight from the Philippines, a weighty past shrugged off, new energies released, people power! But another professor compares it to "the letting down of the pilot," a famous cartoon of Kaiser Wilhelm II—that would be Phil Jordan, I guess—standing at a ship's railing while Bismarck, the shrewd and venerable chancellor, puts off in a small boat.

🌿

"GOOD MORNING," Philip Harding Jordan intones. "I am reasonably happy to see you, and I think you are reasonably happy to see each other. I welcome you back to prickly collegiality after a summer of individuality."

I could have skipped this meeting, which is all about how faculty members are supposed to get students registered for courses. Having no student advisees, I am off the hook. But it's the first meeting of the year and a chance to see the president's first performance, to catch that particular blend of irony and authority, that cheerful, brisk executive tone that makes fun of things other people had better take seriously. The United States has had eighteen twentieth-century presidents. Kenyon College has had six, one of them an interim appointment. Phil Jordan has been Kenyon's president since 1975, arriving from Connecticut College where he'd taught history and served as dean of the faculty.

"I had that wonderful East Coast sense that there are numbers of good colleges out there in Ohio and that Kenyon College was one of them," he recalled for me a couple months ago. On his first visit, coming up from Columbus, he saw a snowy midwestern landscape—"flat and Babbittish"—start to crinkle and roll. And then he drove up the hill to a college he found "enchanted."

"I thought it was exquisite," he reflects. "Just a jewel of a college. The setting was perfect for undergraduate education, a special, magical village. And with Middle Path running end to end, you can't be unknown in Gambier. That's a little scary, maybe, but you can't. The students had an unassuming ease and directness in the way they talked to adults. I thought, 'this is a good place that can be much better. It has not reached its level yet.'"

Jordan had two main competitors for the job that now pays him

$157,000 per year, plus housing and benefits. The search committee was divided. The outgoing president, William Caples, had been a business-man, blunt, bottom-line, no nonsense. Some members of the committee, especially trustees, thought that another president with a business back-ground was what Kenyon needed. Their choice was a lawyer who'd been serving as a trustee at Dartmouth College. Others wanted an academic: they favored a Yale historian, an impressive scholar, who disappointed them by dropping out of the search. They argued about the trustee candidate. "Do we want an academic or do we want this lawyer?" a member of the search committee recalls debating. "It got fairly heated. Then came word that the lawyer was withdrawing his application. By then, we thought that Phil was the person we wanted. We were very happy with that choice."

Phil Jordan has been in office sixteen years, and that, he's the first to admit, is unusual for college presidents these days. His term will soon pass Gordon Keith Chalmers's and he'll then be Kenyon's second most durable president. There the record will stay. Now sixty, Jordan would have to work to age eighty-five to pass William F. Peirce, Kenyon's president from 1896 to 1937. Jordan doesn't plan to go for the gold medal; silver will do.

"The world outside of Gambier is not so sure these days that colleges are to be trusted and faculty members are to be relied upon," Jordan warns the shirt-sleeved, summery crowd. A tall, round-shouldered man with thinning white hair and unfashionably long white sideburns, he seems comfortable and in control behind a podium. "There's a crisis of confidence in education," he warns, "and there are doubts and fears and expressions of anger."

An investor's son, Jordan was born in New York City, raised on the Jersey Shore, attended Lawrenceville (valedictorian), Princeton (Phi Beta Kappa, summa cum laude), and Yale (M.A., Ph.D.). After all his years in Ohio, he still seems a man of the East, Ivy League, New England, a kind of missionary to the Midwest, something like a Spanish aristocrat passing his years in a small Mexican village. He knows the natives' foibles. And they know his: how his eyebrows move when he talks, bouncing up and down his forehead, punctuating, exclaiming. And that presidential laugh, a hearty, three-beat har-har-har that turns heads in dining rooms and, in summer, when doors are open, carries from Crom-well Cottage to Middle Path.

"I've had a love affair with academic institutions, academic life,"

Jordan says. "I've always enjoyed collegiate debates. I just love that interchange, the rhythm of it, and the alternation of activity, the alternation of intensely engaged hours when you're living in people's laps and other times which are intensely private."

He was a good college teacher, he says, but he felt drawn to the college as a whole, "to bring the place together, in the larger sense of helping the faculty trying to find its own tangled way." He wasn't interested in publishing—"learning was a passion, research was not"— and so was drawn to administration, to contending with "ideas in the flesh." What he likes, he says, "is discerning the character and direction of a group, reading the group, the way things get worked out, the right people in the right situation—it's an endless fascination."

Some people have suggested that Jordan has a love-hate relationship with the professoriate, a kind of "loving condescension" toward their demands, their complaints, their knotty proceedings. Sometimes you can catch some of this in the lift of a Jordan eyebrow or the turn of a Jordan phrase. I can sense it in his presentation this morning. He takes a downbeat economy and a hostile cultural mood and uses it as an instrument of control and suasion, grounds for a preemptive warning that goes something like this: You ask whether I have a vision for this place, when what you want is for me to see things your way. You say I don't listen—that means, *listen to you.* When I consider an issue on its merits, you accuse me of improvising. If I don't bend the rules, I'm rigid, if I do, I'm playing favorites. If I move left or right, I'm partisan, if I do both, I'm a hypocrite. If I do neither, I'm a waffling middle-of-the-roader. Remember this, though: you live well, here in Ohio. In Knox County, like it or not, you're an upper-crust elite. You're paid decently, you've got medical coverage, a retirement plan, free college education for your kids, summers off, and a paid sabbatical every seven years. Half of you have tenure already, and half of the rest of you can expect to get it. We send you to a professional meeting once a year, at least, and if you give a paper chances are we paid someone to type it. I'm sorry if you're not as happy as you'd like to be, not as rich or famous. I'm honestly sorry. Now, let's get to work.

After Jordan finishes, the registration meeting bogs down into talk of courses and sections, procedures and permissions, reminders to write legibly on forms, press hard, and don't forget to sign. Jordan lingers a while, affable and confident. I asked him last summer to describe a college president's job, knowing that people are after him all the time about his "vision" for Kenyon. "The job consists of leading the institution, and that's it," Jordan said. "Leading the institution in all of its constituencies, including the two closest, the students and the faculty. Allowing the best possible students and teachers to do the best possible work."

❧

PAMELA LEFT FOR CHICAGO this morning. Max and I will be on our own in academe. I'm glad she got to attend last night's opening banquet, when the faculty of the college, numbering 120, more or less, plus administration and spouses, kicked off another year. Jordan seemed playful and ironic: "We're like Peter Pan. We never grow up." Provost Reed Browning was equally lighthearted, introducing all the new hires, marching them up for a wave and a handshake, these "spectacularly wonderful newcomers to our community." Irony's a tricky thing in small places, winning but corrosive. You never know where it ends. At dinner, Jordan introduced Lewis Hyde, the foundation-funded Luce Professor of Art and Politics, who has just won a MacArthur Foundation "genius grant." Then—shit!—he introduced me. Irony.

The English Department sat together at a couple tables in the far corner of the dining commons. It's a big department, with twenty-three members listed in this year's directory. The only department that's bigger is Maintenance. Subtract a secretary and an emeritus professor, subtract the outside-funded Lewis Hyde, who has no direct connection with the department, and it comes down to twenty. Subtract the president's wife, Sheila Jordan, who runs the Ohio Poetry Circuit, and Karen Edwards, who's managing the department's year-abroad program at Exeter University, and Kim McMullen, who's on sabbatical, and it's down to seventeen, of whom six are tenured, eight are tenure-track, and three are visitors. Of the visitors, one is full-time, one is two-thirds, one is one-third. That last, that's me.

The division into tenured, tenure-track, and visitors is preliminary triage. Looking around the room, I saw people who are mainly teachers and others who have scholarly ambitions. The college insists that the two activities go together; that's the official position. Scholarship invigorates classroom teaching. Teaching experience anchors and strengthens scholarly research. Maybe so, but the odds on finding them in harmonious balance are about the same as locating a perfect hermaphrodite in the buffet line. There are people who'd be happy to stay here forever and others who have a few moves left in them, if they can manage to make them. So: there are lifers, there are candidates for parole, and there are a couple inmates digging tunnels.

I sat across from my classmate in the class of 1964. Once we were lockstep, marching around here, but now, any line I draw has Perry Lentz at one end of it and me at the other. Still, we're connected. We lost touch after graduation, when he headed for Vanderbilt and I went to the University of Chicago. He nonetheless gave me a bad morning a few years later when I saw that the Civil War novel he'd written as a senior exercise for Sutcliffe had been published by Scribner's and garnered a lead review in *Time*. And—damn it!—I was still a journalist, a *Wall Street Journal* reporter. Round one to Lentz. In 1970 he came back to Kenyon, joining the English Department he'd left just six years before. Sitting in New York, working for *Life* magazine, banging out entertainment profiles on my good days, captions and text blocks on my bad ones, I gave him round two, though by a narrower margin.

A funny thing happened to this college rivalry, though. If it didn't die out, it died down. I dropped by Kenyon a few times in the late seventies and early eighties, usually when I was moving from coast to coast, and I looked Lentz up, found him contented, centered, settled. Once celebrated as a writer who taught, he was now highly regarded as a professor who had written. Time was turning yesterday's youthful prodigy into a pillar of the department, a regular at Kenyon football games, a leader of the local church. He'd become a local hero, like Sutcliffe before him, though lacking Sutcliffe's streak of anarchy and anger. Perry Lentz and I weren't competing at all. When I looked at him, I saw someone altogether different, someone living a life I hadn't lived. But I wondered about it. What would it be like to teach, year after year, to believe in a place, to come to it and never leave, to be loyal? What would it mean? What would it cost?

Back from last year's sabbatical, Lentz has just received an endowed position, the McIlvaine chair, which entitles him to a one-third reduction in his teaching load. He won't take advantage of it, though. He's teaching a jumbo American lit survey, year-long, enrollment unlimited, the equivalent of two courses, and a freshman course, English 1–2, the same course we had from Sutcliffe in the fall of 1960. I've asked him for permission to audit it. We'll see. Upstairs, after dinner, they have a band. Jordan was right, nobody ever grows up, not even Jordan. Instantly, the entire faculty of Kenyon College is on the sidelines, back in high school, snickering and gawking while a few bravura types hit the dance floor. There's always someone in a crowd like this who takes the initiative, gets the dancing started. Here it's Phil Jordan, out there doing the Charleston.

🌿

AT MIDMORNING purple-shirted security guys are all over town, directing vehicles toward dormitories. The little village is jammed, there's honest-to-God traffic in Gambier! Cars, vans, station wagons share the lawn outside my window. Suddenly, those beautifully waxed and empty halls are clogged with packing boxes and footlockers and ominous piles of high-decibel, heavy-duty stereo systems. There's one change, right off the bat: today's college students own more stuff. I owned a typewriter-size record player that had a speaker in the lid. These guys have left a grand behind at the Wiz; their rooms look like Mission Control in Houston.

At the college's reception center, freshmen and parents check in, greeted by members of the Admissions Department, John Anderson and his whole youthful crew, smiling plenty, as if they're all finalists for "salesman of the month." Incoming students pick up room keys, schedules, and—if the check arrived—permissions to register. If not, they're diverted to the Business Office to straighten things out: it's a cash-and-carry operation. The bookstore's humming with parents who shop as if one last purchase might spell the difference between success and failure.

Convocation is the big event of the day, academe on parade, all of us in robes, converging in front of Mather Hall, the same place where these incoming students will graduate four years from now. The senior faculty, tenure and tenure-track, flaunt colorful robes, caps, and sashes. The marginal types, myself included, pick our costumes from a ratty, basic-black selection they keep in the bookstore cellar. We stand on both sides of Middle Path, and then the bells in the chapel start ringing berserkly, running wild, joyous, as if the whole sleepy village had hit a triple cherry jackpot, and, from further down the path, the freshman class advances toward us. God, what a white, upper middle–class bunch they seem to be at first, the guys all Ferris Buellers, dressed in baggy Banana Republic shorts or Dockers slacks, spiky just-out-of-the-shower hair. The women are a little better dressed, I guess: blonde-haired daughters of Chicago's North Shore, Wilmette and Winnetka. They shamble in toward us, awkward and embarrassed, as if this ceremony were a form of mild hazing.

It's our first look at the entering class. Weeks from now this pack will break. Individuals will come out of it. Right now, though, en masse, they look like winners bred from winners, lounging past us in shorts and short-sleeve shirts while we wear Indian blankets and sweat bullets. As soon as the last freshman passes between us, it's our turn to parade— process, as they say—in rough order of seniority, pacing through a gamut of camera-toting parents. Impossible not to feel tribally quaint, part of a line of chiefs and braves, vending transcripts instead of tom-toms. And yet, it is moving. There's no denying it. Marching through these beaming parents, I'm ambushed by memories of my own, Walter and Maria, because this is where they left me, let me go; this is where things passed beyond their control. After this, I'd never be home again for good.

We sit on folding chairs, the old-timers—Lentz among them—up front. I'm tucked away a couple rows back, out of sight of the audience, and, though the realization comes too late to help me out today, I see that it's possible to read a magazine back here, if you tuck it under your robe, or work a Sunday *Times* crossword puzzle, no problem.

The speeches are friendly, wise, and long. Provost Browning talks about baseball, baseball and war, baseball and life, closing with a line I've heard in other years, welcoming the freshmen on behalf of "the finest liberal arts faculty in the country." I make a note to remind myself to ask him what on earth he meant by that.

Anne Ponder, dean for academic affairs, brings a motherly approach to the proceedings, bucking up parents for that moment, just a few hours away, when they'll climb in their cars and leave their kids at Kenyon. She speaks for memory. "Surrender to this moment," she counsels. "Be held by it. Here you are beneath these trees. Come to Kenyon and be transformed."

I wonder what the freshmen make of all this. Months later, when I've gotten to know some of them, I'll ask them. "I reflected on living without my parents," one of them will say. "And I thought, this is how I pictured Princeton. Then I pictured graduation, four years away, and I was happy. I remember the way the sun came down through the trees, everybody looked like they had scales on them, the way the shadows hit them. And the faculty—you guys looked like warlocks."

"We're sitting there and it's *hot!*" another will recall, "and there's a long speech about rafting. And I wonder, is there a point? We'd rather be unpacking and he's talking about white-water rafting."

The white-water rafting speech comes from Craig Bradley, dean of students, who takes a summer vacation adventure and turns it into a long, loving metaphor for the four-year passage through college: treacherous rapids, occasional quiet pools, menacing rocks, unseen underwater obstacles. If you saw *Deliverance,* you get the idea. A funny thing happens while all this is going on, though; at first I think it is just me, but later I will find more than one professor who was thinking the same thing. In Bradley's metaphor, we professors are the students' guides and pilots on their risky voyage; when they capsize, founder, get turned around in whirlpools, we're there to rescue them. No way, I think. We *are* the rapids, we are the boulders, and I, personally, am a sunken, rotting log, half in water, half out, with a sharp, infectious branch aimed right at the soft plastic underbelly of a kayak full of summer campers, a cargo of entitlement headed my way! An unworthy thought! Dismiss it. It's a reaction, maybe, to the whole tenor of the afternoon, the suggestion that a deal's been made, an implied entente between college and customers that goes something like this: You freshmen have come to us because you think we're good, and if you think we're good, then you must be good. Conjugate it now: I am good, you are good, we are good. Did we say good? No—it's too fine an afternoon for that, parents looking on, bells tolling for all of us. Let's say *excellent.* At least for now.

Phil Jordan closes the show, noting that this very crop of incoming freshmen is "among the finest entering classes" in Kenyon's history. "The likelihood of disappointment," he says, "is small."

And out we march. Back at the dorms, the parents are pulling out. Roommates' parents exchange farewells the same way in-laws do at weddings: warmly enough, but not so warmly that they'll be stuck if their kids end up hating each other.

※

A WORD about this dormitory apartment I'm paying my alma mater $249 per month for. It's got a bedroom with a linoleum tile floor and one of those off-white acned ceilings you associate with budget motels. It's got a bathroom: I won't need to use the one in the dormitory. There'll be no showering with students, no toilet-to-toilet banter. It's got a living room with a stained, burned orange carpet—not *burnt* orange, as in interior decorator language, but *burned* orange, as in somebody dropped a cigarette before passing out. There's a kitchen area that comes with matching mousetraps. Other than a sign on the refrigerator that holds me responsible for any damage and a sign in the bathroom that advises me not to flush tampons in the toilet, the place is a little on the austere side. I've got a chair and desk, a second green chair with springs hanging out, like a muffler off a clunker car, and a brown couch that's leaking some kind of sawdust on the floor. It's the kind of housing you'd expect to get if you were a failed but unfireable government employee who made one mistake too many and got sent for punishment to Guam.

Max doesn't respond much to this new world of ours. Lethargy perhaps. Not even the students who fuss over him make much of an impression, but, then again, campus dogs are pretty blasé about students. They sense, it seems, how many of them there are, give up on trying to tell them apart, take them for granted, and suspect them of brown-nosing.

At night, Max and I drop in on the evening dorm meeting. I introduce myself and Max and tell them I'm writing a book they might be in. The sooner I tell them, the sooner they forget it, I reason. I tell them that I'm not a college official. I don't work for the dean of students, for campus security forces, for the college counseling service. But I'll be around, and I like to talk. That's about it. I won't be trailing them, especially during the first weeks. I've decided to keep my distance for a while, not to hover. They're sorting each other out now.

After the dorm meeting, there's a hall meeting. The upper-class resident adviser tells the freshmen to avoid drugs absolutely, to avoid alcohol sort of—i.e., don't get caught outside your room with an open container—and never, never, never play with the fire alarms or extinguishers. "It's not worth it, guys."

I go to my room and—since there's no particular preparation for this semester's writing workshop—sit down to reread Fred Exley's *A Fan's Notes*, which I'll be teaching next semester. Dense, self-indulgent, unchronological, unhappy, it figures to be a hard sell: college students have limited patience with losers. I start marking passages, making connections, and it's nice, knowing I'm back where I started, or it would be if I could hear myself think because right outside the window the guys from Lewis Hall, Kenyon's last all-male dorm, are bonding with the women from Norton Hall across the way. The resident advisers have devised "ice breakers." The guys throw neckties into a pile, and the girls take a tie and have to locate its owner, and then they chat. Or they all write down their most embarrassing moment—and bond over that. It goes on till nearly midnight, and then an ice cream truck pulls up on the lawn.

Not much sleep comes to me. After the ice cream, they shift to beer, rampaging up and down the halls. In the morning, the trash cans are filled with empties, cheap brews like Old Style and Old Milwaukee (Old Swill, Old Mill). Right now, it feels like a long time till May. Isn't it strange that an austere stillness pervades our memories of college, like a movie that's lost its soundtrack? But this dormitory is wired for sound; it's like the inside of a jukebox that's got all selections playing at once. Worse yet, we've got guitarists out on the quad, any number of them, and a really bad trumpet player. Now I know why people gave me that look, when I told them where I was living. "Macho hormonal youths," sniffed a female junior. "The nastiest place on campus," the night watchman told me. "A kind of a fraternity-prelude dorm," said the Peirce Hall janitor.

🌿

REPUTATIONS ARE AMAZING THINGS. It's not just how long they last—as in college reputations—but how quickly they get around—as in teacher reputations. These freshmen have been in college for all of three days. Classes don't even start until next week. Yet here they are, out on the lawn between Norton and Lewis, sitting around in Adirondack chairs or shagging that thing—is it a ball?—that lacrosse players throw around, and the whole atmosphere is country club, nineteenth hole, and what they are talking about is professors, English Department professors, colleagues of mine, who's good, who's bad. "People get together," a freshman tells me. "'Who are you gonna take?' someone asks. And someone else will say, 'He's an asshole,' or, 'He's really good,' or, 'He's really, *really* good, but you're going to have to work hard!'" They know that Tim Shutt is lively and friendly, that Lentz is fine but tough, and that another member of the department I hear has been having troubles is a must-to-avoid. "Is it true," they ask me, "that he was asked to leave?"

It's freshman registration day. This is when the dream of walking into a popular course with a legendary professor collides with the reality of alphabet roulette, closed sections, waiting lists, second choices, third choices. Early afternoon, I hang out in Sunset Cottage, watching the computer screen with the English Department secretary, Barb Dupee. It's a lot like watching election returns, results changing throughout the day as we get hourly updates from the Registrar's Office. Some sections of English 1–2 fill up instantly, sometimes with preregistered sophomores. Others barely move. It's a matter of time slots, reading lists, and reputations. The early returns are worth watching, but after that it gets less interesting. Demand exceeds supply, and all thirteen sections of eighteen students eventually fill.

Upper-class registration is trickier. Modern courses and creative writing are snapped up quickly. English majors get preference over other students, and one of the melodramas that results is the effort, often desperate, usually in vain, of a nonmajor to get in. One guy, a chemistry major back from a junior year in Leningrad, keeps dogging me for a place in my fiction writing course, which has twelve people already enrolled and eight on the waiting list. He's just the sort of character I'd like to admit: these non-English majors are often wild cards, loose cannons, and they can light up a room. They don't care about the latest critical dance steps being taught in graduate school English departments; they just like to read and want a chance to write. But my class is full. I send him to another professor, who sends him someplace else, and when I meet him this afternoon and ask how he's done he says he's gotten screwed. He hands me a registration schedule filled with pickup courses he doesn't have the least interest in. Wanting to get away— there's nothing I can do for him—I suggest that this was part of the cost of going abroad, the cost of Leningrad. "No," he shakes his head. "It's not Leningrad. The problem is here. I'm paying $20,000 a year, I'm a senior, and I want to take some English."

Another student is luckier. Phil Church, the department chair, calls me into his office and says he's in a bit of a spot. A student had written to have his name put on the list for my course. It didn't happen somehow, and now Phil is asking if I'd do him a favor: let the student into my course, ahead of the others on the waiting list, and what we'll do is call it independent study, English 94. The student, it turns out, is a childhood cancer victim who's been in and out of Kenyon for years, a tenacious kid who's determined to make the most of the time that he has. It may not be much. He's had a recurrence of cancer, a brain tumor, and now he's just about blind. I saw him sitting in Phil's office the other day, accompanied by a seeing-eye dog, a black Labrador, who may outlive his master. The kid's body, Phil tells me, can't take much more treatment. He wants my course, or a spin-off version of it, to be part of his limited load. I say sure. The kid's name is Mike Stone.

❦

"HOT, SEXY, AND SAFER." The signs are all over campus. The *Kenyon Newscope* offers more: "Hot, Sexy, and Safer presentation by nationally known entertainer Suzi Landolphi on Friday evening, August

30 in Rosse Hall at 7 P.M. This could be the best sexual experience of the year." The place is packed when I arrive, the Fine Young Cannibals pounding out "She Drives Me Crazy." The only seat I can find is in the very last row.

Ms. Landolphi bounds on stage, athletic, lively. She's a performance artist, it turns out, vaudevillian, comedian, and—in large part—evangelist on behalf of understanding AIDS, feminism, honest communication, and condoms. She's against machismo, homophobia, and "society's way of putting people in categories." When a couple walk in late, she jokes about coming late, better coming late than never coming at all, and maybe they didn't even come, they just arrived together. She works the balcony, aiming at guys shouting "yo" and high-fiving each other. She makes the high five herself, shoving her fist in the air. *That,* she says, is dreaming. Then she lowers her fist, mimes a stroking jerk-off motion: *this,* she says, is real life. And so it goes in Rosse Hall: talk about orgasms, cock size, about how HIV positives can live longer if they cut out alcohol, drugs, tobacco, stress. More talk about cocks, called wieners, and vaginas, called nu nus, about AIDS, chlamydia, genital warts. And—the star of the show—condoms. She ends by calling a male student up onstage and asking him to slip a condom over his head, to demonstrate—I guess—how strong condoms are. Another student is asked to taste a condom. He obliges: tastes like toothpaste, he says. Mint flavor, Suzi advises. Banana-flavored condoms are available, too.

❧ *September*

LABOR DAY MONDAY, I drive ten miles down the road to Utica, my favorite small Ohio town. It has a gas station decorated with every Mobil sign ever made, a wall of signs that reminds me of an uncle who covered the inside of his garage with every license plate he was issued, going back to the 1930s. It has Ritchey's—"the luncheonette that time forgot"—where they make brown cows and buffaloes and you sit in booths beneath a stamped-tin ceiling. Marsh Wheeling cigars are for sale at the counter. Sometimes I browse in a wood-floored hardware store, have a beer at a tavern that has shitkicker music on the jukebox, stroll past a grain elevator that advertises "definite feeds for definite needs," eat fried chicken at Watts Restaurant, where they make mashed potatoes from scratch. But not today. Something bad is happening.

I wait outside the vet's office watching Max walk—but slowly, stiffly—on a small patch of grass, both of us wondering what we're doing here. The vet suspects dehydration, exhaustion, change-related upset. A cortisone shot is in order, and some pills. Later that night, Max revives, keeps up with me on a short walk, fetches a stick I throw, not far, outside the dormitory door. But it feels like a short reprieve.

❧

MY CLASS MEETS TONIGHT, September 3. I can feel it all day, in my chest and calves. To blow off my preclass tension, I go running with Lentz. These runs—six miles or so, at an easy ten-minute-per-mile pace—put me back in touch with the country around here. And they add to my sense of how Lentz's life is turning out. Some runs flush out similarities, some bring out differences. He's been teaching here for twenty years. More than half his career is behind him. He's taught thousands of students. This year, getting ready for American literature, he'll reread *Moby-Dick* for the twenty-sixth time. Already he's had a full career, moving from rookie phenom to star regular to designated hitter/first base, where he'll stay, lacking managerial ambitions. If it ended tomorrow, it would have been enough. I can't say I feel the same way about myself.

Odd couple we make. His well-received first novel was followed, a few years later, by a second that did less well, although dozens of Kenyon students still relish the opening pages, an explicit sex scene involving a one-eyed Confederate officer and his obliging wife. The last few years, he's been wrestling with a massive "If the South had won the Civil War . . ." novel that hasn't been published yet: it's as if he'd written those eight hundred pages for himself. Someday, there'll be a Lentz chair, or dorm, or prize, or all three, I predict. But sometimes I worry about the "local hero" syndrome, the way Kenyon simultaneously gilds and embalms. I worry that he might be cast as Kenyon's Mr. Memory. Those are my worries. Not his.

We jog down the college hill, cross Route 229 and the Kokosing River, and turn onto what's left of the railroad that used to run through here. Trains are history now, those midnight whistles gone the way of dormitory maids, commons waiters, polo and flying clubs, literary debating societies, freshman beanies, mandatory assemblies, required chapel, classes meeting on Saturdays. They've pulled up the rails, casting ties left and right, grading the roadbed, and covering it with gravel: the Kokosing Gap Bicycle Trail. It's not open—they haven't paved it yet—but the gravel surface is springy and inviting. We head toward Mount Vernon.

When Lentz graduated from a tiny prep school back in Alabama, he chose Kenyon because he wanted to get out of the South, meet people from other parts of the country. In 1960 you could still travel to college by train: his route went from Birmingham to Chicago to Mount Vernon. Arriving at Kenyon, his reactions weren't so different from mine. "At first," he says, "I was slightly envious of those students who'd gone to famous prep schools. The Gunnery. Phillips Exeter. Places I'd been wondering about ever since reading *The Catcher in the Rye*."

When five hundred males showed up in the middle of nowhere, there was a sense—once the initial shock passed—that you had to make Kenyon work with what was there. What was there was forty faculty members. You justified each other. That was the only way. Running together now, graduates of an all-male school—I had three dates in four years at Kenyon—we can't talk about girls we used to know. And the less said of dance weekends—the crash of chairs through ancient leaded windows—the better. We talk about our teachers.

"The faculty in those days were very powerful, very vivid kinds of personalities, larger than life," Lentz says. "They wore flannel pants, tweed coats, knit ties. The model must have been the Oxford don. They took seriously the idea of providing a kind of social world for us. It's demeaning to say they were parents. But they made sure we had access to adult conversation. Part of their being professors was having a kind of vividness. Not characters but—what's a better word?—personalities. It was less a profession than a kind of calling, less a career than a kind of living."

If someone had stood up at the college's opening banquet last Friday night and suggested that current faculty were less vivid, people would have protested. They'd point to Lentz, who often—inadvertently—cows new faculty and terrorizes students. Just last year, a college guidebook quoted a student describing him as "blindingly brilliant." It was a dubious compliment, Lentz thought, in a trade that aims at making students *see*. What's missing, maybe, is that Lentz once would have been regarded as a central figure, a model. Today he's admired but not necessarily imitated. His loyalty to Kenyon and his commitment to teaching are absolute. And rare. Newcomers look at the college more critically, measuring it against ambitions they might not realize here.

A couple miles down the trail, we spot a shelf of land across the river, a colony of shacks and trailers, junked cars and mean dogs, the sort of place that generates student rumors of incest, idiocy, evil. Lights burning in windows all night long indicate Satan worship, students whisper. By day, though, the place looks tired, it inspires guilt, not fear. We run on, and the talk turns to a major Lentz concern in recent years: students who cheat. I gather from other sources that Kenyon's gotten a user-friendly reputation in dealing with this kind of misconduct. This year, Lentz heads the academic infractions committee, and he hopes to tighten things up.

If a faculty member spots something, it goes to the department head, then to the academic dean, then sometimes to the infractions committee, then back to the academic dean. Penalties range from expulsion to suspension to course failure to failure on the paper. If there's a question, it's usually less about guilt or innocence—we're not dealing with criminal masterminds here—so much as extenuating circumstances. Several years ago, Lentz—who feels personally insulted by such things—pressed charges against a student who'd based two papers on *Cliff's Notes*. The student's papers, Lentz said, showed "a considerable stylistic dexterity in rearranging *Cliff's Notes* into fairly plausible 'term papers,' and virtually no knowledge of the literary texts with which she was supposedly dealing." The student, a stressed senior with a troubled history, showed up at the academic infractions hearing with a couple sympatico professors. When all the pleading was done, Lentz was permitted to give an F on both papers but—stunningly—ordered to award a grade of D for the course. That D was the difference between the student's graduating and not graduating. That D was also the difference between Lentz's attending and not attending commencement ceremonies that year. "I do not believe that the Kenyon degree is to be used as some kind of mental therapy," he wrote the provost, "or that mental distress is one of the things for which the degree is to be awarded."

We come to a railroad trestle and turn back, passing the Appalachian colony again, heading for the college, leaving the zone of hubcaps and harelips, heading for a hill of pink and green. Lentz wants to make sure I don't get the wrong idea from this talk of plagiarism. It's not just Kenyon, it's not even especially Kenyon. He doesn't want to hurt Kenyon, talking honestly with me. Hell, he can't sit through a losing Kenyon football game without dark, fourth-quarter mutterings about how those guys across the field slip under-the-table money to recruits—"behemoths"—we wouldn't consider accepting. It's not about the college, this cheating business, it's what's happened to the business of being a professor.

"Faculty have been encouraged to remove themselves, to disengage somewhat from a full, complete, intense commitment to students," he says. "We're teaching less, there's less emphasis on faculty keeping office hours and attending meetings, more celebration of publication and other accomplishments. Students are aware of that, aware of it when you go from asking for four papers to asking for one, aware of it when you go from ten office hours a week to two. That suggests disengagement. Things slide, a student gets in a bind . . ."

❧

I VISITED Denham Sutcliffe's grave a couple days ago. He's not buried on campus, in the college cemetery. He ended up in a less imposing place on the outskirts of town, a place where farmers repose, the same names you see on mailboxes and county road signs. The dates don't get revised: 1913–1964. I wondered why he picked this place. Was he saving money? He'd been poor, the kind of poor you never forget. Maybe that was it. Or was he keeping his distance, at last, on the college he had served? I'd give a lot to know how he saw his life here, whether the commitment he made, that Lentz is making now, worked out for him. Another thing: I realize there's still part of me that fears getting called into his office and asked to explain what I've done with my life, all those years since then. He was never an easy grader.

Two photos of Denham Sutcliffe hang over the fireplace in the Sutcliffe Room, where my writing seminar meets tonight. One of them, from well before my time, shows him sitting at the counter of a used-book store he used to run. The other shows the man I remember, sitting in his office, leaning back in his chair, ready to launch a sentence, something devastating, maybe about the preposterous idea of spending one's junior college year in Europe. "Studying natural history," Sutcliffe used to say, "is not the same thing as going to the zoo." About half the junior class goes overseas these days.

Photos of Kenyon professors line the walls, joined by a whole gallery of writers who've been associated with the place: John Crowe Ransom, Robert Lowell, E. L. Doctorow, Randall Jarrell, William Gass, Peter Taylor, and others. There's a connection, I suppose, between those photographs and this "English 3: Introduction to Fiction Writing" course that's about to begin. But it's tricky. How do you match the expectations generated by those pictures with the reality of a department that is mainly a teaching department and definitely not a nest of heavyweight critics, poets, writers? Can you risk disappointing those kids who come to Kenyon expecting to learn to write from writers? Can you risk obliging them? How many creative writing courses can you— should you—offer? And how do you balance the demand for elite writing courses against the screaming need for basic composition courses?

There's a lot of looking each other over after I walk in. It's like a blind date, times twelve: *Am I in for a bummer?* I try to mix firmness and good humor. I warn that this is not a conventional academic course, that their notes won't amount to anything, there's no test, no final exam, no required reading. It's not a skills course either, like pottery or baking, that you move through step by step, beginner, intermediate, and beyond. It's immersion in a process that will raise them up and take them down. There'll be vast mood swings. There'll be advice that sounds contradictory: I'll be telling some people to slow down, others to speed up. I'll want less of one thing and more of something else. I'll say different things at different times, and I won't always be right. They may be more talented than I am. I grant that possibility. They may be luckier. That's easy to concede. They may be just as smart. But I've been smart longer. That's all.

I suggest they keep journals, which will put them in the habit of writing, but I've decided not to require journals or ask that they be turned in: in the past, I've had beefs about privacy. Add to this the fact—which I tell them—that I'm writing a book and the journals are unworkable. I tell them that this course is writing for an audience. If they're out for therapy, catharsis, self-expression, they might as well stay home and get well there. Fellow students are an audience, even the stupid ones; they're all readers, and if writers hear dumb, resentful things, well, that's how it is outside Gambier. Take the necessary hits. And don't be dismayed if, early on, someone writes something I love. That happens. Usually it's something from a drama major, glibly familiar with dialogue, able to improvise a scene. But things even out. Don't worry about talent yet; don't wait for inspiration, ever. Write. Don't aspire to perfect openings. If you do, you'll never finish. Just write.

Interest perks when I offer what I say will be my only comments about grading. The first thing I say is that everyone has to be in it for a grade; pass-fail students are slimy. Grade inflation has gotten out of hand, I declare, and eventually someone will have to call in all this debased paper that colleges are printing and issue some solid, gold-based currency. But not me. Not here. Not now. Because I don't think I should begin reform by beating up on my students, especially when they're taking a chance on a workshop class that doesn't respond to conventional academic stimuli. So, get right down to it, my grades will probably land where everybody else's do, in that crowded zone from A minus to C plus.

We'll begin in the shallow end of the pool, doing exercises. I ask them to write something that happens in Gambier, a scene, a vignette, whatever. Next, I'll hand out copies of the classified personal ads from *New York* magazine and ask them to imagine the conversation that a response to one of those ads would generate. That's for dialogue. Later, I'll ask them to give me a "day in the life" of someone they worked with in a summer job. I'm interested in patterns of a workday, the lingo, the tricks of a trade, the goofing off, relations with coworkers, customers, bosses. Exercises like this will take up half the course.

Memory of our first session is dominated by Mike Stone. We talked afterwards. He has terminal cancer, he says, wiggling quotation marks with his fingers as he says those awful words. It first showed up at the age of seven—rhabdomyosarcoma—a tumor in the skeletal muscle around an eye. Large doses of radiation cured the tumor but led to complications, stroke, vision loss, paralysis, speech difficulty. Stone coped. Two years ago cancer was back in a new form, fibromyosarcoma, which led to eleven hours of experimental surgery. "Worrying about dying wasn't bad enough," Stone says. "I looked up during the operation and I was in a theater, with people looking down at me from above. I'm a guinea pig."

The operation worked, and Stone has returned to Gambier, a short, beat-up kid with the manners of a middle-American humorist, low-key and understated. He's deaf in one ear, blind in one eye, almost blind in the other, which affords him a narrow tunnel of vision that has the clarity of plate glass in a shower door. His body can't take much more. "If the cancer comes back again," he says, "I'll pop off." Meanwhile, he wants to try writing, wants to be challenged. "I want to turn out something that's not an essay Professor Sharp can say he's seen twenty-five times before."

❧

STONE SAYS he came to Kenyon because he could memorize the place: it is small, manageable, easy for an almost blind man to get to know. A small world that is getting smaller, by the day, for my dog. First the English Department was too far to go, then the History building, where I have my office this year, and now all he can manage is a slow, lurching circuit around Lewis Hall. The least irregularity in the ground, a ditch or a rise, even a scattering of tiny crab apples, throws him off balance. Spinalytis deformans, arthritis basically, a spur of bone coming off the cervical vertebra behind that much petted head. Not treatable, not curable. So I scan my appointment book and look for a day, a little later in the week, that will be the day he dies. A day with no office hours, no teaching.

❧

"THIS IS MY TWENTY-SECOND YEAR of teaching 'Tintern Abbey,'" Ron Sharp remarks. We're sitting with a couple other faculty members at the regular Thursday lunch—$2.25 for all you can eat—in a function room below Peirce Hall. It's only been a couple weeks, but already the food is getting me down, fried chicken, fried everything, boiled-to-death vegetables, library paste gravies, hockey puck muffins, coffee that you can see through, down to the bottom of the cup. Still, I enjoy talking shop with Sharp. Just named John Crowe Ransom Professor of English, Sharp has a solid reputation as a teacher, specializing in the romantics, and he's kept publishing, just recently coediting the *Norton Anthology of Friendship* with Eudora Welty. Phil Jordan puts Sharp on a short list of Kenyon faculty who've managed to reconcile teaching and research.

"The crisis came in my tenth or twelfth year when another member of the department says, 'It's great, but come on, how many fucking years can you go out and teach it?' He said he couldn't do it anymore, he just couldn't teach 'Tintern Abbey' again. I understood what he meant. So the next year I went in and I said, 'Let's start fresh.' I threw away all my notes. I just read the poem, went into class with a few sketchy notes, trying to establish a new relationship with the poem. I went in there, and I was really impressing myself. I was flying! I was impressed that I was thinking on my feet, allowing myself to take such a risk, and to such a profit! And then, almost in midsentence, I had this sudden sinking feeling. I realized that what I was saying was old stuff that I'd said before."

Eventually, Sharp says, he realized that this sense of repetition, year in year out, was unavoidable. "There are no elaborate strategies to avoid it. 'Tintern Abbey' is an important work, it has to be taught. It's my problem, not the students'. There's this very inflated notion, a piety in our field, that great texts can stand multiple readings, that you can always find something new. Shakespeare for me is the one writer who, everytime I read, I have new ideas. 'Tintern Abbey,' though, you're not going to come up with a new way of teaching. I'd be suspicious of it if I did."

I ask Sharp about something that's been dogging me. If texts don't change and lectures come to resemble each other, what accounts for the differences we feel, from class to class? Why is it that one day, primed and pumped, your teaching goes flat? And why is it that sullen, harassed days can be unexpectedly redeemed? There are all kinds of notions about why classes do and don't work. Monday classes are often bad, Lentz thinks, and Friday classes are usually good. And Bill Klein, another English professor, prefers the fifty-minute classes we teach on Monday-Wednesday-Friday to our Tuesday-Thursday eighty-minute sessions. He compares classroom epiphanies to bedroom climaxes: you can accomplish one in fifty minutes but you can't necessarily manage two in eighty minutes.

"To me it's the single most noteworthy thing about teaching," Sharp declares. "You can go into a class incredibly distracted—maybe by illness or a meeting with the provost—and you think, oh shit, and often those are your best classes. Other times you're perfectly prepared, all geared up, and it falls apart, it doesn't fly. The number of variables is astonishing—the weather, the number of colds in a room, the moods. If you have twenty-five kids in a room and if persons A and L are pissed off on a given day—about grades, about a girlfriend, they just don't want to be there—that's picked up by the whole class. If it's a little dark out, if the heat's on too high and everybody's groggy, if I don't smile as I come in the door . . ."

Talking to Sharp, I realize my arrangement with Kenyon—one course per semester, this year—saves me from the worst fluctuations he describes. I can't imagine what it's like to teach three courses at a time. I operate on adrenalin and angst. I can tell stories once and not have to hear myself tell them again. How long would it be, teaching three courses a semester, year in year out, before burnout?

"In the beginning, teaching is so exciting," Sharp says, "you're totally inside the experience. You don't see what you're doing. In retrospect, you realize there's a kind of ego trip which feels grand. You feel witty, brilliant, passionate, intense. You see those adoring eyes. You like that, you want that, you mistake that for success as a teacher. But then something happens—it happened to me. It's almost an instinctual thing. After a while, I just began to feel myself passing up opportunities, prohibiting myself from making certain moves, from telling that hilarious anecdote to drive home a point, using the example which involved my knowing someone famous. I was holding back, and I wondered why. Not out of perversity. Out of an instinctive sense that I had to deepen my abilities. Those clinching anecdotes and illustrative stories are important, but I didn't want to depend on them as much. It has to do with being loved: I didn't want that to be my shtick.

"Two things started to emerge. One was clarity, which is hard. It's hard to be clear as a teacher. We're all verbally adept. We can throw up language that sounds impressive, fog up a subject. My goal was to be lucid, to be clear, so students could grasp distinctions. Also, I wanted to ask more theoretical questions, to think about literature systematically. I wanted students to be more reflective."

Listening to Sharp makes me feel like a rookie. It's as though I'm joyriding downhill in a kid's toy wagon while he, a far more serious pedagogue, labors uphill in a larger vehicle that's got gears, gauges, dials, and pedals I don't even want to know about. He's watching the miles per gallon, making sure the engine doesn't overheat, the windshield wipers work, and the tires hold the road, and here I come toodling past, wind in my hair, every chance I'll go flying into the bushes.

"I have this romantic idea of teaching as gift exchange," he tells me. "What matters is if I reach a few students at a level that transforms them and gets them to see the world in a different way. Gift exchange. Sure, teaching is method and information, but it's something else, a gift, an enrichment of your life, a transformation that you spend the rest of your life discovering. I'm not saying that I put method over substance, that what we teach doesn't matter. But what Perry Lentz got from Denham Sutcliffe wasn't mainly stuff he said in class about *Moby-Dick*. It was a posture about books and living, new categories, relations to larger realities and questions. That kind of teaching only happens with a relatively small number of students, and you do the best you can with the others."

🌿

MAX DIED THIS MORNING, around ten o'clock. I borrowed a car and took him into Mount Vernon and watched, touching him, as a couple syringes of what looked like pink lemonade went into him. He made a half-hearted try at lifting himself off the table. There was some labored breathing, four or five times, as though he'd gotten tired after a run, and then our thirteen years and nine months together were over. When I got back to Gambier, I went running out on Caves Road, nine miles, crying, calling his name, looking for him. Just a few weeks ago, I'd decided that the only emotions worth having were mixed emotions, but I was thinking about Kenyon then. I have mixed emotions about this place and about my friends and my work and myself. Not Max. My feelings for him were unequivocal.

We've had some late rain, too late to save the crops, but the Kokosing is moving again. It still feels like summer, black-eyed susans, daisies, grape, and sumac along the road, butterflies around my head, crows further above, searching for dead things in the fields that farmers are plowing under. I pass abandoned churches—Mount Zion and Quarry Chapel—graveyards remaining after the churches close forever, though markers are broken, weathered to illegibility, some sunken into the ground. A second death. I can smell apples along the road, cow shit, plowed fields. A farmer pulls his pickup to the side of the road, picks hickory nuts off the pavement. A little later on, I see a woman kneeling by a garden at the edge of a barn, listening to Paul Harvey on the radio while she weeds. It seems to me that there are more beer cans along the road now that the students are back.

🌿

"THE BOTTOM LINE," Phil Jordan says, "is that we're no longer holy. Colleges and universities have become the same sort of messy, vulgar, misbehaving institutions that America is used to. Or, at least, they're perceived that way."

It's the morning after Max died, and I'd thought of canceling my appointment with Kenyon's president. Then I decided I needed to be out of the dorm room with the stippled ceiling and burned orange carpet. Everyone's been decent. When I stopped by Sunset Cottage, Phil Church, our department chair, came up to the balcony where I was sitting, not wanting to be seen, and I fell apart in front of him. "You've got to remember, they live faster than we do," he told me softly. And invited me over for dinner on Saturday night. Condolences fill my mailbox. Sheila Jordan quotes a poem by Czeslaw Milosz. But I still keep looking for Max. Phil Jordan's just returned from a retreat on the Georgia coast, a meeting with trustees and senior staff. Evidently, they spent a lot of time talking about money. Tough times are coming. "We're not talking about going broke," Jordan says, "but we're going to hunker down through lean times."

Almost all talk about Kenyon turns into money talk. It's almost as if some law were at work: the less money you have, the more you talk about it. Conversations that start by being about something else—food quality in Peirce Hall, closed courses, high prices in the bookstore, the paucity of black students, the college's flabbergasting inability to induce someone like Colin Powell to address graduating seniors—all turn on money. You can't not be aware of it.

The college has three sources of money. One is the income from its endowment of about $35 million, $25 million of which is actively managed, the rest tied up in various ways. That $35 million is low. It's low by Ohio standards: Denison, down the road, has $82 million, Oberlin nearly a quarter billion. Amherst and Haverford, the two eastern schools that topped Kenyon in that ancient *Chicago Tribune* survey, respectively, have endowments of $273 million and $84 million.

No one's really clear on how things got this way. Granted, when a railroad engine turns a Deke pledge into sashimi and enrollments drop for ten years, that hurts. When your central dormitory goes up in flames, that costs you. Disasters aside, though, it seems that Kenyon has been contentedly small and poor for much of its history. That was its character, and character is fate. Aggressive fund-raising violated Kenyon's sense of itself. "For a long time, the board of trustees didn't care about raising money," a college official tells me. "They wrote checks. And the older faculty let it be known that fund-raising was hokey. Kenyon was so good that people ought to come forward with checkbooks in hand."

Kenyon no longer minds asking for money, but the gap between it and other schools that asked earlier and received sooner threatens to widen as the rich get richer, faster, and Kenyon struggles to hold its modest position, aiming—with a recent change of investment managers—for a return of 5 percent, after inflation.

Gifts are next: bequests, charity, alumni donations, the kindness of strangers. There are Cinderella stories all through the liberal arts gulag about how a pharmaceutical tycoon, an investment banker, an aluminum magnate descended upon a small college and enriched it beyond imagining. That's what it takes, multimillion-dollar gifts, to move a college up a notch. Small gifts help a college keep pace, monster gifts move it forward.

These days, Kenyon receives between $4 million and $5 million a year in gifts, about half from trustees and alumni. That figure should keep growing, if past experience holds. Kenyon keeps track of its 11,000 graduates, as well as of parents and friends. There's a list of 863 "major donors," and a shorter list of 150 people who might be good for $100,000 or more. Those are the ones who get what's called "the treatment." The five "I"s. It begins with Identification—a name—and goes to Information—files, clippings, real estate records—and from there to Interest. What does the donor care about? Poetry? Theater? Football? Steps four and five are Involvement and Investment. The donor serves on something—the board of trustees, the alumni council, a committee or a panel—and makes a gift. But competition for gifts is getting tougher. Education competes with other nonprofit sectors, religion, environment, human services, health. And the gift-givers themselves aren't exactly a day at the beach. They have opinions about coeducation, diversity, gender studies, political correctness, fraternities, college architecture. They like being listened to. When the college disappoints them, they warn that they're revising their wills.

What the customers pay is the third source of money. And with endowment remaining small and return on endowment being . . . well . . . just okay, with gifts climbing an increasingly steep slope, I get a feeling that the customers are about to take a hosing. This year, Kenyon's tuition and room and board came to $19,425. That's before books, beer, transportation, popcorn, pizza, which add a couple thousand to the bill. Though not up there with Bennington or Sarah Lawrence, both above $23,000, it's uncomfortably high. And Jordan signals that it's going higher.

"When we lose kids, we lose them to more expensive places," he tells me. "It's tricky—public attitudes are so ambivalent—but there's something to the connection between price and quality. Our price increases in the past have not attracted a lot of comment. When a child comes to Kenyon and lights up and says, 'This is the place!' parents don't say, 'I'm sorry, it's $500 more than your second choice.' Or $2,000 more."

After I leave Jordan, the prospect of a price hike nags at me. An expensive college is getting more expensive. The administration will defend the boost in tuition, and it'll do so successfully; what's more, I don't doubt that they need the money and will spend it wisely. Still, the implications are disturbing: Kenyon's low endowment and resulting 78 percent tuition dependence—i.e., paying for this year's college out of this year's money—mean the college is obliged to educate the people who can afford it, to humanize the rich rather than enrich the poor. "Kids with scholarships and demonstrable need are in the minority," one former Kenyon professor, John Ward, told me last summer. "And that defines Kenyon's teaching position, which is trying to challenge the assumptions and principles of the upper middle class. What results is a dialogue between America's upper middle class and the imperatives of academe."

There's more. Customers start looking at the college they're paying for critically, even cynically. They resent parking tickets, registration fees, the five dollars per box the college charges them to store their stuff over the summer. They start to wonder about these scholarship students the college fusses over. It's called the Robin Hood factor: robbing the rich to pay the poor. The college's annual budget of $35 million includes $6 million for scholarships, and—well, you figure it out—wouldn't it be a couple thousand less per student if no one rode for free? These are unworthy thoughts, but they occur. Check out that group of black students, sitting together at a table in Peirce Hall, almost all of them on college aid, laughing and whispering, not that they don't have a right to do that—hell, fraternities sit together—but when you're the one who's paying, the question comes up: is this diversity worth it?

🌿

KENYON'S BLACKS — a couple dozen of them, and a handful of Hispanics—huddle around a fireplace at the end of a daylong orientation-retreat at a Girl Scout summer camp a couple miles out of town. The day's been organized by Mila Collins, a black assistant dean of students who's director of multicultural affairs. She knows about adjustment here. "I cried every night for a week or two after I arrived," she says. "It was a beautiful campus, with offices in houses, but it reminded me of Mr. Rogers' neighborhood." Besides Collins, Kenyon's minority student apparatus includes a part-timer, Frank Hale, who is something called "executive assistant to the president for multicultural affairs," and a black admissions officer, Matt Davis. They're all supposed to get black students to come to Kenyon and stay.

It's not an easy sell. A costly rural college with limited scholarship money and an overwhelmingly white student body and faculty—four black faculty members—has the odds against it. There are lots of blacker colleges blacks can go to, and better colleges for better blacks. That's the conventional wisdom anyway: a black who can succeed at Kenyon has what it takes to succeed at Amherst or Harvard. So why come here, playing Jackie Robinson, if you can go to a cheaper place that's more congenial or get a free ride at someplace more prestigious?

There were just three blacks in my class at Kenyon, and though that sounds like a prescription for loneliness, they were judged as individuals. That's all they were. No retreats like this for them. What I see in front of me now is a group, but a small one, well short of that healthy "critical mass" that turns up whenever people talk about minority students at Kenyon. About a hundred blacks would feel right, they say, and Kenyon has around forty. I wonder if it's not just as hard—and lonely—to be part of a small group than to be by yourself. It's the difference between being in a room, alone, and going to a ragged, underattended party. Isn't that the kind of company that misery loves?

I stand around with a couple other professors, chewing room-temperature hamburgers the college food service trucked in. Then it's camp-fire time. The students go around the circle, giving names and hometowns, one by one. It's easy to spot differences: inner city and suburbs; well-adjusted preppies and not-so-sure high school graduates;

kids who are used to dealing with whites, and others who aren't; the ones who'll date anybody, and the ones who'll date only blacks, and others who'll be spending a lot of time by themselves. "I tell students that if you feel you're going to come here and fall in love with a black man or woman," Mila Collins says, "that's probably not going to happen."

After introducing themselves, the students perform skits. They sing "Row, Row, Row Your Boat" and "Lean on Me." They toast marshmallows. And then, while the fire is still blazing, they pile into jeeps and vans and head back to Kenyon. It's as if they want to sort things out at large, back on campus, before they decide how—or whether—to connect with other minority students.

I drive home with Ted Mason, a black English professor, and since it's still early, still daylight, we cruise around in his pickup truck, prospecting the roads that we might want to go running on. And we talk about blacks at Kenyon. Mason's take on black students surprises me, and if the black students round the campfire had heard it, it might surprise them. There's something about the confluence of black students and Kenyon College that bothers the hell out of him.

"There are ways that blacks and many other students come here unprepared," he grants. Blame it on the decline of public schools, the impact of television, the overall dumbing-down of America, but Mason estimates that, over the past ten years, entering students have lost about a grade, i.e., the level of preparedness has slipped down to that of a high school junior. But instead of remedying these problems—with a take-no-prisoners course in grammar, say—we schmooze, we sympathize. "We read problems of blacks primarily as problems of psychological adjustment. There's a kind of presumption that black students are going to have trouble, that academic problems are related to adjustment. It's an attitude that sees black experience as dysfunctional from the get-go."

What happens next is predictable: the college that coddles is the college that gets conned. Black students develop what Mason calls "trickster strategies" to get by: "an odd combination of self-deprecation and gamesmanship" that wouldn't play at Harvard or Yale but works well enough at a place that factors misery into grades, anticipates depression, opens itself to special pleading, and, if you're black, enables you "to perpetuate the mythology of your own isolation."

And it's not necessary. That, to Mason, is the saddest part of all. These students can survive, playing straight up, meeting the college on its own rather lenient terms. "They come here not expecting to do well," he says. "It's an estranged environment, they think. 'What am I doing here?' And the damnable thing is that, except for the top 5 percent of the class, most students don't work very hard. Black students fool themselves. They think that other students are doing well, that they're world beaters, and that's not true."

After Mason drops me off in Lewis Hall, I sit outside for a while, watching students toss a frisbee through the twilight. Someone carries a case of Old Milwaukee into the dorm. "We can't enforce drinking rules," an assistant dean of students told me. "We don't have the people to check rooms or take fingerprints off door knobs." Sitting there, I decide that someone should erect billboards in black neighborhoods across America, the same billboards that now advertise Nike shoes or Colt-45 malt liquor. The signs would show a place like Kenyon, in all its autumn beauty, and pass along this message in six-foot letters: YO! IT'S NOT THAT HARD.

❧

I RUN THE AIR CONDITIONER all night, not because it's hot in Lewis Hall. Actually, nights are fairly cool, and, even if they sweltered, the air conditioner wouldn't make a degree of difference. It's only good for noise, a wheezing rattling sound that screens me from the doings outside my window or inside, up and down the hall. Still, I hear things. Giggles, footsteps, a sudden bellow of outrage: "*Who the fuck was in Gund 105!*"

We had a close call in Gund the other night when a freshman put his fist through the plate glass covering a fire extinguisher, severing an artery. There was an astonishing amount of blood all over the carpet, just about impossible to clean, the maids complain, and a dark stain on the steps leading down to the parking lot. The kid—one of the sweetest dispositioned on the hall, so far as I can tell—is going to be okay. He'd been drinking, and it was something about a girl. This morning, I sign a card for Mike Stone, who's in the hospital. He was having headaches, and at first they suspected sinus trouble. But there's a tumor in his frontal lobe, in back of the right eye, and Stone's going in for surgery he probably won't survive. Before going to the hospital, Stone made his way into the Church of the Holy Spirit, where he knew they'd be having a prayer service for him. He left his cane behind, on the altar, and a poem.

Here I leave my staff
For on You shall I lean;
Your guidance shall I follow;
Lead on, All-Mighty Shepherd!

🌿

"I KNEW ABOUT LENTZ because everyone knows about Lentz," a
freshman tells me, a kid named George who lives down the hall in
Lewis. "Perry Lentz sounds like a professor in a movie or something.
You hear he's the hardest, he's the best English teacher. Now I'm not
one to jump into an uphill situation, but I signed up for the class.
Having the best English teacher at a school that's among the best,
whatever grade I got, I'd feel good about myself."

Lentz decided it would be okay if I sat in on his English 1–2 course.
When I first asked his permission, I didn't realize how touchy professors
are about visitors. It's as if you were setting up a camera in their
bedrooms—no, make that bathrooms—recording the groans, farts, and
flushings that accompany the passage of classics through students' di-
gestive tracts. But Lentz said yes, on the condition that I wait a couple
weeks, until he'd gotten preliminaries out of the way. That was all right
with me, but I wondered what those first classes were like. I ask around.

"Oh, God, that first day," George complains. "I don't know what he
took for breakfast. He was so hardball that first day, with his *rubrics*.
I'd never heard the word before. What's a *rubric?* No hats in class, if
you're late don't come in at all, not even if it's 10:31. Plagiarism went
on for half a page. And then he asks us to sign this agreement. If you
can't live with these rubrics, he says, I'll help place you in another class.
He's almost asking us to leave. That's when I knew I would stay. He's
giving us all these ways out. 'I'd still respect you, if you left. I'd be more
than happy to help you.' It was the scariest thing. That first day is
frightening. I tried not to let him know I was intimidated. I would look
pensive, and I sat upright. I wouldn't let him know I was a wreck."

"Everybody looked around that first day, and it was, holy shit, this is
like military school," says Matt, who sits next to George. "You say to
yourself, 'I'm not going to wimp out,' so you stay. But from the first
class I've always been in awe of him. One of the reasons I don't feel bad
about spending $20,000 a year to go here is because I have Perry Lentz
as a teacher. To see this staid conservative person get excited and pace

the room and pound the table and yell—it's a weird dichotomy. It's not what you'd expect from a man who wears the same black tie everyday."

Three days a week, I walk from my office in the History Department to Sunset Cottage, knocking on Lentz's office door to let him know I'll be part of his audience. Downstairs, I drink coffee and sort the departmental mail, wanting to see who's flirting with the University of Virginia, the National Endowment for the Humanities, the Guggenheim Foundation. One day, Ron Sharp hits a trifecta at the mailbox: letters from George Steiner, Martin Esslin, Maynard Mack. Mostly it's junk—publishers hustling textbooks—and I should be ashamed of myself, nosing around like this. At twenty minutes after ten, Lentz steps out of his office, and we head out across campus, past the college cemetery, so crowded these days that you have to be cremated before they let you in. We enter Ascension, the same building where Sutcliffe taught English 1–2, although—like many other places—it's been prettified. The classrooms are air-conditioned and carpeted, the chairs are molded plastic, the blackboard is divided into panels that move on rollers, and the ivy that once covered Ascension is gone. All Kenyon's ivy is gone: they said it was destroying the stonework. It's as though the whole campus had chemotherapy. I enter class first, Lentz pauses for a drink of water and follows.

"He wears all black ties," George says. "Black ties with a plain white shirt or a shirt with black and white pinstripes. He's got a seersucker jacket and a plain jacket and a green 1960s avocado thing, I don't know where he got it. Tan slacks and black slacks. He's got glasses hanging off him, he's got to put them on to read, but he takes them off to look at students. His hair doesn't move. I don't think it could move. I remember his first haircut. It was pitiful. I'd been intimidated by him, but it was pitiful. He got sheared. He looked like a cadet."

Lentz starts talking as soon as he enters, while he moves a lectern up onto the table, opens the window, erases the blackboard. His beginnings tend to be formal. When he throws a pop quiz—what he calls a "recitation"—he asks students to "affix your signature" to a corner of the paper. Giving an assignment, he'll say: "Next Monday, I expect to be in the presence of people who have read the first five chapters of *Gulliver's Travels.*" Turning to text, he'll ask the students to "cast your powerful imaginations on the middle paragraph of page 162."

Having surrounded himself with an aura of authority and discipline, he often, unpredictably, shifts into another mode, personal and vernacular, drawing examples from sports, television, college life. When a student gives an answer that's way off the mark, he'll burst out with, "Oh, give me a break!" And when an answer is wrong but interesting, he'll say, "You're in the right town, but the wrong state." Coming up against a tricky passage, he'll say, "Let's disentangle that in language appropriate to the *National Enquirer* as you stand in the checkout line at Kroger." Soliciting an easy answer, he'll advise, "I'm only looking for a one-yard plunge."

The course began with "The Dead," moved on to some Flannery O'Connor stories. Now he comes to *Gulliver's Travels,* which he's been having some trouble with in recent years. Students these days don't seem to catch Swift's satiric force. The sectarian disputes he ridiculed are, a priori, ridiculous to them. They're not hung up on politics and religion. Satire is a literature of attack, but they have a hard time seeing themselves as targets. Lentz starts the first class with a recitation. What does the term "Big Endian" mean? From there, it's an inventory of the number of Lilliputians—41,000—killed in a dispute about which end of an egg to crack. Why is the war ridiculous? Why is it that Gulliver doesn't see the absurdity of it? "Gulliver doesn't have to—in your term—kiss up to the Emperor" Lentz says. "Why does he do it?"

He establishes the difference between satire and realistic fiction, how fiction draws you into a world and how satire—usually through a fantastic device or premise—obliges you to stand back and take an ironic perspective. Irony compels the reader to state the truth that is not given in the text, and irony is tricky, especially when cultural bearings change. You can't count on Gulliver to set you straight; he's a naive narrator, not a full character, certainly not a hero. Back then to irony, varieties of irony: verbal, dramatic, situational. Sometimes Lentz draws stick figures on the blackboard to make his point. Sometimes he acts out parts, falling into the teensy voice that Mr. Bill used on "Saturday Night Live," then going into a roar to mock the Emperor. Some things work, some don't. More often than he would like, he finds that an attempt at humor—his or Jonathan Swift's—falls flat. He listens in vain for a laugh, a chuckle. *Hello? Anybody out there?* And when he presses the point, explaining *why* something is comical, that makes it worse. *Oh yeah, whatever,* the class sighs, and those are times the McIlvaine Professor of English looks like a kid in a grammar school show-and-tell period who brought in a bird's nest and nobody cared.

Sometimes he's onstage, it seems, sometimes at a lectern, sometimes at a pulpit, but he takes them through the book—the close examination of classic texts that Kenyon's English Department is still known for. He likes to set traps for students, drawing them into agreements that they later regret. He talks, for instance, about those grotesque experiments Swift describes—shoving a hose up a dog's ass, pumping air in, blowing it to pieces—to suggest science gone awry.

"Twenty-five years ago, most students at Kenyon would have been offended by this book," he says. "Most students thought humanity had progressed and that science was part of that. How do you feel now?"

Well, yeah, the students kind of think that sometimes science does get out of hand, and they allow that maybe Swift has a point. Then Lentz pivots. "Swift is driven insane by headaches that could have been cured by . . ." He pauses, drops his voice, a trick that he uses too often, I think, but it works today. ". . . an aspirin. How about that? Do you realize the advantages you are enjoying are unimaginable through most of history? And that they are the results of the science that Swift satirizes?"

On the last day, Lentz tries to pull it all together. "What would Swift's target be today?" he wonders. "Materialism? Self-interest? Self-pity? Perhaps it's the search for power without responsibility. The right to have rights with no concomitant sense of responsibility." He talks about kids in Washington, D.C., averaging ten sexual partners by the age of sixteen. He warns the kids in front of him about insistence on "our godlike rights to enjoy what we want whenever we can enjoy it." He looks at the students. "Watch the unfolding landscape of your college experience. What are your rights? Who are your gods?"

❧

AT LAST the college begins to feel like home. Mornings are lovely, especially on weekends, when all the students sleep late and it's as though someone had dropped a neutron bomb in Gambier. There are more kitchen workers than students at breakfast. Later in the morning, there's a farmers' market on Middle Path, apples and tomatoes, pies and—small miracle—baklava. No place I'd rather be.

In late morning, students start to stir. I'm not forcing friendship, but the dorm is getting used to me. Some of the guys are getting curious. A couple freshmen down the hall show me a copy of *Eddie and the Cruisers* they took out of the library. Another wants to know whether it's possible to write good poetry while you're drunk. I wouldn't know, I say. I've never written good poetry. Someone else is excited about a paper he's writing that compares Ajax to Saddam Hussein, Zeus to

Hitler. The afternoon turns golden and crisp, first leaves falling, and Kenyon loses a football game to Albion in front of a cheerful crowd that's far smaller than what you'd see at an average high school football game. The setting overwhelms them, those warm brown hills beyond the field.

Bit by bit, I grow accustomed to living with students. One of them tells me about booting, which is drinking beer out of athletic shoes. Used, well-worn athletic shoes, aged and ripened and full of beer. "The first bootful tends to be kind of funky," I'm told, "but after that it's not bad." Another student elaborates on "boot tag": As a verb, to boot is to vomit. As a noun, boot *is* vomit. To play boot tag is to vomit on someone, who becomes "it" until he—or she—vomits on someone else. More silly stuff: a junior political science major talks to me about goldfish swallowing.

"The record is forty-four," she says. "They buy them in pet shops."

"Did they stay down?" I ask.

"No."

"Well, did they come up alive?"

"No, the stomach acid gets them, I guess. And when they come up, they come up without eyes."

"Oh."

"Yeah. The eyes are the first to go."

On Sunday, I run into Lewis Hyde, fingering a *New York Times* at the bookstore, not sure whether to spend three dollars for the national edition. He decides to sit down and read the bookstore's copy for nothing. Nice to see that getting a MacArthur Foundation genius grant—$50,000 per year for five years—doesn't change a guy in any important way. There's some other reading in the bookstore that's going to piss people off around here. *U.S. News and World Report*'s much-detested, much-read annual college ranking shows Kenyon slipping. Last year it was in the first decile of national liberal arts colleges, the group that follows just behind the leading twenty-five. Now we've landed in the second decile, slipping into parity with Denison and falling further behind our prestigious albeit crunchy-liberal neighbor, Oberlin.

Ticked off, the college reacts, cranking out a statement that deplores the vulgarity of it all, hints that some other places may be cooking their figures, and argues that as long as a college's financial resources are taken into account, poor Kenyon will never get the respect it deserves. The trouble is, Kenyon was also poor last year, when it ranked higher. Phil Jordan tells visiting Kenyon parents that the survey is "one of the sillier enterprises," a journalistic snapshot, pandering to a natural love of rankings, something designed to sell magazines. And so forth. "In the end, we're sort of mystified as to why this happened," he says, confessing to "a sense of wounded pride." The admissions director, John Anderson, compares the survey to football polls. "I have no objection to someone saying Williams is better than Kenyon, Swarthmore is better than Kenyon, looking at things objectively," he tells me later. "But I do object to someone saying Williams is twenty-seven places better."

※

IN GUND HALL, three students enter the men's room, block the door with garbage cans, put candles around a photograph on the floor, perch on the ledge above the sinks, their feet in water, and conduct a séance in honor of Allen Ginsberg. And at dinnertime, the object of their prayers, tired and travel-worn, walks into a faculty parlor to meet some English Department people who'll dine with him before his performance in Rosse Hall. Conversation is a little stiff at first. We talk about what students have and have not read these days. At Brooklyn College, Ginsberg gives students a list of his favorite authors and then assigns the least-read names. I find myself next to him at dinner—some kind of kosher fish soup, spiceless and punitive—and get him talking about Jack Kerouac. I'll be teaching On the Road next semester, and I can't help wondering why Kerouac's works stick around, even as time takes away writers as good or better, Algren, Dos Passos, Farrell, all squeezed out of the canon, slipping out of cultural recall, while Kerouac resurges in biographies, memoirs, new editions. Ginsberg speaks warmly about his friend: his subtlety as a writer, his personal and stylistic beauty, his vulnerability, and—what he feels has been underrated—his dedication to craft. Comparing him to Fitzgerald, who did not survive his personal crack-up, Ginsberg says that Kerouac kept writing and reading through all his bad times.

What a mutual admiration society they must have been, Neal Cassady, Kerouac, and Ginsberg: the Colorado hustler, the Canuck athlete writer, the homosexual Jew from New Jersey. And, now, look how it turns out: Cassady dead on a railroad track in San Miguel de Allende in 1968; a year later, at home with his mother in St. Petersburg, Kerouac hemorrhages fatally while sitting on a toilet. And this balmy night in September 1991, Allen Ginsberg walks into Rosse Hall—which hasn't been this crowded since the condom lady came to town—and puts on a show. He camps out onstage with a sunflower he picked up along the road. He invites students onstage. He plays a harmonium, sings songs of William Blake and an anti-Reagan calypso of his own composing. He mixes songs and sutras, poems and doggerel. Acknowledging a request from a member of the English Department to read a gay poem, he grosses out the fraternity guys with an ode to pederasty. He charges up the hot crowded hall, loving it and—Kenyon is generous with its standing ovations—getting his love returned. I know there's a lot of showmanship in Ginsberg's performance. But for a little while, Kenyon is what it once was and could be again: a small place that finds glory in writers.

❧

AUTUMN HAS FINALLY COME. I can see right where it landed. Down on Route 229, on a maple tree in front of Hall Farm, suddenly flashing flame-red leaves, starting from the top.

❧ *October*

A NOVELIST FRIEND of mine who teaches writing at another Ohio college divides his students into three groups, the way military medics sort through battlefield casualties. The best students are the slightly wounded: an injection, a bandage, and a splint are all they need. The middling group, more seriously wounded, require immediate help to be saved. They take time. And then there's the back of the pack—"the sucking chest wounds." For them, you can't do more than ease the pain.

This group in English 3 is middling and tightly bunched. There's no one who absolutely has to be in the course and no one who certainly shouldn't. One woman hasn't done anything special in her other classes, I gather, but is discovering a talent for writing, a knack for getting into other people's lives and capturing their voices. And I've got a man who's catching the writing bug right in front of me, authoring a fine early piece about two women deciding to make love, a hard topic but he handled it in a controlled, genial, understated way. Another fellow has written a thoughtful piece set in Malawi. And there's another student, a classic fraternity dude—laid back but talented—who could drive me crazy. He missed a seminar, seems to take off every weekend to hunt something— he was shooting doves in Pennsylvania last weekend. He's facile and nonchalant, but he might be the best-read student in class, and he turns out clean copy. The rest are okay, often lively and vigorous. A lot of them have the same problem I'd have had, taking a fiction writing course at age twenty-one: a love of writing and not much to write about.

The Gambier-based sense-of-place essays went from just okay to pretty good. I'm struck by how wised-up these kids are. More of them have seen *Terminator* than *Citizen Kane*, more have read Stephen King than Updike, but their writing isn't naive, it's prematurely jaded. Forget boy meets girl, loses girl, gets girl back. Or girl gets boy, etc. The more typical pattern is boy snubs girl, girl goes to dorm, binges on food, and bitches, guy gets drunk, vandalizes some college property, and walks home in the rain. Jake and Hannah are popular fictional first names.

There are good things, though. One piece describes a football player who "wedged a wad of paper under the water fountain to make it stay on and stuck his foot up in it, cleaning his toes." Another recounts two women's adventures: "Tonight started as a regular booze binge for us, two girls out on the town, flashing our fake i.d.'s with authority, like g-women on a quest for the most wanted beer in the country." And this, from a story told—alas—from the point of view of a fly, describing college students with "silver bangles and bandannas, their ripped, worn and ancient out-of-style, in-style but always clean clothes."

🌿

CATFISH HUNTER. The Village Market closes at six. What people don't see, looking in at academe, is the life-destroying amount of time we spend in meetings. These meetings are always scheduled after classes, around 4:00 P.M., so while the rest of the world goes home, plays with kids, rakes leaves, we stay behind; teachers, not students, kept after school for punishment. There's always a collective intention to keep things moving—the Village Market closes at 6:00 P.M., remember—and yet we fail. *Rabbit Maranville.* It's good to have something else to do during meetings. You can't read—that's rude—or grade papers. So I make lists. Today I'm listing all the baseball players I can think of with animal nicknames. *Mudcat Grant.* It's our second English Department meeting. Consider this an example of how people who are individually smart act feebly as a group *because they are smart.* The first issue is the reading of ten or so five-page senior honors essay proposals. Last year, I gather, there was agreement that the honors program was disorganized and ought to be shaped up, and the first idea today is that we should *all* read *all* of the proposals. But some people start to wince. Fifteen people reading and commenting on every proposal? That's work. Do we all have to get into the act? Maybe so, it is work, comes the reply, but shouldn't we all at least know who our honors majors are and what they're working on? Yes, someone says, but if we all comment, there's bound to be dissent because there's not enough consensus around this table about what good literary work amounts to and somebody might turn down a project that three other people think is great. Someone then suggests that half the department do the reading. Or five people, or four.

Or—wait a minute—what do we have an honors chairman for? Why not let her do it, her and a couple others maybe. *Andre "the Hawk" Dawson.* Suddenly, we're like a jukebox, overloaded with coins, listening to other people's selections forever before our own tune is played. What are we going to do about some members of the department who've been asked to mentor two or three of these essays while some other members of the department haven't been approached at all? How do we make it up to the people doing double, or triple, duty? Release them from other duties later on? It goes on that way. *Goose Gossage, Goose Goslin, Birdy Tebbets.* We'll have to make extra copies of student proposals, so we all can read them in time. *Ducky Medwick.* That brings us to the use of the xerox machine that sits downstairs, outside the department secretary's office. Phil Church, our chair this year, has calculated that at current rates, we're going way over budget on xeroxing. *Hawk Harrelson.* Last year we were 23 percent over. Some professors are letting creative writing students use the machine to duplicate work that gets passed around in class. Not me. *Phil "the Vulture" Regan.* Others are probably reproducing copyrighted stuff that the college copy center won't touch, since their interpretation of copyright law is strict. *Ron "the Penguin" Cey.* Last year the copy center wouldn't even reproduce a chunk of *King Lear! Moose Haas, Moose Moryn, Moose Skowron, Hoss Radbourne.* It's a phony issue, a colleague exclaims, one of those things that can drive you crazy around here, getting nickel-and-dimed by the administration, which charges us a dime a page when everybody knows it costs maybe two cents. *Harry "the Cat" Brycheen.* Our chair comes up with a few modest proposals about curtailing student xeroxing that we'll end up adopting in another half hour, but meanwhile, we keep rolling along. *Pepper Martin, "Wild Horse of the Osage."* This is the administration's way of getting the chair to do its dirty work for it, policing the department, and that's not right. Let's just keep on doing what we've been doing, and if the administration has a problem, they should come over and meet with *all* of us. *Hippo Vaughn.* "What do they think we're doing?" someone asks. "Xeroxing invitations to Halloween parties?" *Mark "the Bird" Fidrych.* The Village Market closes at six. *Doug "Rooster" Rader . . .*

❧

THESE DAYS the English Department offices are in something called Sunset Cottage, a two-story red-brick building on the edge of campus. It used to house senior professors. Even today, after its conversion into a warren of offices, it retains traces of the old gentility: a dark wood–lined study, a fireplace in today's seminar room, a luxuriant second-story porch I spend lots of time on, in nice weather. This year, there was no office space for me in Sunset Cottage, though. They put me across campus, in a similar residence, headquarters of the History Department. But I check in at Sunset Cottage twice a day, to pick up mail, to drink coffee, and, late this Friday afternoon, to talk to Ron Sharp. As it happens, he's the only one in the whole building. It's just an impression, but it's not just my impression, that the building is less social, the halls less alive, the offices less tenanted than in other years. People used to hang around more, that's all, and I know it probably got annoying, all that hearty intramural bantering, but now people schedule themselves more carefully, maybe because they have more things to do, but I don't like walking into a college building in broad daylight, seeing all those doors closed and locked, sometimes a whole row of them, not even the hall light on, and the place is spooky, like a scene out of *The Shining*.

At our department meeting, Sharp was the one who said there wasn't much agreement in our department about what good work in literature amounts to. I've been wondering what he meant by that, and he begins by telling me about meetings—"torture exercises," he calls them—that the English Department used to have.

"This is back in the days when we were all teaching common texts in English 1–2," he says. English 1–2 used to have a common reading list, I know; now teachers pick the texts they want to teach. "We wanted to see how we were grading, whether anybody was off-base, too tough, too easy. So we'd xerox two or three papers and pass them out. And one guy would give a paper an A and one a D. There was some unanimity in the B-C range, but we almost never gave the same grade, and frequently it went from A minus to D plus."

Some people favored style, others looked past style to substance. That was only the beginning, because there were arguments about substance itself. "One guy is an old-style, formalist New Critic," Sharp says, i.e., long on close-in textual analysis, disdainful of historical, psychological, biographical approaches. "That's not a literary theory he has. To him, that's *the truth*. So when he'd make an objection he'd say, this is not a *literary* argument, this is history, sociology, politics. Rubbish, someone else would say: you can't understand poetry without context. You could meet till kingdom come and not agree. The fallacy is there's a middle ground, but there isn't."

While Sharp talks, in my mind I picture the English Department, which was once a department store, an orderly place with polite help and sometimes snooty managers; now it's become a bazaar, a melee of wares and fashions, customer-oriented and market-driven, shopkeepers outside every stall. Gender, gender, gender, someone shouts. Special on "Cross-dressing in Shakespeare," get it while it lasts. "Wordsworth and the Imagination" over here. Black women, "Sisterhood in Victorian Literature." Christian themes. "Friendship in Literature," "Landscape in Literature," "Form in the Sonnet." I grant that the dissolution of consensus in this department is minor compared to turmoil in other places, where people trade insults and sue. Here, we still believe in reading and marking what our students write, in making ourselves available to them. Our very smallness keeps us together. Still, what I'm asking myself is this: if we have gone from a time when everybody taught the same books the same way to a later time when people taught the same books differently and then—always for the best of reasons, mind you—to a time when people teach different books in different ways, what next? Is the movement outward, forever? Or is there a turning point someplace, a reaction and return? When will that happen? Will anybody like it? Will I?

"We've confronted this disintegration of consensus about what we're doing pretty successfully," Sharp says. "We have a modus operandi, getting by without pitched battles. What this means is that you do your shtick and I do my shtick. But there's a real problem—and I don't know what the solution is—if you get the department together to really talk turkey. There isn't world enough and time."

※

"THE ASSUMPTION IS that an alumnus is a boob," Bob Price says to me, "and I'm not a boob."

Kenyon's most celebrated alumnus is Rutherford B. Hayes. Its most famous, surely, is Paul Newman. Its funniest, though he didn't stick around long enough to graduate, is Jonathan Winters. But, for now, Bob Price is its most controversial. Mention his name in college offices and eyes roll. You hear speculation about his character, his style, his motives.

The object of this scorn is a Philadelphia lawyer, a tax expert whose office nickname, he tells me, is "the Professor." He's back at Kenyon for homecoming weekend, an autumn nostalgia festival for alumni, many of whom are now down at the football field. Bob Price takes pride in never having attended a Kenyon athletic event, and he's not about to start. He's here on another mission. After sitting with me outside, smoking a closely rationed cigar—one a week, on a doctor's orders—he steps inside my office, offers me a swig out of a vest pocket whiskey flask, takes a nip himself, and explains the series of events—betrayals, he would say—that may lead him and a number of other alumni to sue Kenyon College.

The issue came up a few weeks ago, in September, during something called reunion planning weekend, when representatives of those classes with major anniversaries coming up in May gathered for dinner—airline food: chicken, rice, carrots—and Phil Jordan got up to address them. He was in fine form. "Where memory dwells past sweet supposing," he began, quoting and repeating a quote from "Kokosing Farewell," the best of Kenyon's songs, up there with "Shenandoah" and "Danny Boy." I can't listen to the thing with dry eyes. Proceeding smoothly, he extolled the importance and power of memory, which—even though we edit what we recall—is central to the character of Kenyon, a distinctive liberal arts college in a setting that's "human scale and extraordinarily beautiful." God, he was good. He turned to the college's history, evoking Philander Chase, "an irascible, impetuous nineteenth-century clergyman who fought with everyone here and moved on to fight with someone else." Then he segued into talk of change at Kenyon, how change must blend with continuity, and how Kenyon has always reached out to others, even before diversity became popular. He was pulling a fairly thin thread here, I thought, citing a handful of American Indian students, a Ghanaian "prince" who's buried in back of Rosse Hall, then the first American blacks who showed up after World War II, but never mind. When he turned to recent changes in Kenyon's student housing policy, I sensed a wavelet of tension. The old system was "problematic," he said. And so it was: fraternities, in some cases for a century and a half, held housing rights in specific wings of the three great old dormitories on the south end of campus. They had their pick of rooms. They controlled the lounges. Independent students got what was left, often ground-floor rooms near doorways. That was annoying but tolerable when 90 percent of the students belonged to fraternities. Now more than half the students are female, and only half the males belong to fraternities. I'm condensing a story that's a little longer than *War and Remembrance*, but a few years ago the college decided that lounges were everybody's territory, that half the rooms in former fraternity areas—divisions, they were called—would be open to independents, and that sophomore fraternity members would not be guaranteed a place in the divisions. That settlement wasn't the end of the war; it was a beginning. Jordan's speech drew to a close with talk of how rough times are—rising costs, fewer high school graduates, fiercer competition for philanthropic dollars—but the college was in decent shape, financially sound, a wide range of views on the faculty, etc.

"We all remember Kenyon is not Utopia," Jordan said, circling back to the memory theme. "It never was. We all remember February." A round of laughter and applause, and Jordan stood for questions. That's when it happened. An older alumnus asked whether the college has additional plans that will affect fraternities. "Is there more coming?" he asked. "Is another shoe going to drop?" No, no, no, Jordan shook his head, we're just making provisions for the future. "I think you've broken a covenant with the past," the alum retorted.

That was several weeks ago. This morning, there was a meeting of concerned fraternity alumni in Ascension Hall. Bill Ranney was running the meeting, a former trustee who's second only to Price on the college's least wanted list. Ranney went out of his way to set a constructive tone: how much we all love Kenyon, what a faithful and generous constituency fraternity alumni are. But the anger breaks through nonetheless. "I've always known that fraternities would have to compete to survive, adapt to society's changes," he says. "That's my middle-of-the-road voice. My other voice said I'm pissed."

There were maybe three dozen people sitting around. I spotted current fraternity members, recent and not-so-recent graduates, and—right next to me—two faculty members who act as fraternity advisers: Tim Shutt (Delta Kappa Epsilon) and John Macionis (Delta Tau Delta). They're in a minority on the faculty, no doubt about it. History's Peter Rutkoff probably speaks for the majority when he argues that Kenyon will never be a first-rate place until fraternities are gone: "They're discriminatory. They're inimical to the goals of the college. They encourage stupid behavior. The most important thing is, they're fuck-ups."

Ranney kept the meeting moving, eliciting complaints about administration policy, adding a few of his own. There was a lot of disgruntlement in the room, people who felt they'd been jerked around, people who believed that the presence of fraternities is integral to Kenyon's character, at the heart of the college they remember. Hostility mounted. Then, suddenly, there was an outburst to my left. It was Tim Shutt, my colleague in the English Department, clearly distressed. He pleaded to the alumni not to make a bad situation worse, but the thrust of his edgy, highly charged speech was that things are pretty bad already.

"It costs someone who is a conservative and a Republican to be here at all," he declared. "There are people in my department who would write against me if they knew I was here at all. I am here at risk. The more you institute hostility, the harder you're going to make it. There are unfair individuals out there."

Around then, Bob Price took the podium, a dark-suited, portly man with a battered briefcase full of documents, a whole chain of documents going back to the turn of the century, documents that he said demonstrate that Kenyon accepted money from some fraternities, money that went for dormitory renovations and repairs and, in exchange, granted those fraternities "perpetual exclusive housing rights" in Kenyon's three "historic" dormitories, Old Kenyon, Hanna, and Leonard. These documents were headed to a law firm for an advisory opinion, Price told the meeting. If the lawyers saw merit, the alumni might ask the college to concede. They might sue for a declaratory judgment or—most seriously—sue the college for breach of contract.

Someone asked whether Price had discussed all this with Phil Jordan. "He heard me, but he didn't heed me," Price responded. A little later, straining to maintain a loyalist tone, Ranney declared: "I don't think alumni are particularly litigious. We're just trying to find a two-by-four that gets the donkey's attention."

"Are fraternities worth defending?" Sitting in my office, Bob Price repeats my question before he answers it. He tells me about coming from a Philadelphia public school to Kenyon. He was an outsider here, a Jew at an Episcopalian school. He had a wonderful time here, and fraternities were part of his acceptance. He joined two of them, Alpha Delta Phi and Delta Kappa Epsilon. "This was a way for me to become part of a group that was very supportive. It taught me to hunt as part of a pack—something I found useful later at large law firms. In groups, deciding what are the subgroups, where are the leaders. It forces you to learn how to work with people in a cooperative group for an end—whether it's giving a party or rushing freshmen. And if you make a mistake at this level—you're an undergraduate—you're forgiven."

Price's passion for fraternities is something I don't share. I didn't like the hammerlock they had on housing, but then again, they gave parties that were open to everyone, and if a bunch of upper middle–class kids wanted to initiate each other, to bond and buy me a beer, so what? Fraternities did some good around campus and could be relied upon for a certain amount of nonsense, dumb ceremonies involving costumes, and coffins. Their members had a lower grade average as college students and a higher donation rate as alumni. That, pretty much, was it. Now fraternities are at the center of a much larger fight, not just at Kenyon. Nationally, Dean of Students Craig Bradley tells me, they've been in overall decline for a quarter- century, though there was a modest—and temporary—uptick in the Reagan years. Some colleges have abolished them. At others, fraternities have been obliged to accept women. Elsewhere, they've just faded away. At Kenyon the stakes are high because fraternities don't own their own residences: they occupy college housing. That's part of their appeal. It's also what renders them vulnerable, even though, defenders insist, there's more at stake than dormitory rooms and lounges.

"This isn't about housing," Bob Price tells me. "That's the purest bullshit. If it's about housing, we could fix it." Price agrees that Kenyon's housing should be upgraded and equitably distributed. If some fraternities have to move, in a block, to new dorms, so be it; if new dorms are needed, he's got a wealthy grad who's all ready to lead the fund-raising campaign. It's not about housing. It's about political correctness, left-liberal capture of the academy, feminism and multiculturalism on the rampage. "Phil Jordan's goal," Bob Price says, "is to convert this place into Oberlin without leaving tracks." He's given up on Jordan, though. Before the year is out, he expects to take his case to the board of trustees. If that appeal fails, he may take his alma mater to court.

🌿

CELL BY CELL, a human body replaces itself in seven years. A college takes longer. Death, retirement, and departure have accounted for all the rest of my teachers, but Bill McCulloh still teaches classics in Gambier. He's the only professor still here whom I took a course from: "Greek Literature in Translation." He was a rookie then, just arrived from Wesleyan, chain-smoking cigarettes, lecturing on Sophocles and Sappho, courtly, thoughtful, and committed. You could tell he'd be around here forever.

I had supper with McCulloh the other night, wondering how he measured the years, the coming, the staying, the not leaving. He wasn't comfortable talking to "the press," he told his wife. "It's only old Fred," Pat McCulloh assured him. He seemed tired, overwhelmed by work, and it was almost as if the questions I was asking him about his life were good questions, things that he'd never had a chance to think about. At least, he made it feel that way. He was always the politest of men. And—politeness aside—the most thoughtful. He measured the good things: "the chance to teach classics at Kenyon and spend my time with Greek, which is my lifeblood, in a setting that I relish, the chance to teach advanced classes with six or seven students, or even one." He described his discontents. The almost total neglect of one's higher scholarship and research and the collegial sharing of ideas came first. Next: too little time for writing and reading, for music and lectures, for travel, even for family. It pleases him that forty or fifty students keep in touch with him, across the years, and pains him that he's too busy to answer their salutations. He pointed to the offprint of an article a former student, now a professor, had contributed to a scholarly magazine, an article dedicated to McCulloh that came in the mail six weeks before. "He got it to arrive on my sixtieth birthday," McCulloh said, "and I have not responded."

What struck me most, though, was McCulloh's account of his rookie year here, 1961, his falling in love with a small, plain, run-down little college in the middle of nowhere. Assigned to an office in Ascension Hall, McCulloh remembers nervously facing his first class, only to see the English professor Gerrit Roelofs walk by the open door and flip him the finger, cheerfully, as if to say, "Give 'em hell." And whenever Denham Sutcliffe walked by McCulloh's office, he would start chanting the *Iliad* . . . in Greek. "I feel the shortfall now," McCulloh says. "People were always dropping by. Sometimes it was a pain in the neck. But people who come now don't get that kind of welcome."

You can't talk to anyone who's been around the college a while without sensing that, though a lot was gained when the place tripled in size and admitted women, something else was lost. The old-timers always mention the years when most of the humanities and social sciences were packed together in one building, Ascension Hall, before departments moved into houses and became quasi-independent principalities. A longtime Kenyon psychology professor, Chuck Rice, believes that "centrifugal spin-offs of departments were the biggest single cause in the decline of the ethos of Kenyon." Rice had a basement office in Ascension Hall. One night, working late, he heard an "awful crash." And then a shout. "No, you goddamned fool, no!" Rice rushed out to intervene and found Kenyon's philosophy professor, Virgil Aldrich, gentle, pipe-smoking Aldrich, two-time head of the American Philosophical

Association, in his office, working late. Alone, thinking, arguing with himself.

Now, putting together a sense of things, marching from one place to another, talking to people who have stopped talking to each other, I discover a campus divided into territories, defined by fields and force, shadowed by the memory of old feuds, the Hatfields of History versus (the real) McCoys of Political Science. And almost every morning, I bullshit with a man who completely disagrees with all of this talk of lost community.

"I came here in 1971 for an interview, and the place was the ideal image of the liberal arts college, overwhelming, beautiful, tranquil, all that crap," the History Department chair, Peter Rutkoff, says. Now a balding, spindly guy, a Jewish New Yorker trailing memories of Brooklyn, Rutkoff was startled to discover at his first faculty meeting that people were debating whether sociology was a discipline. "I heard that debate and I thought I was on another planet," he says. "There was an excessive rhetoric of the liberal arts. People were talking passionately about disinterested inquiry . . . during Cambodia."

In 1971 the college still made an effort to "socialize" newcomers. Older professors asked new hires to receptions and dinners. Rutkoff wasn't impressed. "It was a funny high-WASP culture which I had no experience of and no affection for. Really foreign. I'd have been just as happy if I'd never been invited."

The Gambier that others look back on and miss was a place that was due—past due—for change, Rutkoff thinks. The school's concentration on textual analysis of great books was narrow and constrained, overlooking "the rich plurality of historical inquiry, ignoring political, social, and cultural issues." And in its all-out commitment to teaching, Kenyon stinted scholarship and research. "Good teachers didn't do research," Rutkoff says. "It was looked down upon. It wasn't rewarded. It was a Mr. Chipsy kind of place." The town was uptight, insecure, rumor-ridden. "They said, 'Don't build a house because that's a sign of arrogance.' Or, 'Do build a house because it shows you want to belong.'"

If, like Rutkoff, you wanted change at Kenyon, the early eighties were your time. The college was racist and sexist, said Bruce Haywood's successor as provost, Jerry Irish. Education was political. Irish aimed to reshape the institution, bonding with younger faculty members while the old-timers, many of them, bailed out. It was surprising, once things started, how easily the old order yielded. "They'd degenerated," one professor tells me. "They were decent people but not great thinkers. Too genteel to get involved in curricular fights." For Rutkoff, though, it was a time marked by advances on all fronts. "In terms of what was important, we had the votes," he remembers. "Non-Western curriculum, diversity, the student body, women, reducing the teaching load. We were all doing fine."

The run of victories ended, though, when Provost Irish came up against the political science professors, a group of neoconservative University of Chicago graduates who fought off his efforts to diversify their department. "He vetoed some candidates, pressed others," says Harry Clor, a survivor of those days. "He wanted to upset the balance of the department, to change the character of a department he perceived as conservative, sexist, and racist, and which we perceived as one of the best political science departments in the country."

The conflict involved trustees, alumni, faculty and students, insiders and outsiders, before it was over; it was a fight for the soul of the college, and no one won. In 1986 Irish left. The next year, his main antagonist, the Political Science chair, Robert Horwitz, died, embittered and exhausted. The battle for Kenyon was over, and both sides rushed to claim defeat. Liberals lamented the loss of their leader, the conservatives deplored what Irish had managed to do before he left. The people who were attached to the past sensed its irrecoverable loss, and those with their own vision of the future suspected that, early victories notwithstanding, it might never quite arrive in Gambier.

Put Rutkoff in the second group. He misses the momentum of the Irish years and thinks it's been replaced by a waffling, visionless centrism. A combination of administrative cynicism and fiscal restraint is reversing earlier gains and preventing new ones, he thinks. "The administration now doesn't know where it's going. Making do, making bandaids, reacting, doing nothing except responding to this asshole or that asshole. And, to me, Jordan's become someone who manages problems as they arise politically, but he doesn't address problems. Phil doesn't hear what he doesn't want to hear."

❦

I'LL NEVER AGAIN make the mistake of thinking of dormitories as part of the college. They are the anticollege, college refuted, an opposing universe, negative and opposite, a building-beast where animals play golf hockey, swinging golf clubs, using the ball like a hockey puck, racketing at midnight right above my head, a place where animals nest in cages filled with comic books, video games, pizza boxes, unwashed clothing, and endless noise. The other night, I walked down the hall to a room in uproar and found a student sitting in front of a stereo with more nobs, dials, and meters than a nuclear submarine.

"That's really loud!" I told him.

"Thank you," he replied. I walked away, wondering what life is coming to. It's funny, though, how the dorm is drawing me in. I kept my distance at the start, entering and leaving by the outside door. Now I come and go through the inside hall, passing rooms, savoring noise, smells, arguments. It can be a relief, coming back here after, say, a Kenyon College faculty meeting.

🌿

FOR THE FIRST THIRD of the twentieth century, Kenyon College faculty meetings began with the president, William Peirce, on his knees, leading the tiny group in prayer. Later, when Gordon Keith Chalmers was president, the whole faculty arose as he entered the Campbell-Meeker Room in Ascension Hall. "Good afternoon, gentlemen," he snapped. Later still, when F. Edward Lund was president, people were shocked to see an English professor come sauntering into the faculty meeting in tennis shorts. He was never tenured, but what he started kept on happening. Buck Lund's successor, Bill Caples, a former vice president of Inland Steel, presided over meetings in a corporate style, relishing exchanges with faculty, giving as well as he took, muttering an aside when someone said something he thought was dumb.

These days, half or a little more of the faculty meet in the Biology auditorium, a modern arena with movie screens and blackboards down in front and TV monitors appended to the sidewalls, where windows ought to be. Like students, we take seats in the back rows first, near the exits; meetings that start a little after four begin thinning out at five. Slowly, the room half fills. There's a funny look on people's faces, an air of "here we go again," like they're all at a carnival, sitting in dodge 'em cars, waiting for the current to come on.

I used to think that these faculty meetings would be like Oxford Union debates, bristling and witty. Failing that, I hoped for battles royal, rousing and cathartic free-for-alls. Lately, though, it's seemed like opera. Bad opera: incomprehensible plotting, endless recitatives with barely a whiff of aria. The longer you sit, the more it feels like you're in an opera crowd, up high, in the cheap seats, where folks in rumpled clothing noisily unwrap lemon sour balls and clutch librettos that they follow with pocket flashlights.

Bad opera. No Aristotelian structure here, beginning, middle, and end, no unities, no performance that is over in an afternoon. You have to think of this as an ongoing opera, one year long at least. Meetings in early fall are noted for their deceptive calm, a misleading appearance of efficiency. The second semester is when things happen, when reports come out of committees, action can't be postponed, and professors' moods get sandpapery. "The season of fret," they call it, "the silly season."

Three leitmotifs will likely dominate the opera this year, three issues upon which the faculty might—I said *might*—take action. The first is about power, kind of. There's a proposal that the faculty form a tenure and promotion committee, which will make recommendations to the president and provost. Most other colleges have such a committee; the administration would like to have one here. It's hard for an outsider to understand how important people here believe this is. They insist that faculty should take a hand in hiring and firing. It's about democracy, it's about personal responsibility. It's about protecting academe from pressure and manipulation. That's what the advocates of a tenure and promotion committee say. Other faculty members, just as stalwart, argue that hiring and firing is administration business and not something that colleagues should do in committee. Kenyon's faculty has voted tenure and promotion committees down twice in recent years. You can read this turn-down in two different ways. The administration has a way of claiming that half a glass of water is half full, even if the glass is cracked; they say that the current system must be working pretty well, thanks, if faculty decline to alter it. The competing interpretation is that faculty are uneasier about each other than they are about the provost and the president.

The second issue is a double whammy: two potentially controversial hiring searches. After long argument, a Women's and Gender Studies Department was set up here a few years ago. That was the end of one argument. Kenyon chose a man, Harry Brod, as interim department head. That was the start of a new argument. Now Brod and his wife, Maria Papacostaki, have applied to become joint tenure-track department heads. Buckle your seat belts. The other search to watch is in the Integrated Program in Human Studies. IPHS started years ago as a kind of British-model great-books tutorial, in which Kenyon professors from other departments would address the enduring questions—Man in Nature, Man in Society, that kind of stuff. The idea was that the professors would be invigorated, their students enriched. It's had some good years, by all accounts; some of the college's best teachers have been in IPHS at one time or another. Still, like any program that depends on people who volunteer, or get volunteered, there've been bad seasons, too: out-of-field professors teaching out-of-context books to out-of-depth students. It's a potentially showy, student-attracting program, though, and now the college wants to appoint a tenure-track director. Among the applicants: Harry Brod. He seems likely to have an interesting year.

The third issue is the most important, I think. Also the most elusive. It turns up in phrases like "residentiality" and "professional responsibility" and "the character of the college." What it means is that, as a result of decisions almost everybody applauded when they were made, Kenyon College is beginning, just beginning, to change in ways that make people uncomfortable. Philander Chase chose a remote site for this college because he thought isolation was a good thing, ideal for a college community. More than other colleges, Kenyon has defined itself by its isolation. Those miles of unbroken country, those bleak wintry fields, those dark nights made us, and maybe they made us different. For years, residence was required. You had to live here. Bit by bit, the requirement eroded; the three-mile rule became a seven-mile rule and later a ten-mile rule, a rule that became a joke. They stopped measuring as the roads run and started estimating as the crows fly, and then they stopped measuring and estimating and enforcing altogether. "It was an insult," one professor says. You can't dictate where professionals should live. You can't legislate community. Some of those people living right in town weren't worth a damn, and some of those who lived far out went out of their way to maintain an active presence around campus. So they buried the rule. But now there are new problems. A handful of faculty commute from Columbus to Gambier—an hour's drive—and more are thinking about moving. Columbus has things Gambier lacks: better elementary schools, a Jewish community, jobs for spouses, a university research library at Ohio State, restaurants with liquor licenses and spice cabinets, movie houses that don't show *Wayne's World*. You can't blame people for moving. And, sure enough, it's possible to arrange your schedule so that you spend just two days a week in Gambier, holding great classes, supportive office hours; you can do all of that in two days and leave. But Kenyon markets itself as a residential college, human scale and personal touch, the kind of place where you run into professors at the bookstore, bank, and post office, where you bullshit and baby-sit for them, pray, play, and . . . well . . . live together in the same small place. If you care about things like that, if you think they're essential and not merely cosmetic, you start to worry about whether what's happening is the beginning of a tide that could carry the college out to sea. This is the flip side of my worry about Columbus moving in on Gambier; this is Gambier moving to Columbus.

Tenure and promotion, a couple testy hiring searches, and the beginnings of a concern about residentiality: those are three issues that might enliven things around here. The hiring is done by search committees and may not come directly before the faculty meeting. Residentiality is too diffuse to generate much more than talk, if that: they're not going to bring back the ten-mile rule, not this bunch. Tenure and promotion might get interesting. You never know, though. "Directing faculty," someone says, "is like herding cats."

At this opera house, performers, chorus, audience, all sit together. Relaxed and alert, Phil Jordan enters, wearing the forbearing expression of someone attending an event that could very well get silly before it's over. Reed Browning and Anne Ponder appear, provost and dean of academic affairs, collegial and polite, not looking for trouble but knowing that if the show requires a villain, they will do. Jordan, I suspect, carries a warranted confidence that he can handle whatever happens here. His assistants don't have that kind of immunity.

Now, the featured players. That sandy-haired cherubic figure in a sports coat, striped shirt, and bow tie, who looks like Ted Koppel's older brother, is John Macionis of the Sociology Department. Macionis considers himself a reasonable man, a centrist; his enemies charge he's a disguised conservative. Thanks to the royalties on a couple of much-used textbooks that he wrote, Macionis drives a Jaguar or two and lives in a mansion outside town, sixty-five acres with tennis court and swimming pool and a second house that he's turning into a bed-and-break-fast. I had dinner there a couple weeks ago and heard Macionis deplore the loss of center and loss of civility at Kenyon.

"I'm disturbed by the fact—to be damn honest—that my friendships now make more sense politically than they did ten years ago," he said. "There are people I've liked and then, after a committee squabble, if you disagreed, they distance themselves, and the people you agreed with nuzzle up to you. I used to have friends for all sorts of reasons. Now it's 80 percent explainable in terms of politics."

He reviewed the things that divide professors: the role of race and gender in curriculum; interdisciplinary programs; whether you see teaching as a purveying of eternal truths or the servant of some kind of political agenda; whether you're concerned with or even interested in the character and traditions of this particular college or regard all that as so much irrelevant baggage; whether you think fraternities have a place at Kenyon or—like what Macionis estimates is 80 percent of the faculty—would cheerfully vote to abolish them tomorrow.

"People don't know how to engage with each other and disagree," he complains. "We don't know how to do what we claim we're doing. In classroom we can all claim to be Socrates. Outside, we have no language, no emotional skills. Step one: you say something, I think what you said sucks. Step two: you suck. It's ironic and bewildering. We don't expect to learn anything from anybody else."

As if to underscore what he takes to be his centrist position, Macionis usually sits near the middle of the auditorium at these faculty meetings. In back—usually all the way in back—are the old-timers. That's Carl Brehm back there, a jovial, potbellied economist who loves playing the role of campus curmudgeon. All this talk about more power for faculty is a charade, he tells me, "not unlike high school student council." He's got some problems with younger faculty, he grants, charging that some of them have "little idea of or respect for the idea of a liberal arts college." He admits to missing the ten-mile rule. "When people talk about moving to Columbus, we're no goddamned different from Columbia University."

That older gent with close-cropped hair and a stingy-brimmed hat is Harry Clor from Political Science, the surviving third of a campus conservative trio, Tom (Short, of Political Science), Dick (Hoppe, of Psychology), and Harry himself. Short left to edit a conservative journal, *Academic Questions,* at Princeton. Hoppe commutes between Gambier and Chicago, where he now works for a commodity trader. That leaves Clor, living through a period of lull, a kind of sitzkrieg. Having endured the presence of a "radicalizing provost," he's careful not to exaggerate how bad things are at Kenyon. "The worst things haven't happened yet," he allows, "but every year there's a new agenda, a demand for a new program that the academic left wants." This year, he's keeping an eye on the IPHS hiring search, and he opposes the proposed faculty committee on tenure and promotion. "I'd rather take my chances with a weak and unimpressive administration," he says, "than a gang of ideologues who have wanted this for years, for reasons that aren't very hard to figure out."

Now, some voices from the other side of the aisle. There's Rita Kipp,

Sociology Department chair, wearing a batik shawl she surely brought back from fieldwork in Indonesia. She'll be heading the Women's and Gender Studies search. She's one of the professors who've been worrying about residentiality. "I guess I feel guilty," she tells me. "When I first came I was one of the strongest advocates of doing away with the ten-mile rule. I think I was justified, I'm not sorry, but I don't think we've replaced it with sufficient ways to socialize people into what it means to be a faculty member. We do a better job with students than with faculty. When people live elsewhere, there are fewer here to give receptions, do committee work. I ask myself, 'Why the hell am I doing all this work? Is it just because I live within walking distance of campus?'"

Is there any end to students' ingenuity with nicknames? They call her "Zewskers," Joan Slonczewski, biologist, another representative of the left-liberal side of things, though she might argue with such coarse categories. An intense, busy woman who writes science fiction late at night, she involves herself in Quaker causes and is widely rumored to actually *enjoy* committee and faculty meetings. That kind of scares people. "I'll talk to anyone, go to anyone's office," she cheerfully admits. "It comes from the Quaker experience. It's refreshing to interact." I guess that scares people, too. She deplores intramural feuding, calls it "the date rape model at Kenyon: you assume the worst about each other." These days, the college is being run by junior faculty in alliance with the president, she says, and the upcoming tenure-promotion debate is "the last battle of the old order."

Two other players from the left side of the aisle. There's David Lynn, a Kenyon graduate of the seventies, a self-described "blonde, blue-eyed Jew who went to an Episcopal school." Now he's tenure-track in the English Department, and he's immersed himself in campus disputes. His opinions are many and vehement. He wishes they'd gotten rid of fraternities ten years ago, he insists that a grown-up faculty has to take charge of its own affairs, and he wishes those graybeards in the back row would realize how times have changed. "The conservatives have lost," he declares, "and they haven't lost because of numbers. The problem is, there's simply no defense for many of their positions. If you follow developments of the life of the mind, of scholarship, their positions don't hold water. It's not a matter of creating a Marxist society. It's a question of being honest about what makes sense, and they aren't the ones who make the most sense. It was a hard fight, but it's an intellectual battle that is over. What lost was the notion that there was a coherent Western tradition based on excellence and merit and greatness, something that—all other considerations apart—matters most in life, makes us what we are, has shaped us as a culture, and makes life worth living. *There are other positions,* other traditions that have been suppressed. To be honest, we have to realize we are more and more diverse."

Then there's Vernon Schubel, Religion Department, consensus choice for campus radical. Dressed like a Third World road warrior in duster raincoat and sunglasses, black vest, black jeans, brown sandals, the dread Schubel plays an electric guitar, named his dog Uli after the terrorist Ulrike Meinhoff, and has a reputation for looking through, or past, administration people when he meets them on Gambier sidewalks.

"I didn't come here to be labeled as a crazy," he protests, when I ask him about his reputation. He professes to love Kenyon, a place he finds "right on the edge of being spectacular." Those old complaints about loss of community are bogus, he says. "It's not that we share a space, it's that we're engaged in the same enterprise." He likes living away from Gambier, in Mount Vernon. "That four miles gives me just enough distance to remind me that, though I teach in Plato's community, I'm here where there's a Big Bear and people who work." Schubel's wife, Donna Heizer, is a part-timer in IPHS—about as tenuous a hold as you can have around here—and this leads Schubel to add a fourth item to my list of smoldering campus issues: the college's policy, or lack of policy, on spousal hiring. "Spousal hiring is going to blow this place up," Schubel predicts. "If you're going to have a liberal arts college in the middle of nowhere, you have to find a way to say, in some kind of writing, if there are possibilities or no possibilities." Kenyon belongs to a consortium of colleges that share spousal applications, but that's "a joke," Schubel says. "The only reason I would leave is if it became certain my wife had no future here. I'm not going to stay here and let my wife bake cookies."

If I'm correct in thinking of all this as an opera, then last month's meeting was an overture, though it's hard to tell when the tuning-up ends—those odd trills, booms, riffs, and tinkles—and the real music begins. There was a little skirmish about IPHS, people wondering just how the decision to make the directorship a tenure-track post was made, and others—Rutkoff was one—applauding the idea of taking the program "into the mainstream." Later, outside the meeting, one professor suggested there is a plot afoot to make sure Harry Brod gets the position, and another professor intimated that all this talk about a plot on behalf of Harry Brod is anti-Semitic. In the meeting, faculty members worried about the disappointing performance of the Ganter Fund, the earnings of which constitute part of a tenured professor's pay. Others pressed the administration on providing child care for faculty members, an issue that's been cooking for some time. The administration is trying to work something out, here in Knox County, but it's tricky finding partners for a child care project. Kenyon's faculty, the president pointedly noted, are among the top 10 percent of local wage-earners. No one reacted to that: this was supposed to be about what the faculty wants, not—please—about what it already has. This is *next* Christmas, not *last* Christmas!

This month was a little livelier, with a short but spirited duet between Vernon Schubel and Carl Brehm. They were talking about a proposed faculty executive committee, which is supposed to increase professors' involvement in college governance. Schubel was for it, Brehm against it. "This is the same idea that's been discussed before," groused Brehm, "the same language, meaning more power and less work, and it won't work." They clashed again on whether nontenured faculty should serve on committees. Schubel was for it: "Today's junior faculty are tomorrow's senior faculty." Brehm countered: "There's something to be said for people having been here a while rather than just walking through the door and revolutionizing the place."

All these are preliminaries. If anything major happens it'll come later in the year, in the springtime, when the faculty rushes toward anticlimax. Still, I've seen enough to begin to feel a little island-crazy, measuring divisions between tenured and not tenured, old and new, male and female, conservative and liberal, progressive and traditional, teaching and research, on and on. These divisions aren't consistent; they are variable, erratic, sometimes principled, often self-serving. These people aren't clowns either; they're mostly smart, articulate people who have more in common than they realize. Nonetheless, I begin to understand why some people around here never attend faculty meetings. Lentz, quoting Melville, calls them "isolatoes." And my thoughts turn to a troubling conversation I had with one such isolato, just the other day.

AT NIGHT—it was specified that we meet at night, when fewer people are around—I'm with a professor who loves Kenyon and Kenyon loves back, a professor who's popular with students and been given teaching awards by peers; an engaged, lively professor who's always been cordial to me, curious about my work, and has invited me to dinner at least once every year I've been back here. When I proposed an interview, the professor acceded, but nervously, and after the ninth or tenth time I'm asked for assurance that what's being said is not for attribution, I decide the whole interview will have to be that way. You'd think a tenured professor would let things fly: tenure safeguards freedom of speech. But this is a small town, a company town, and you have to be careful. "You come and go," Rita Kipp told me the other day. "We all stay here. You can't get away from the messes that you make and the messes that others make around you." So I decide, gender-neutral language being the order of the day, to call the professor not he, not she, but, combining the two and adding a capital letter, Hesh.

"I wanted an institution which emphasized teaching," Hesh says when I ask about coming to Kenyon. "To work with people and ideas in a good environment, away from cities. I never worked harder than my first seven years here. It's a blur—it was like having a new child at home. I gave it every ounce of energy, and I was always happy." To be sure, some students were arrogant—"the ones who talked about faculty as though they were servants at a country club"—but they became Hesh's reclamation projects. Hesh's energy and enthusiasm engulfed them. "A good teaching situation was . . . and is . . . the gift of Kenyon."

As soon as we turn to faculty life, though, Hesh's mood darkens. The wars of the eighties are over, Hesh says, but what remains is "quiet, subtle, but discernible guerrilla warfare, and the faculty are the guerrillas, alienated warriors whom no one will listen to off the hill, in Mount Vernon or in Los Angeles. Only in academe . . ."

Hesh walks on eggshells around Gambier; to hear Hesh describe it, this peaceful village is downtown Mogadishu. "I avoid curricular issues, women's and gender studies, IPHS, area studies. I keep my distance. Also, I choose my own colleagues and friends. At times it's not a very friendly place. It's not Jordan's fault, or Browning's, it's the faculty themselves. There's a viciousness, an ugliness that shouldn't be, a fighting for turf and dominance, fighting with egalitarian rhetoric when they're not egalitarian or democratic at all. It's a censorial society. We're talking Yugoslavia plus."

Hesh pauses. The anger, which surprises me, may have surprised

Hesh as well. Believe me, most days, seeing Hesh on campus, you'd say there goes a happy professor, a perennial candidate for Mr. or Mrs. Kenyon.

"Thank God I love teaching," Hesh says. "And I love the kids. Otherwise it would be a fucking zoo here."

SALVATION. MIRACLE. SAVING GRACE. The college rolls along some-how. Tangled and bitter as things get, the life of the college proceeds, adequately, vitally, sometimes wonderfully. You leave behind the messes you find in offices and enter classrooms that are like sanctuaries and a dormitory that—would you believe it?—is a safe house. That's the pattern I find in these October days, all crisp and golden and smelling of apples.

I love the mornings, walking past the Peoples Bank, birds twittering in a wall of vines turning red and brown. I check the upward progress of the red column rising in a painted thermometer that marks the progress of the United Way campaign, temperature rising as winter nears. I walk with Lentz to class; he's doing *Walden,* which fits this season well. This morning, he's annoyed. Four students came late to "American Literature." He turned all of them away. And he's got an-other guy who routinely falls asleep. Walking across to Ascension, he wonders how to handle the nap-taker, and that gets him thinking about another student, a woman from a few years ago, who was routinely late to every class. She always seemed harassed and anxious. He gave her the benefit of the doubt; maybe she had a problem, alarm clock dyslexia or something. Then, while lecturing one morning, he looked down onto the road that runs past Ascension Hall, and there she was, "calculated and contemptuous," because she wasn't sprinting toward his lecture, she was moseying into Peirce Hall for breakfast, before dashing into class, late again. Years later—she's surely forgotten by now—Lentz thinks of her. She's on his mind as he starts lecturing on *Walden.* He tells his class about the student who sleeps in American Lit, how that student preoccupied him as he walked to school this morning, so that he'd almost missed the sunrise. "The sun was absolutely glowing with a rose color," he says. "I've never seen that color in a sunrise. I wasn't paying attention to Thoreau's lesson, I was obsessed by shams and delusions. I was thinking about this student. But students come and go.

This one may come and go a little more quickly. . . ." The class laughs gamely. "And then I worried about late students. Five, ten, twelve, twenty minutes late. And I saw cedar waxwings, a whole flock of them. The point—Thoreau's point—is that we need to concentrate on what is real, on what nature provides, on the magic quality of this world . . ."

I can't imagine what the students' notes on all this amount to. Lentz's version of English 1–2 is not the version others teach. All the professors go their own way with this course. Lentz regrets the change, I know: he believes a common list of books gave students something in common and—almost as important—forced professors outside their specialties, obliging them to teach—in some cases to read—works they'd never have touched. English 1–2 with Lentz is long on examination of text, on historical background, on the moral underpinnings of writers' visions. It's light on critical theory, not breathlessly abreast of current scholarship. It's the sort of course that's meant as a preparation for life, not for graduate school. In lesser hands, it's the sort of course others criticize as "S and S": summary and sermon. It's not "cutting edge," in the current phrase.

"I've seen more cutting edges come and go than—what's an assemblage of cutting edges?—a Cuisinart," Lentz counters. "In twenty years I've seen a sweeping new kind of conception every four or five years. The new historicism, deconstruction before that, feminist literary theory, reader-response criticism, structuralism before that, one after another of them, these waves that engaged people profoundly and honorably, for the most part. To me, they were constantly reinventing the wheel." He doesn't spend much time reading literary criticism. "The pearls are so few," he says, "the ocean so vast." He reads history, psychology, fiction. And he rereads the books he teaches, rereads them every year, with a doggedness and diligence that's made him locally famous. He rereads because the books keep changing. These days he finds there's something "terribly bruised," rather than stoic and fine, about the love affair in *A Farewell to Arms*. He finds it's harder and harder to make a case for the greatness of Ahab's quest in *Moby-Dick*: time has turned him into more of a Richard III than a Hamlet. He even attempts to defend those terribly disappointing final chapters in *Huckleberry Finn*, those Tom Sawyerish capers that send the lovely tale hurtling downhill. Those chapters demonstrate, he says, how Twain's characters are trapped in a cultural matrix. To leave them free would be a Hollywood cop-out; Tom Sawyer's annoying hegemony over Huckleberry Finn is prophetic. The Civil War was all about "hundreds of Tom Sawyers leading hundreds of thousands of Huck Finns into Yankee artillery."

🌿

"DO YOU VIEW John Adams as a hero?" Phil Jordan asks. In jocular moments, he refers to himself as someone who teaches history and does other things as well, and tonight I find him facing a seminar on the American Revolution, the sixteenth president of Kenyon College assessing the character of the man who became second president of the United States.

I sit in the living room of Cromwell Cottage, watching Jordan elicit reactions to Adams. What do they make of him? he asks. What can they tell from their readings from Adams's journal, letters to his wife, and other texts? Do they admire him? The initial answer is: not much.

"If it were not for the revolution, he'd have been an upwardly mobile social climber," says the first student who speaks, a guy I had in class a couple years ago. I'm surprised to find him taking a leading part in discussion. "He wanted to get where he was going, no matter how he got there."

Adams was an opportunist, others agree, self-seeking, compulsive, "open to discussion, to a point, but he was the one who was going to lead the discussion." Jordan hears out all these complaints. He sits in a chair, facing the students, legs crossed, books at his side, but he doesn't touch a book all night. He knows the material cold, I sense. He takes the seminar through Adams's personal history, emphasizing how his marriage may have changed him, a "companionate marriage . . . remarkable for the era . . . perhaps for any era." He wonders what propelled Adams into public life, or whether he propelled himself.

"What I'm getting to," he says, "is one of those questions historians love to deal with when there are major figures in history. To what extent are they articulating actors, giving shape and character to events, or to what extent are they swept along by events over which they have no control?"

The most interesting questions you can ask a class are the ones that don't have easy answers. Forget those rhetorical gambits that compel the class to guess the right response, the one the teacher wants to hear. It's the big questions, the ones that hang in air, hedged by silence—

thoughtful silence, you hope—that pay off. This is one of those. Patiently, Jordan takes the class through Adams's career, its seeming inconsistencies and changes, its mixture of principle and self-interest, his actions sometimes contrary to public opinion, sometimes riding along with it. It's a mixed record, the class agrees, and that's probably the point: public lives don't come pure and simple. Sometimes, argues Jordan, a man can be self-interested, self-promoting, and nonetheless have an idealistic side. "I ask again," Jordan presses, "how much moral commitment do we have to expect in order to argue that there are principles at stake at some level in Adams's career?"

After almost two hours, Jordan pours cider, breaks out cheese and crackers, Pepperidge Farm cookies. His dogs wrestle on the floor. It's the very picture of a small liberal arts college—seminar at the president's house, and a good seminar at that. By now, I've seen Phil Jordan perform in a variety of venues, in front of faculty, parents, alumni, always poised, articulate, a little self-mocking, and I've begun to see why, in spite of those qualities, or rather *because* of them, his appearances are often regarded with cynicism. After sixteen years, people take his strengths for granted. What a pleasure this must be, facing a new audience, lively and interested, that won't stick around too long. During break, Jordan tells me he likes this class, its willingness to talk, not just to him but to each other, so that two- or three-sided discussions arise and sometimes the seminar has a life of its own. Sometimes, it feels as though the seminar might be reaching that ecstatic point professors dream about, something that's right up there with the Cubs winning the Series: you could leave the room and discussion would continue without you. During the first half, Jordan's seminar felt that way. Not after the break, though. The class turns sluggish; responses slow. There's a kind of pause, two beats too long, between question and answer that suggests that no one has done all the reading. "Come on, guys," Jordan prods them. "Did I feed you too much?"

Working toward closure, Jordan cites Adams's attendance at the Continental Congress, his travel through the colonies, the merging of personal ambition and larger cause, a provincial politician becoming a national leader. He asks, near the end, what would have been the course of Adams's life if he'd been born earlier, in 1730, say, or 1710. "A royal sycophant," says one student. "Harvard Law!" another. "The revolution would have happened fifty years earlier," a third argues. "No, he'd probably have gone for the money." All of this is lively and good-natured. Then one student—the one I'd predict an A for—senses how tricky and important is the confluence of a man and a moment: "Circumstances enable us," she says.

After all the others have spoken, Jordan sums things up. I've been told that the kind of politics he teaches in this seminar is the kind of politics he practices in his office, across Middle Path, a style that his friends find enlightened and pragmatic, his critics deem voguish and opportunistic. "My own view," he says, "is that Adams was much shaped by events which were singular to his era. But he was able to seize them and, to some extent, for a time, to lead them."

🌿

No cider and cookies in English 3, no texts to read, no John Adams to ponder, only the fragmentary efforts of beginning writers. Still, I look forward to these one-night-a-week sessions. So, I think, does the class. I try to keep things good-humored, and so do they; I don't sense any of the personal antagonisms I've seen in other years, i.e., she trashed my paper about a fraternity party so wait until I get into her thing about clubbing seals to death.

By now, I sense two or three standouts, but they keep making errors that keep them in touch with the pack. For one thing, I haven't seen a paper yet that wouldn't have been improved by a final going-over, a last proofreading and markup. It's as if they hesitate to attack a paper with a pencil, changing things and crossing them out, once it's been printed. Week in, week out, you see annoying errors repeated: abrupt changes in tense, garbled punctuation around quotes, misplaced clauses ("Driving down the street, the rain kept spattering"). Not this again, you say, and you get to a point where you can't say anything more than, get better, damn it, just get better.

Our pattern is simple. They turn in work a week before class, they read some or all of it aloud, and we talk about it. The healthy work gets criticized more vigorously than utterly botched efforts, which elicit sympathy and condolence. Sometimes it feels as though I'm a doctor running an open clinic, never knowing what kind of problem will come walking through the door.

"Kenny could feel the heat begin to singe the white-blonde hair that richly blanketed his burly auburn arms."

"Maria came to the small shop with its three little tables at 4:30 or thereabouts every day but Wednesday. She would talk or more likely argue with her mother until 5. Maria got pregnant when she was 20 and had the baby."

"Mime. He hated that word. It was as quiet and meaningless as himself, the mime, the non-person."

"Marla took a deep breath and wiped her hands on the little green apron around her flat waist."

There are mistakes by the thousands waiting for writers to make them, a thousand bad ideas in ambush. What can you do with a Central American peasant who's described as having "worn and blistered hands"? Sometimes, if just for a paragraph, they get things exactly, wonderfully right. That happened the other night, smack in the middle of an otherwise disorganized piece. A black woman muses about going out with a black MD, whom she sees wearing white, clinical clothing. "The contrast made him look very much like a piece of white movie candy, half-sucked, exposing the black licorice inside. Good and plenty."

Wow! And damn! I wish I'd thought of that.

❧

It's hunting season now, herds of deer stirred up by the annual slaughter, panicked and on the run, coming close to campus. All the trees have turned, all except the oaks. Balls of hay sit rolled up in the middle of now-barren fields, like carpets taken up at the end of a ballroom season. Fields of soybeans that were Van Gogh golden a few days ago are brown and empty, erased like blackboards at the end of class.

Can I admit it? I'm happy. My life is rich and full. Coming back here was not a mistake. Granted, attaching yourself to a college is a lot like rooting for a baseball team. It takes a lot to keep you going into middle age, a suspension of disbelief, almost, as teams roll by, as players grow more mercenary, owners more bullying and predatory, as franchises themselves change towns, leaving faithful fans behind. You have to wonder what you're being loyal to. But once the season starts, the game itself just carries you away.

❧ *November*

THE MOOD CHANGES when autumn is over, and autumn is over in a wink. The skies turn gray, the fields are empty brown, and those trees that waved leaves at freshmen and their parents in August stand out now, black and skeletal, like pickets in a fence that holds us in.

You can feel it in the classroom. In Lentz's English 1–2 the other day, while he was elaborating on "Tintern Abbey," I timed the sniffs and coughs and hawking sounds from student throats and noses, never more than a few seconds apart, as if there were an invisible ball of snot bouncing around the room, like a beach ball in a stadium, landing first on one student, then another.

My colleagues feel November, too. At the bookstore, I run into Jennifer Clarvoe, of the English Department, just back from California, her system in metabolic shock after three consecutive Thai meals. She glances outside at our tiny, block-long street, much less charming than in autumn. "I go home," she says with a sigh. "I watch 'Star Trek' at six o'clock with my cat. I eat my frozen dinner . . ."

The dormitory starts to feel, and smell, like a cage, especially after weekends, when the carpet is mud-tracked, beer-soaked, and the maids' Monday morning revenge on inmates is to vacuum hard and early, banging the machine into every door.

We all face it now: the long haul.

❧

"I HATE IT, I just hate it," Cyrus Banning says. White-bearded, ruddy, and bespectacled, he sits in a Philosophy Department office in the basement of Ascension Hall. "A lot of work, detailed work, is involved.

Peoples' feelings run high. What I regard as civility, other people regard as intrusiveness and coldness. It's an anxious time for everybody. One reason I don't like it is I know people are agitated and uncomfortable and scared. I try to put them at ease, and I don't know if I'm acting as uncomfortable and stupid from their point of view. What do the candidates see when they see me? A tired old man with a white beard?"

There's a tenure-track position open in the Philosophy Department, and Banning, a Kenyon professor since 1962, chairing the search committee, is at the beginning of a process that's an ordeal. It's a process being replicated in a dozen other places around the college, in contested areas like IPHS and Women's and Gender Studies as well as in relatively quiet departments like his own. The English Department isn't hiring this year, but I'm following the Philosophy Department search: the sifting of applications, the composition of lists for interviews at the East Coast meeting of the American Philosophical Association in New York next month, the invitation of candidates to campus for interviews and auditions. I've even arranged to sit in on the final meetings, when the searchers decide on who they want, and I'll wait with them to see if the people Kenyon chooses want Kenyon in return. I'll see if they get their first choice, their second, or if, mood darkening, expenses rising, time growing short, they're forced further down their list of candidates, far enough down, maybe, that they abort the tenure-track search and settle for a stopgap visiting appointment. Or—this is an unlikely worst-case scenario—they piss on the fire, call in the dogs, call off the hunt, and decide to try their luck next season.

It's a lengthy process and costly—about $3,000 per search, sometimes more—in which often differing ideas of what the college should be confront the reality of what the college is. Part of the problem with searches is sheer numbers. The jobs that Kenyon advertises attract hundreds of applications. It's fair to say that, most years, as many people apply to teach at Kenyon as to study here. All this gives Cyrus Banning the appearance of a reluctant passenger on a roller coaster. The fact that he's ridden before—maybe ten search committees over the course of his career—doesn't make the trip any more appealing.

It wasn't always this way. In my student days, and on through the seventies, Kenyon hired via the now much-derided "old boy network." If you had an opening you called a friendly chairman back in someone's graduate school, asking whether he had a likely rookie who might be right for Kenyon. When the prospect showed up in Gambier, what he—later, she—went through was more like a fraternity initiation than a job interview.

"I arrived on a sultry May afternoon," an English Department colleague recalls. "The mood was very much end-of-year. At the Alumni House, there's a note from the chair, Bob Daniel: welcome to Gambier, I should make myself comfortable, he'd fetch me at 4:00 P.M., which he does, and we drive to his house, which is all of one hundred yards away. 'Would you like a drink?' he asks. I say, Scotch. He brings me a tumbler, it must have been ten or twelve ounces, with a *few* cubes of ice in it, a quadruple, a quintuple shot of Scotch. I wouldn't know how to begin to describe it. After half an hour, I'm nursing it. He asks would I like a refill, he asks me two or three times, and I get the idea I'm supposed to have a refill. Meanwhile, we're talking about literature, about teaching. I have no idea how much Scotch I've drunk. I was in awe of Bob Daniel. Here's a guy who knew Allen Tate!

"Then, around six, the doorbell rings and it's Gal and Joan Crump. I remember standing up to meet this next member of the department and his wife and thinking, *Holy shit, I'm completely smashed.* We go to the Alcove Restaurant in Mount Vernon, and it's two drinks before, wine with, brandy afterwards. I remember it as clear as yesterday, thinking: *I'm shit-faced, falling-all-over-myself, undergraduate drunk, and I hope I can hold it together until we get back to the hotel.*

"But we're not going back to the hotel. It comes out we're going back to the Daniels' where the rest of the department is waiting to meet the candidate. *It's over,* it occurs to me. *I don't have a prayer.* I walk in, and the whole department is sitting around, pouring themselves their first drink . . ."

The old boy network is history now, condemned as elitist, clubby, possibly discriminatory. What's replaced it is supposedly more open, more rigorous, more carefully regulated, but not necessarily more efficient. There are at least two problems. The first is a paradox: that a diligent search entails a higher risk of failure than a phone call to some grad school chairman. You tend to spot the same fine candidates that other schools identify, and some of those other schools can offer more money, or a lower teaching load, or a bigger library, or a better chance of a job for the candidate's spouse. This is a problem that Kenyon's English Department runs into. Like it or not—and there are people in other departments who definitely don't like it—the English Department still has a national reputation. Its openings are likely to attract hotshots who may also be looking at Chicago and Stanford—and end up going there.

The other problem with national searches is that they aren't. Not every candidate is unknown, coming in from far away. Often, applications have Gambier postmarks. They come from visiting professors trying to snag a tenured berth. That makes things tricky. "The worry with internal candidates," says Provost Reed Browning, "is that friendship and convenience and wondering what to do over the next four months with a candidate who hasn't been selected will cloud the vision." Or they come from a professor's spouse, and when this happens, watch the melodrama begin, lobbying and whispering that give the supposedly national search an inflamed local angle, so acute you could start to miss the old boy network. Suddenly, local careers and reputations are on the line. And everybody knows it.

Spousal hiring is the black hole of the small liberal arts college. There's not a department in town that hasn't been affected by it. Spousal hiring turns scholars into influence peddlers, colleagues into co-conspirators. It strains marriages, stresses departments. It's bad enough when someone's spouse isn't such a hot candidate. Turn them down and the damage is limited to one unhappy household. It's worse when the spouse candidate is good, as good or maybe better, fresher, more congenial than someone who already holds the coveted position. And it's even worse when the spouse candidate fills in for a year while the incumbent is on sabbatical, then gets shunted to the sidelines when the old goat returns. When that happens, the pain doesn't go away. There's not a year here that doesn't have one or more such melodramas in progress; every one is different, and every case is special. Those disinterested national star searches are fine, in principle. But wait until someone you know is a candidate and, well, yesterday's advocate of coast-to-coast talent hunts starts talking about neighborhood values, known quantities, keeping folks happy at a residential college.

At the start of the Philosophy search, Banning is optimistic, to a point. There are two internal candidates, both currently visiting professors in the Philosophy Department: no way of knowing how messy that will be. But he feels confident that the department may not have to travel too far down its list of candidates. "What we would like to get," he says, "is a bright, congenial, cheerful colleague. Obviously, the best candidate would be a black woman, but that's not going to happen. They're just not out there." Short of that, he feels the right kinds of candidates will find their way to Kenyon.

"There's a greater degree of self-selection in Philosophy," he says. "The people who apply to Princeton, Harvard, and Stanford will not apply to Kenyon. The very best people, we don't get. We make clear it's not a research position. You must teach in order to hold a position here. It's a teaching institution. You must do research, but it's known you don't have to do six articles and a book to survive at Kenyon."

The job pays $33,000 or so a year; there's a little room to negotiate, not much, and Banning doesn't think that money, alone, is that much of an issue in hiring. "Philosophy's not a money field," he says. "A Ph.D. in philosophy isn't going to make a lot of money. You can't go into private practice as a philosopher, into industry or government or consulting work. The only way you can do philosophy is to teach it."

🌿

"WELL, WE'RE ON the John C. Templeton Honor Roll for Character-building Colleges," Phil Jordan announces at his weekly senior staff breakfast. Jordan and his subordinates—some deans, the chair of the faculty, some people from the business side—meet like this once a week. The *U.S. News and World Report* survey still rankles, and this lesser survey, from a neoconservative no one's heard of, doesn't so much balance that annoyance as suggest that all surveys are part of the same silly pack.

"How *is* John?" someone asks, kiddingly.

"*Who* is John?" someone else inquires.

"Some guy who has money and has a foundation which evaluates colleges for character building. We made that list. He evaluates them for teaching free enterprise, too. That's another list."

"Did anybody make *both* lists?"

"We made another list for being among America's thirty-five prettiest colleges," John Anderson, the dean of admissions, volunteers. "They're really going crazy out there with lists and rankings."

Surveys aside, the senior staff chats about Peter Rutkoff, my History Department buddy. He's had a heart attack. I stopped in at the Mount Vernon hospital yesterday, found him resting in bed with the *New York Post*. They chat about how colleges are doing financially—"grim all over"—and about fund-raising: "too early to tell." A much-liked security guy has testicular cancer, a senior trustee is recovering from surgery. Then they turn to the fall meeting of the board of trustees, two weeks away.

"What is it we hope to have accomplished by the end of the meeting?" Jordan asks. They start putting their agenda together. They want to adjust the payout on the endowment, reducing what goes into college operations and slightly increasing what is added to the endowment principal. They want the college to remain the same size, at least until the midnineties. They want the trustees to commit to adding a faculty member per year. But the biggest item is "pricing policy." What it amounts to is, Kenyon wants to raise its fees by 9 percent. That might be tricky, since some trustees want the college to hold prices down.

They rehearse some arguments. Compared to price rises at public institutions—admittedly, much cheaper places to start with—Kenyon's 9 percent hike is "minuscule." Still, among private colleges, it may be on the high side. They talk about "price tolerance." They mull over the impact on scholarships: they'll have to go up, too, to keep pace with tuition. Anticipating arguments, guessing at individual reactions, listing key trustees to turn to, if the meeting goes off course, they rough out their plan of attack. "The trustees," warns Jordan, "are not a group given to a high degree of self-discipline or even focus. We need a pretty highly structured discussion."

❧

MARKING PAPERS IS, without a doubt, the hardest thing we do. How compromised and imprisoned you feel when you see that stack of undergraduate papers sitting on your desk, like a dozen unfiled income tax returns! They turn your life into one long April 15. Dozens, hundreds of pages, and I'm just teaching one little seminar; imagine what it's like for someone with a full three-course load, 45 students in one class, 30 in another, a dozen more in a seminar, 87 students generating, let's say, 25 pages per semester, that's 3,480 pages per semester, 6,960 per year, excluding final exams and honors essays. It gets worse, because unless you're very good or very bad, you're going to have to read those papers twice, once to get a feeling for them—how they rate as a group and where they stand individually—and then you're going to have to go through them again, red marking pen in hand, filling the margins with enough ink for the students to know they're getting their money's worth, topping things off with a closing note that nicely balances encouragement and reproof.

Say goodbye, then, to the idea of leisure reading. Your eyeballs belong to the college: that's 6,960 pages per year, read twice: 13,920 pages. My

Modern Library *War and Peace,* translated by Constance Garnett, runs 1,136 pages. But we're not talking Leo Tolstoy, we're not talking Constance Garnett. You can't just curl up in an easy chair, pour a drink, and grade student papers from eight till midnight. After three or four papers, terrible things happen to you, a wave of disabling reactions. Mistakes that were merely annoying in the first paper are maddening in the third. Judgments darken, comments get bitterly ad hominem. The first time you see *conscience* spelled with a "t" and ending in "ious" you merely circle it; before long, you're forecasting death. And then you start dying a little yourself. Is it *me,* you wonder, is it something wrong with me? This thing about misspellings . . . is it my funny little hangup? What am I doing here? Reaching out and squeezing the pimples on someone else's face? Hey, get wise, the spell-checker broke down. Okay?

Eventually, you see some errors repeated so often you go back to the dictionary, checking *harass, embarrass, weird,* just to make sure you're not going crazy, that they haven't changed spellings lately. A Ph.D., literate, intellectual, you sit at your desk writing "awk" for "awkward," you write it so often—awk, awk, awk—you feel like a bird shitting on a statue. You lean forward, late at night, mumbling grade school lessons, eternal truths like "*i* before *e,* except after *c*" and "there is a *rat* in *separate.*" This is what all your dreams have come to, and since you can't whip through it, you divide hell into pieces, manageable chunks. You try to accompany grading papers with useful labor—soaking beans or doing laundry. You interrupt yourself with small, pathetic rewards: one more paper and I'll floss my teeth! One more paper and I'll walk around the dormitory!

It's the hardest thing we do. It's also the most important: a one-on-one transaction between teacher and student, writer and reader, performer and audience. There's no ducking it: no student assistants to do the grunt work. There are moments when you miss the perquisites of stardom: walking out of a lecture hall while a graduate student collects undergraduate prose. But that's not Kenyon: we owe them the hours we spend spreading red ink around their papers. My only doubts are at the other end of the equation: whether the messages we send are received. Splattering comments on papers, you sense you are working harder on grading than they ever did on writing, that you are obliged to take seriously what they took casually.

Watch a class, any class, when papers are returned. Watch how they approach the front of the room at the end of the period, grab their paper off the table, turn right to the last page, glance at the grade, then, like factory workers just making sure that the right amount is on their weekly paycheck, no unexpected deductions, shove the things in their pockets and leave. Those painstaking comments are for later. Do they ever get to them? I wonder. Sometimes, near the end of a semester, professors put out that last batch of corrected papers on a chair in front of their offices, so students can retrieve their final efforts. The pile goes down, granted, but it never goes away. There's always a handful that stay there, on into summer, till someone throws them out.

❦

"THERE ARE TWO WAYS of getting through Kenyon College," my pal Mike informs me. This was right after classes started and we were sitting at the bar of the Village Inn, renewing a friendship that began a couple years ago, when he took both courses I was teaching. He's had his ups and downs around here: he's a six-year man at Kenyon. He spent last year as an oil rig diver in the Gulf of Mexico.

"You can go to class and not do the work," Mike declares. "Or you can not go to class and do the work. Either way, you get a B minus." He pauses, reflecting back on wilder years. "Or you can not do either one, like I did. Then you get a C minus." We sit a moment longer, contemplating our beers—he drinks Beck's, I drink Rolling Rock—and suddenly we enter hypothetical realms. We're out there among quasars, black holes, novas. "Or you could . . ."—I sense the hesitation of a thinker on the edge of discovery, the charity of an aging gardener planting the seedlings of fruit trees he will never live to harvest—". . . go to classes *and* do the work. A minus."

I haven't been putting letter grades on my writing students' papers, so far. Letter grades would lead to comparisons and rivalries and a kind of caste system, dividing students between Brahmins and untouchables. Instead, I make comments that I hope are helpful. But I'm only buying time. Before long, everyone in this class will be getting a grade from me, and then I will have to face one of the oddest and most quietly disturbing elements of college life: grade inflation.

Who doesn't remember how things used to be? On paper, in the Kenyon faculty handbook, the rules haven't changed:

GRADES. Instructors are required to report one of the following grades for students enrolled for credit.

A—Excellent
B—Good

C—Average
D—Poor
F—Failing

"The faculty has established broad guidelines for grade distribution," the handbook continues. "Though not required in specific courses, it is desirable for 20 percent of all grades to be A, 30 percent B, 30 percent C, 8 percent D and 2 percent F."

That's policy, not practice. A confidential 1990–91 grading survey of nineteen selected liberal arts institutions, Kenyon included, showed that As and Bs accounted for 75 percent of all grades. The gentleman's C has become the gentleman's—and gentlewoman's—B.

Perhaps because the phenomenon is so widespread—i.e., we're all in it together—no one seems to be losing sleep about grade inflation. When you ask about it, you're quickly made to feel a little simple. Press on and the first line of defense is that it's good news, after all, that so many of our students do so well. They do well because we admit them carefully, teach them diligently, counsel them wisely if they get in trouble. At Kenyon, if a student does below-average work—i.e., C minus or less—he or she gets pulled in for a chat, possibly placed on "conditional enrollment." Life support systems are readied, safety nets go up, an ambulance is waiting. Who would want it otherwise? What kind of reactionary creep defines the quality of an institution with a body count of the number of people who fail there? What's my problem anyway?

My problem is that I'm bothered when there's a discrepancy between what a place says and what it does, when disinterested judgment based on a full, fair reading gets replaced by a clubby chuckle. It's not that anyone says, let's compromise, let's make it easier on our customers, let's water the wine. But colleges have drifted away from their stated standards. Our generosity discredits us. What starts as a small concession becomes an institutional cop-out; today's favor is tomorrow's entitlement. Before long, people get cynical. If our grades are written on inflated paper, what about our diplomas? And the more students I talk to about grading, the more cynical the system seems.

"B is blah, B minus is eeech, and C is: you suck," explains an English major named Amy, who's done well here. "It's too easy to get a B, and you have to sell your soul to get an A." A student who gets As pretty regularly is Becky, a junior English major. She's the kind of student Kenyon likes to crow about. She chose Kenyon over Princeton and Dartmouth. But her reading of Kenyon's grading system is, if anything, more skeptical than what my friend Mike told me at the Village Inn. "A large number of students are English majors by default," she says. "It's not the toughest department. You can slide through, say nothing for the entire semester, and get away with it. I guess it's possible to flunk out of here, but you've got to try hard to do it."

So much for jaded upper-class students. Come with me now to the freshman dorms. I'm sitting outside one sunny day, enjoying autumn sunlight, and a student spots me, changes direction, and sits down beside me. He looks at me glumly, offers no small talk. "I just found out how easy this place is," he says. "I turned in a paper I wrote in forty-five minutes at two in the morning. I got an A minus. And it was a bad paper." A few days later, another freshman accosts me in front of the post office. "I'm tired of not doing the work and getting straight As."

In Lewis Hall, I encounter one of the more thoughtful students, by no means a nerd but I've noticed he has a serious side. He only drinks on weekends. "You have very bright students here," he says, "and some who aren't into studying at all. I've always been told I'm bright, but I do stuff half-assed, at the last minute, and get by on what I already know. I find there are some people here I honestly can't believe got in. I've been asked to look over papers and the grammar was terrible. Who taught these people? What have they been teaching themselves? And this is college! I kind of wish that the administration—this is pompous— would be a little stricter with the kind of people they let in."

Then there's a guy down the hall who, in no time at all, has become a legend. The biggest scammer and goof-off in the hall, his classmates say. He spends all his time sleeping, watching TV, eating pizza, visiting other dorms. If he goes to the library at all he gets no further than the atrium, where he flirts with girls. And—because he's shrewd—he gets away with it! I seek this kid out, find him immediately likable, the kind of student Kenyon should turn inside out. I ask him how hard he works here.

"You really want to know?" he asks. I nod. "If I don't have a paper due, I probably put in half an hour a week. If I have a paper due, I stay up the whole night before and write the paper."

"What kind of grades are you pulling?" I ask. I know a candidate for a gentleman's C when I see one. Maybe even a D, that would shake him up.

"It's embarrassing. B plus, across the board."

"So what do you think about that?"

"The type of student who comes here . . ." The kid pauses. He's the kind who always has an engaging take on things. ". . . if they'd worked harder they would be in an Ivy League school. That's my first complaint. The procrastinators and fuck-ups. If I saw a student like myself, I would talk to that student and I'd say, you should have proofread that paper and maybe you'd have seen you wrote half a sentence . . ."

His voice trails off. I wait, wishing he hadn't been so quick to find out that, when you lift the college's lips, you find more tongue and gum than bite.

"And I still get a B plus."

As disarmingly frank as students are about grades, faculty members are disingenuous. They'll talk about how tough they are, tell you about the Cs they've handed out, sounding prouder of them than of the As they give. Sometimes they sound like people bragging about their prowess in bed: like Sicilian husbands hanging sheets stained with their brides' hymenal blood out of the window the morning after they get married. But, in the long run, it's only talk. They may begin a course with a scattering of Cs and Ds, but everyone knows that this is a scare tactic. In the end, Bs prevail.

"I don't know how to account for it," one professor tells me. "There's an almost visceral sense when you're grading a paper: *It's not that bad, so give it a B*. It's hard to say, *Look, this isn't what we want, this is a C*. It's very hard to say that. Grades are coded, and you're sending a message with a C that this is disastrous. You give up responsibility, feeling that the forces against you are colossal. Every year I say, *Asshole, grade harder*. But I can't do it."

I drop in on another professor, someone who says he aims to be "a moderately hard grader" but fails, the way almost all of us do. "It's a lot easier to give a higher grade," he says. "Hard grades cause upset, and you have to be able to defend your grade when they come in angry. You give someone a C plus, they think you're saying they're a C plus person. It's indelible. And college is haunted in a gruesome way by high school teachers who made people straight A students and got them into the habit of thinking extremely well of themselves."

I go where the grades go, to the Registrar's Office, because I'm still puzzled. C is average, right? That's what the college faculty handbook says. Average means that a certain number of students are above and a certain balancing number below. But at Kenyon, everybody's average or above: if you do prolonged less-than-average work, you can't graduate. So, okay, everybody who graduates is above average. Well, wait a minute, where are the below-average students? Down the road at Mount Vernon's College of the Nazarene? In Columbus, at Zero State? At Moler Barber College?

"Where are the below-average students?" Rich Switzer, the lanky, good-humored registrar, repeats my question. He's like a student called on in class, improvising. "That's a good question," he concedes. We look at each other. He smiles, I smile back. It's a delicious moment. It reminds me of the time an income tax guy explained business deductions to me, advised me to save movie admission stubs because, hey, I might write a movie someday, I had to keep up with what was on the screen, right, and if I forgot about the stubs, no sweat. He opened a desk drawer, riffled through a confetti of theater and movie tickets going back to the opening night of *South Pacific*. "I've got plenty," he said. Now Rich Switzer gives me a peek into the world of college accounting.

"We have to tell the world you can't have a Kenyon degree unless you're doing at least average work?" he says. It comes out like a question, not an answer, something we're just trying out together. "Yes?"

I nod, yes. We both laugh. Then I ask whether it is possible to flunk out of college. Granted, subpar work gets you on conditional enrollment; keep it up, you can be advised, or required, to withdraw. At any given moment, there are a couple dozen students on conditional enrollment, Switzer tells me. Around half of those may withdraw, usually with the understanding that they can come back if they clean up their act. It's not like anyone's hopelessly dumb, Switzer says: he can't remember more than one or two of those, over the years. It's behavior problems, drugs, alcohol, family trouble, homesickness.

"Basically, they almost always tend to be spoiled kids from Connecticut," he says. "You wouldn't believe the number from Greenwich!"

It's a wonderful island we've got here, I conclude, where no one fails, where everyone is average or above, where—as Woody Allen remarks—80 percent of life is just showing up. Who wouldn't want to live in such a place? Twenty thousand dollars per year is cheap insurance against failure. True, it doesn't insure from cradle to grave; it's a four-year policy, convocation to graduation. But that's four good years. Maybe not as good as they could be, however, if we did what we said we do, if we really marked the difference between excellent, good, average, and below. This is naive, I suppose. The college won't die of grade inflation. Still, something valuable is lost in the land of the universal B: intellectual honesty. "Every kid a winner," someone said to me the other day. That's the slogan of the Little League.

🌿

YOU SEE THE FLAG at half-mast behind Ransom Hall and your first impulse is to hope that it wasn't someone local. Let it be their president, Bush, not our president, Jordan. Better a pope or a politician, far away, than a well-liked janitor, an ancient trustee, a student slamming into a tree. But death has made a local stop, it turns out. Bob Baker, a splendid history professor in my time, died after years of ill health. I'm supposed to say something about him at a memorial service. What I'll say is that, it's awkward for professors and students to see each other grow old. Maybe we should never meet again after we graduate, just move on, leaving classroom memories in place, without considering what does, or doesn't, happen later. Another thing I might say is that it's not the future, the darkness in front, that bothers me. It's the lights going out in back, the darkness behind.

🌿

BEGINNING FICTION WRITERS tend to present narrators who are scarcely disguised—if wishful—versions of themselves. You get sardonic, lonely young men, jaded, ironical women, all living through the aftermath of something tragic that happened before this particular story begins. To parry this, I ask the class to think back to their summer jobs and to build a story around a day in the life of a coworker—not some upwardly mobile college kid but a full-timer who wouldn't be taking off at Labor Day. I succeed only partially. Instead of getting into the lives of people they know, the students resort to redneck, blue-collar working-class clichés. I get a lot of waitresses-with-attitude, right out of "Alice." One of my better writers turns in a piece set in a waterfront seafood joint in Maine. There's lots of hot grease on "the fucking grill," lots of pudgy tourists, whining kids, pissed-off employees. After the class finishes commenting, I sum things up—lack of color and atmosphere, perfunctory, predictable characters, a sense of a writer as bored at the typewriter as her waitress is at the deep fryer. Then I take a chance and ask the student to tell us about summer in Maine. The result is spectacular: an eccentric town, lively, gay restaurant owners, customers, and characters all over the place, plus underlying tensions between yearlong residents and moneyed summer residents. All this and a mouth-watering description of lobster rolls, the fresh white meat picked out of the shell, mixed with not too much mayonnaise, wrapped in white bread. We're all hungry when she gets done, and I hope my lesson has gotten across. There's a story in there, someplace.

❧

OUR LATEST ENGLISH DEPARTMENT MEETING is a cheerful, feisty session, galvanized by a threat from outside that is reported to us by a colleague, Ted Mason. It seems that some folks in other departments are pressing for the college to offer minors. Minors would give students a chance to dress up their résumés, but this isn't really about students. It's this: minors might enable small departments to expand their enrollments and, if that happened, to add faculty. Some Kenyon departments are close to becoming "service departments": lots of students in introductory courses but just a handful of majors. They're like well-situated restaurants where customers stop by for a drink-with-a-view at sunset but no one stays for dinner. Offering minors might help them.

All this is hypothetical. No one really knows whether minors would lead to fewer majors in English or lots more English minors, whether the net effect would be to increase our teaching load, reduce it, or not make any difference at all. But our consensus is that we don't want to be pushed around on this, that we need to defend ourselves against people who resent our size, our reputation, or both. So we try out various arguments against minors in English: that we're overburdened already, that we'd have to load up on introductory courses and cut down on electives, that there's no pedagogical coherence in an English minor. It would be a mish-mash, what Phil Church calls "a dip and doodle thing." Finally, one colleague comes up with an answer aimed at jealous competitors in other departments. "Try this on them," she suggests to Mason. "We hire good junior people, the best available, and they get bozos, and that's it."

From there, we get into a discussion of the department's reputation. Some people see it as an empire, pure and simple, an Evil Empire. Some see it as an Ottoman Empire, overrated and riding on the past. Others portray us as an Easy Empire, we hear. We mull this one over a while. In other courses, Tim Shutt says, you learn science, which is hard; you learn a foreign language, which is also hard. In English, the impression is, "you just read books and emote."

❧

THE ROAST BEEF has turned into pot roast by the time it arrives at my table at the trustees' dinner. Forget the vegetables. "Every time I see squash on my plate, I feel they're asking for money," one benefactor confides. "Phil probably wanted to send a message," a senior administrator remarks, glumly glancing down at his plate. "This is by far the least lavish trustees' dinner I've seen." Word is that the trustees' meeting went well, the administration got what it was asking for—permission to raise the prices being item number one. Tonight is social, congenial, even self-congratulatory. "It's nice being respected in a place society respects," a trustee tells me. Everything's pleasant. Granted, it hasn't always been that way. There have been—what shall we call them?—incidents. Loose hands, loose lips, one drink too many, that sort of thing. Not surprising. Some professors have an attitude, skeptical and haughty, toward people who make it big on the outside, and trustees, in turn, don't like being condescended to by academics. "I've found some of the trustees to be bright and interesting, as well-read as academics," says a professor seated nearby. "It's gotten better in recent years. There used to be incidents, guys getting looped, slurring, stumbling, arms around female faculty, faculty wives, all in a sort of bush league way. You want to say, 'Look, you drunken old fart . . . .'"

Tonight, everyone behaves well. I've arranged to be seated next to Charles Davison, a Connecticut greeting card company owner who's reputed to be something of a loose cannon. I test him early, ask how he'd feel about sending a kid to Kenyon. This is before I learn that he *has* sent a kid to Kenyon. "To this bucket of nothing?!" he retorts, and my interest perks up instantly; this love-in might turn lively after all. But no, Davison turns out to be a loyalist, in his nineteenth-hole-at-the-golf-course way. Elsewhere, around the room, I spot three trustees—Gerry Fields, John Buckley, Harvey Lodish—who were students in my time. That feels old, like the first time I noticed that men younger than I am were being nominated to the Supreme Court.

The only critical note all weekend came from Bill Ranney, after the Kenyon football game. We adjourned to the oxymoronically named Gambier Deli. He took off a blazer with a Kenyon coat of arms on it, revealing a sweater with a Kenyon coat of arms below, and—while I was wondering about his undershirt—assured me that the alumni campaigning for fraternities look forward to Jordan's departure. "We measure his insincerity by the level of his laughter," he said. Unless I'm way wrong, though, these gents aren't going to get far with the board of trustees. It may be different at other colleges; it's been different at this college, in the past. At least three college presidents, including its founder, have been ushered out by trustees. But that's not in the cards now.

"The administration runs the college," a classmate trustee, David Banks, tells me. The paradox of being a trustee, he explains, is that you have hands-on business types operating part-time and at some remove from the college. Lines must be drawn, decisions made about how far to get involved. "Once you interfere, you'll do it only once," Banks warns, "because then you've got a dead president."

This evening's president is alive and well, thanks. He arises to present our entertainment, a singing group of female students—all white—who announce they are about to do their version of the Pointer Sisters' "He's So Shy." Instantly, I reach for my wineglass: this upcoming madrigal and the mystery meat that preceded it will need some washing down. Sure enough, what comes my way sounds like something from the Vienna Boys' Choir. I'm sitting there, wondering why my life turned out this way, and a trustee wife leans over toward me. She senses my reaction to the evening's entertainment. "What's wrong with being a WASP bastion?" she asks. "Is there something wrong with that?" I tell her yes.

☙

IT'S SNOWING OUTSIDE—winter's first snow—as if nature itself conspired to underscore the whiteness of the campus, when John Anderson welcomes a couple dozen high school admissions counselors, half of them black, and urges them to send minority students to Kenyon. Anderson describes the goals of a liberal arts college—"learning to think, gather, analyze, evaluate." He summons up Kenyon's "long and illustrious literary tradition," touts its "we try harder" science departments, acknowledges its $20,000 plus per year cost, describes available scholarship aid. He introduces two smiling student guides, one black, one Hispanic, and sends the whole bunch out for a tour of the campus.

I tag along. The counselors are a slow-moving, gabby group, anxious to go inside. Once they're in the bookstore, souvenir shopping, it's hard to get them back to Peirce Hall in time for lunch. At lunch—croissant sandwiches, salad, cheese-broccoli soup, chocolate chip cookies—Frank Hale, executive assistant for multicultural affairs, and Phil Jordan renew the plea for minority applicants. It's a gallant effort, but I sense the problem: most of their students want safer choices, closer to home, while the superstars are headed for the Ivies.

What I've been most curious about is a session that's scheduled after lunch, when three black students are supposed to have an unconstrained chat with these visitors, upstairs in the Black Student Union lounge. I'm barely seated, though, when John Anderson announces that college policy is to leave students alone with outsiders. It's a decent idea, I guess, and risky. I leave, glancing at the three students waiting to talk. Two of them are gamely smiling; I suspect they'll speak well of Kenyon. I'm less sure about the third: she seems unhappy, angry, glaring. This student is named Reida, and later I learn that I read her expression correctly. At least two of the high school counselors called John Anderson and wondered why he let her on the panel; they felt her criticism all but erased the welcoming impression the college was straining to create. Later still, I invite Reida to drop by my office and talk about what happened that afternoon.

"They know I have problems with Kenyon," Reida tells me, and, yes, she wasn't happy finding herself on a panel with two other students who are "basically cheerleaders for Kenyon."

A resident of Newark, New Jersey, Reida came "blind" to Kenyon. A counselor at a boarding school she'd attended praised her, said she was articulate, knew how to deal with white people, could handle Kenyon. Now, she thinks, she was badly misled. "I don't like this place," she says. "I don't want to tell people to come here, and I don't want to feel guilty about getting people to come here."

Her problems with Kenyon are complicated. For one thing, she doesn't drink or smoke and doesn't like being around people who do. She thinks that the courses she's taken here have stinted black authors: "I always feel I'm getting a 'black week' or a 'women's week,' and then it's back to the mainstream." She charges that the college's efforts at diversity are inadequate, short on curricular change and support services. And, while fraternities routinely sit down to eat together at Peirce Hall, a table of black students gets regarded with suspicion, she says. "They make you feel paranoid about sitting with your own." Fraternities have—or have had—lounges; some of them have off-campus lodges. But black students are begrudged the key to the Black Student Union, a room in Peirce Hall that they want to lock and open at will. "We need a home, a place where you can put your feet up, relax, not be bothered, hang out without being stared at, watch 'Cosby' without people getting emotional about switching to 'The Simpsons.' That's the issue. Other Great Lakes College Association schools have black houses. They don't have ten students fighting for a little room."

What bothers her most, I think, is the role that she feels a black student is asked to play here: ambassador, spokesperson, exhibit A. She's tired of the word *multicultural,* tired of hearing about "qualified" blacks. "If you want me to educate white students about black students, pay me a salary like everyone else on this campus," she says. "My mom pays for me to be educated about Europeans. Someone can pay me to educate them about blacks."

I can recognize very little of a place I know and usually like in Reida's account of Kenyon. It seems to me she's constructed the harshest possible case, often mistaking awkwardness for arrogance. And, it's fair to add, other black students tell a different story. Still, her testimony remains in mind, with all the indelible authority of a sour note.

Blacks have a simplistic view of Kenyon and Kenyon has a simplistic view of blacks, Ted Mason remarks when I bring this up as we run along the Kokosing. There are blunders on both sides. "Sometimes you want to say, look, you didn't go to Howard or Spellman," Mason says. "You didn't go to Wilberforce or O.S.U. You went to Kenyon. Does that mean anything to you?"

🌿

RAW, RESTLESS NOVEMBER. Restless faculty. Sometimes at night you can almost sense it, like owls hooting along the Kokosing or dogs barking at distant farms—it's odd, how far the sound of a barking dog carries at night—and I can hear the sound of colleagues reworking vitas, old hot-shit transcripts being dusted off by once-promising top-gun graduate students, aging letters of recommendation reread, recopied, the scanning of job lists, forlorn requests for Guggenheim and Fulbright applications, NEH and NEA grants, a collective chorus of "Rescue me, rescue me!" The calls come from all over, all directions, incoming and outgoing, hundreds of applications piling up in the Philosophy Department for one tenure-track job, hundreds of smart, desperate people for whom a call from Gambier would spell joy: a small place, a house with a yard, better-than-average students, a job that's as close to lifetime employment as you can get.

I wondered about restlessness when I was talking to Phil Jordan. I asked about it twice, to the point where he must have wondered whether I was harping on the down side of things, but I really wasn't. I was wondering why people aren't happier, not just here but at colleges everywhere.

"We have every reason, all of us, to be disappointed with the way we carry on our careers," he answered. "We were all bright students, we all had senses of high promise as graduate students. We saw ourselves making contributions to the higher world of scholarship, as well as teaching. There are fantasies: I will change this field. My contributions will be significant and recognized. I have energies which will lead to work that will make me acknowledged. And here you come into a situation where you can do *something* of all you had hoped for, but you wish you could do it at a faster pace, more of it. It's hard to sustain yourself. You think, I should be farther along. I should have accomplished something. I ordered my life wrong. And then, what happens when your graduate school mentor comes and gives a lecture, someone who writes, gets awards, is being recognized? And what are you doing?"

He knows, I think, as I listen to Phil Jordan give what will turn out to be the warmest and most empathetic response I'll have from him all year. *He knows.* In the same way that Goethe said he'd never heard of a crime he could not imagine himself committing, so Jordan has never heard a complaint about college life that would surprise him.

"Everything's on the line when you teach," he says. "You can prepare for hours and be terrible. Then, after grading papers, advising students, you find yourself wondering, *Does anybody know? Does anybody care?* You're isolated. The work's repetitive. The utter predictability of the future can give you comfort—or it can be dismal. You can have terrific days, feel you're part of a terrific department, gorgeous days, a wonderful feeling of freedom. Or you can have black moods, when you feel like a kept woman."

❦ *December*

I RETURN FROM CHICAGO, though only for a couple weeks. People around here can go on for hours about theories of academic scheduling, factoring in transportation costs, heating bills, you name it, but the bottom line is that Thanksgiving comes too close to Christmas, and, as long as we celebrate both holidays, we condemn ourselves to this little rump of time in December, two weeks under gray blanketing skies, a time of cold rain, puddles on Middle Path, and all the color in the landscape concentrated in the lights of a Christmas tree in front of the Kenyon Inn that you can see for miles away, coming in from offshore. In no time, the place surrounds me.

I begin to understand why so many writers come to roost in academe. It's not just the money and the medical benefits. It's not just a cynical decision to cash in whatever reputation we've acquired outside. It's because the writing life is lonely. I sensed it, over Thanksgiving break: whole days by myself, no conversation between my wife's departure in the morning and return home at night, day after day that even the most productive writing and reading can't more than half fill. In Gambier the days are crowded and there are people all around.

In Peirce Hall, at breakfast, I notice the dark oil paintings of college presidents and benefactors have been covered over with black cloth. This, it turns out, is a "day without art," sponsored by AIDS Awareness Week. Couldn't they have found some other art to cover? And what is it about Gambier that makes worthy causes seem ridiculous by the time they arrive here?

The most highly charged confrontation I can remember from my own student days in Peirce Hall was a food riot. I can still see the shower of sugar bags that greeted the food supervisor the night he served Polish sausage, can still picture the guy who jumped on a table, a pitcher of milk in one hand, a pitcher of lemonade in the other, walking the length of the table, pouring out the contents of both pitchers on diners' heads, like a gardener watering two rows of flowers.

These newer battles are less good-humored. They battle about the tables in the dining hall. Fraternities sit together at tables, and the other day a hundred women and independent men decided to change that. Putting up a sign announcing "open seating," they sat at fraternity tables. Some frat guys moved to other tables, some left, others sat where they always sat, tolerating the outsiders, sort of. "The Dekes lined up behind us and sat on the heater," one sit-in participant tells me. "They refused to sit with us. 'Why not sit with us?' we asked. One started yelling, called a woman a bitch. Then they sat at one end of the bench and started moving in, till we were all squished."

In the afternoon, I dropped in at a presentation by the first candidate invited here for the Women's and Gender Studies search, a lightly and belatedly publicized appearance that kicked off all sorts of conspiracy theories about the motive and methods of the search committee. The underlying debate seems to be whether the Women's and Gender Studies chair should be a scholar—academic, nonpartisan—or a sixties-style activist committed to feminism as a resonant, grass-roots movement. Today's candidate was the activist type, jovial and clearly partisan, whose speech described codependency as a concept used, conspiratorially, to depoliticize feminism. The idea seems to be that, by subscribing to the concept of codependency, women embark on therapy, which can lead to personal peace but deflects them from changing a society that is "a racist, capitalist, heteropatriarchy." Postlecture questions related to the fascist leanings of the Alcoholics Anonymous founders, the possible lesbianism of the Women's Christian Temperance Union founder, and something about genital mutilation. Afterwards, the scholarly types around the room said that they were "appalled." The activists seemed pleased. Anywhere else—outside of academe, that is—people would decide what they wanted, settle their disagreements, go out and get what they needed. Not here. They put representatives of both camps on the search committee and let them soldier on.

The English Department has received a petition signed by dozens of English majors who say they are "concerned about the current state of the English Department." We call a meeting and, after a certain amount of harrumphing, consider their complaint. It's not about the quality of classes, thank God, but about what the signers say is "a breakdown in communications in the department," a sense of feeling out of touch, a loss of contact with professors. The small, hands-on college is not quite living up to its intimate reputation.

"There's no ill will, ill temper, indignation, or outrage," says Phil Church. Our chair had met with some of the plaintiffs. "It's just that they want to find some way to work out more . . . how shall I say? . . . congenial opportunities to get together somehow."

"I buy into this," Ron Sharp says. "I think we underestimate the importance of hanging out with faculty members for ten minutes once a semester. These days we have labyrinthine procedures, we have faculty leave, study abroad, we've grown in size, and all of these things are innocent in themselves, but students have a legitimate feeling of not being a part of something. We used to have this party and that party. Now we have nothing."

We talk for a while about possibilities: turning the Sutcliffe Room into a lounge, about parties with sherry, hot chocolate, cider. "Anthropology has barbecues," someone volunteers. In the end, we form a committee.

AIDS at breakfast, date rape for lunch, gender studies in the afternoon. Fraternities. Hiring searches. There are these little dramas all over campus you can immerse yourself in, joining one team or another. The constant pressure is to choose sides: then you're a known quantity, friend or foe. If you don't choose sides, you're a soldier out of uniform, a spy maybe, and no one will trust you. It's easy to blunder, in these unforbearing times. On good days, I sense this is because we've grown up, we're more sensitive than we used to be. On bad days, I suspect this isn't about being sensitive at all. It's about being touchy.

What is anyone supposed to do? Move carefully, advises one colleague; move quickly, says another; don't move at all, says a third. But nothing works in a small place that's divided. I talked about this with Bill Klein a while ago. A member of the English Department since the 1960s, Klein suggested I take the comic view.

"There's no sense in viewing it any other way," he said. "We're sheltered from responsibilities here. Our foibles and our petulance are indulged. The place indulges us the way we indulge our students. They're eccentrics, even in their costume, a cross between the Comédie Française and street bums. I walked across campus the other day, and I couldn't decide whether it more resembled a prison or a mental hospital! We indulge ourselves in being human, in being selfish. We indulge ourselves in scholarship, which is costly, on sabbaticals, and the results are so tiny in comparison to the investment. We speculate about the nature of the self, and we don't know about twiddling thumbs. This is a special form of the barnyard."

❦

THE PHILADELPHIA COUNTRY CLUB, way out in the suburbs of that Pennsylvania city, is decorated for Christmas. There are five of us in the party from Kenyon College: Phil and Sheila Jordan, Lisa Schott and Doug Campbell from the Alumni Office, and me, tagging along at my own expense for a taste of life on the alumni trail. It might be interesting, I thought, seeing representatives of the present college meet with agents of the past. I suppose I pictured us entering a crowded room where we'd be swept up in a wave of affection and nostalgia, memory and argument.

The function room is empty when we enter it, except for a bartender and a waitress. We aren't just early. We're the first to arrive, and my heart sinks, not for myself but for the Jordans, and for Kenyon. Gamely, we stand by the fireplace and admire the flames, compliment but pass on the hors d'oeuvres, check the view out the window, across an empty pool and wintery greens, and I wonder if anyone will show up. What if it's only two or three?

Eventually, people do come. Some people. About twenty of them, alumni and spouses and a few pairs of Kenyon parents. Instantly, Jordan is in form. His day began early, in Gambier, and while I ate lunch, browsed in bookstores, napped, he was schmoozing a pair of Kenyon parents connected to the Du Ponts, urging them—what was the delicious phrase he used?—"to engage with the college." On the endless ride out here, I saw him nodding off. But now he's restored and vigorous. "Those downbeat articles about higher education." He stands tall, works the room. "College is no longer a sanctified special place." He describes a crisis while leaving little doubt of his ability to face it. "Gambier is an intense, intimate, occasionally quarrelsome setting." He personalizes his speech, seeking eye contact with listeners. "A bright entering class." His eyebrows bounce. "Twenty-three years of operating surpluses." Does he ever regret having not moved on? There was a flirtation with Brown several years ago, I hear. "A challenging period now—reduced projected income from endowment, reduced projected rate of increase of gifts and grants." He could be a corporate president facing a room of financial analysts. "Heavy dependence on tuition . . .

low endowment, need for college to sustain its essential character." Figures at his fingertips. "Solid confidence, strong sense of purpose, real belief in the nineties." End of speech, happy to answer any questions. Political correctness at Kenyon? "It's more a media event than an actual event," he responds. "There's no prevailing orthodoxy. It's simply not occurring at Kenyon."

After a while, we head back downtown for a late dinner. Wide awake, Jordan speculates about the low turnout. Something about the holidays? Or the remote location? What about alumni anger about fraternity housing? Philadelphia is Bob Price's town, and he was conspicuously absent tonight. At the edge of the crowd, though, I heard a couple of alums grumbling about housing and political correctness and about withholding donations. They passed around copies of an interview with the departed philosophy professor Tom Short that appeared in the campus conservative magazine, the *Kenyon Observer.* Short charged Jordan with radicalizing the campus. "Every year, politicized teaching takes a bigger bite out of Kenyon's curriculum." Sitting with the Jordans now, I speculate that the fraternity loyalists, most of them, had steered clear of his appearance here.

"The college has made up its mind," he says of the fraternity question. "There's no going back. But I'm willing to talk."

"It's gotten beyond talk," I say. Jordan believes in dialogue, reason, and persuasion, but his enemies are beyond that. "In a way," I suggest, "a lawsuit is a kind of conversation."

"If they want to go to war, we're ready," he responds.

In New York, the following night, Kenyon alumni meet at the Holiday Inn Crown Plaza at Forty-ninth and Broadway. Later, I learn, Jordan complained about the "triple-X-rated" nature of the location, a puzzling reaction to a tourist hotel in the heart of the theater district, *Cats* playing just a block away. Here, Kenyon College occupies just one end of a crowded bar, maybe three dozen of us this time, about half of whom remain for dinner. Another upbeat, gallant speech from Jordan, but now the fragility of the whole enterprise gets to me, traveling so far to see such a relative handful of people. Other colleges and universities have their own clubs and rooms, checkrooms, libraries, and easy chairs, and Kenyon gets the end of a bar at the Holiday Inn. I've never felt so loyal. I hate those other places!

The next day, Phil Jordan is scheduled for lunch at the University Club at Fifty-fourth and Fifth, with Ray Grebey, class of '49, a retired labor negotiator. He represented major league baseball owners when Marvin Miller handled the players' union. Now, I gather, he's one of the "Greek" alumni and wants to talk to Jordan about the college's housing policy. Jordan's invited me to sit in, and we wait together for Grebey to arrive, watching a steady parade of sleek, moneyed college graduates in Burberrys and London Fogs, marching through a revolving door, proceeding with familiar ease toward the coat-check desk, lots of nods and greetings, as if they all went to the same large, well-endowed university.

Ray Grebey turns out to be a ruddy, sharp-featured gent with the initially reasonable, unprepossessing manner of a professional negotiator, prepared to match courtesy with courtesy and—only if it comes to that—blow for blow. At lunch upstairs, the two men chat about friends in common. Grebey was in Paul Newman's class at Kenyon and later sent a son and daughter there. They talk about the endowment. Then Grebey remarks that he wants fraternities to survive. "So do we," Jordan assures him promptly. They turn to what Jordan calls "those ancient agreements" that may or may not entitle fraternities to a perpetual place in college-owned housing. Grebey indicates how unfortunate it would be if alumni ended up suing the college. That would be a shame, Jordan agrees. But, adds Grebey, in a negotiating situation you do what you can to get the other side's attention. It's surely sad, but there you have it. "People I talk to," he continues, "feel there's a conspiracy to get rid of fraternities." I ask him if fraternities can survive under current conditions, sans housing monopoly and control of dormitory lounges. "People I talk to," he says, "feel they can't."

The conversation doesn't go much further: the whole session feels like a coin toss at the beginning of a football game, fraternity alums kicking off into the wind, college administration waiting to receive. The two men agree to talk some more sometime, in Gambier or Washington. Jordan has to leave: he's meeting a Wall Street trustee whose nonattendance at meetings has caused some concern. I stay behind with Grebey, lingering over coffee. We're both cigar smokers, it turns out, which is a hard thing to be these days, more endangering than fraternity membership perhaps. I tell him about a tobacconist I know on Thirty-ninth Street, and we walk there together, down Fifth Avenue. "The people I talk to," Grebey says, "they're real pissed off." He recalls working with other fraternity members on the lounges that the college has taken from them. "We sanded the floors, we varnished, we painted the furniture—which alumni donated—we lemon oiled, down on our hands and knees."

❦

"DID YOU HEAR what happened in Lentz's class?"

I've just unpacked from New York, I'm cruising the hall for the first time, checking the cages and animals. I confess that my view of the dorm has changed. At first, I was at Lewis Hall out of duty. It felt like a place of penance and exile, a joke I'd played on myself. But now I look forward to plugging back into it, to rooting around for gossip, and here's something they can't wait to tell me. And it's about Lentz! It seems Lentz is hard at work on *The French Lieutenant's Woman* when suddenly there's a noise outside, in the hall. This is a good fifteen minutes after class has started. It can't be a student, not this late; they've been warned not even to think about such a tardy arrival. So the door opens and a hand pokes through, pointing at Lentz, and crooks a finger, beckoning him outside. So far, it's roughly how I imagine the Mac-Arthur Foundation coming into my life with a genius grant, only I can never decide whether to resume class, not missing a beat, or just walk away from it. When Lentz returns, he's followed by fifteen prospective black students he had—or had not—been warned about. They jam into the classroom. Discussion wilts, Lentz is flummoxed. There are lots of good qualities I find in my old classmate, but the catlike ability to improvise on his feet isn't one of them. He's a man of habits and patterns. He always wears black ties—one less decision to make each morning, he says. He prepares his lectures point by point, at the level of detail you'd expect in a recipe. He checks the classroom he teaches in every day, right after breakfast, making sure everything's in order, that the room's not too hot or too cold. Now, one of the visitors wields a camcorder, goes to the front of the class, pans over the room, friends waving at him. Class ends early. "It was the most embarrassing incident in my professional career," Lentz tells me later, "and that's saying something."

This morning I walked with him from Sunset to Ascension, wanting to see how he handles Fowles, but it's something that happens at the start of the class that grabs my attention. As usual, Lentz takes attendance. He doesn't call names aloud. Instead, he has seating charts. Every class, he glances around the room, circles unoccupied chairs on his chart. Later, he records the absences in his grade book. This morning, it is clear, there are some problems.

"If we've learned anything in the literature we've read in this course, from Flannery O'Connor's profoundly Christian vision to John Fowles's existentialist, what they have in common is the need for honesty." He sounds grim. He's got the class's attention all right. If being honest means a student admits he hates Lentz, can't stand his course, so be it. He'll help them find another section of English 1–2. "You have to be honest with yourself."

For a course that's met three times a week since September, three absences is not an exceptional figure, he says. But one student has been absent six times in three weeks, another has seven absences altogether, a third has twelve.

"There must be something wrong," he declares. "I can only assume there is something actively distressing you in this class. I urge you to consider transferring to another section. We'll work something out. I'll respect you for making that decision about yourself and about me. Please take this advice seriously."

The class is clearly chagrined. What they don't know is that it could be worse. Every once in a while—once a year maybe—Lentz finds a class that hasn't done the reading. This offends him: it turns a cooperative enterprise into a kind of theater, turns the professor into an entertainer. When that happens, he cancels the class, walks out, sometimes cancels the next class, too. One of my seminar students saw that happen and hasn't forgotten.

"We were in class one day," he recalls, "and then something happens that happens all the time. The teacher stands up and asks some question that's obvious and broad. But this time, everybody plays that I've-got-something-more-important-going-on-in-my-notebook game. There were two or three moments of silence. 'If you're not interested in reading it, I'm not interested in teaching it,' he says. End of class."

❧

MY WRITING STUDENTS have been a good group, I think, with three or four who'll continue writing seriously, one way or another, and the rest can say that they've had a taste of the process, of what it's like writing for an audience, and they'll be better writers, too, even if it's only in letters and memos, and better readers. I succumb to repeated requests to turn the last seminar into a party, in a trailer one of them occupies with some other students. When I drop off a case of beer at four in the afternoon, the place is messy and empty and I regret having agreed to this: students can be awfully half-assed. But by seven the place is full of hors d'oeuvres, salad, lasagna. I'm surprised, and pleased. For a little while, I offer a sort of valedictory lecture in which I try to sum up how the class has worked, saving my best wisdom for last: that writing isn't just a way of saying things, it's a way of seeing them. Maybe they'd figured that out already. This last meeting is harder for me to take than I let on. It's only December, I know, and I'll be seeing these students around campus until May. But they'll never be together again like this, never again in the same room at the same time. It's a captive audience, I know, but I'd gotten used to it. I close by passing out my card, telling them that if they're ever in the city I live in—New York until two years ago, Chicago now, Manila in the years to come—I'd like to hear from them. I'll buy them a meal—at the restaurant of my choice, not theirs. Short of that, I'd welcome Christmas cards, postcards, phone calls, whatever. As they leave, I try to guess which students might drive ten miles out of their way to visit me in a nursing home, thirty years from now.

As it turns out, I hear from four students in the year that follows. One of them sends a cheerful note from San Francisco, where she's working for a publisher for not a lot of money. I get a phone call from another student, working as a gofer in a Washington, D.C., law firm, and hating it. He wonders about graduate school, also fiddles with a book proposal that will spring him out of the law offices. I get several chipper calls from a student who's a reporter on a newspaper in Little Rock, pondering a move to Washington with Clinton and Company. And one March morning, I glance up and see a game, lively would-be writer who's had a rough year, living with his parents, working nights at a supermarket for $13,000 per year. "I wish Kenyon had been tougher on me," he says. He doesn't have the knockout grades that would propel him into graduate school. He doesn't know what's next. "I was in New York last week," he says, anger surging into his voice, "and I went into the men's room in Grand Central Station, into the toilet. There were no doors on the stall, and I watched all these homeless people walking by. And I said to myself while I sat there, Kenyon was supposed to separate me from all this!"

Now, calculating grades, I review their final efforts. There's a story about two boyhood friends, divided by social class, struggling against that separation, winning a temporary victory. The style goes lame at points, and the ending trails off, but it's a game effort. Next story: a woman, a rape victim, moves to Brazil, but traumatic memories follow. Nice local color, no drama: it's all in her head, and the flashbacks are awkward. Then there's a winning story told in an adolescent, Lily Tomlinish voice, but it needs more work, and how many times do I have to say that "alot" is two words, not one, and that talent isn't license to make dumb, little mistakes? The fourth paper is an expanded version of the day in the life of a summer lobster shack in Maine, still short on character and action, but she certainly got into describing what makes a good lobster roll. Small victories. Next, there's a piece about high school kids cruising a small town, a piece that, like its characters, has no place to go. Two accounts of a parent's death, one about the breakup of a friendship, one about the death of a dog, another about sibling rivalry, all deeply felt, obviously; if only deep feelings were all it took. One movie-influenced account of a black blues singer, another of an American rock and roller in England. There's an intriguing, Hemingwayish piece about a falling-apart marriage in Africa: the wife attempts suicide when the husband philanders, is saved by a transfusion of blood that might be AIDS-tainted, and the husband, faced with making love to his possibly infected wife, patching things up, can't tell whether this lovemaking is reconciliation or revenge. And last, there's an account of a turbulent marriage, told from the children's point of view, but how am I supposed to react to: *ectatic, rythmn, macoroni, liscense?*

So it's one A minus, four B plusses, three Bs, five B minuses, two C plusses. I'm not so tough, after all: everybody's above average, all fourteen. There's no final grade for Mike Stone.

❧

HE SURVIVED THE SURGERY he didn't expect to survive but paid a price he cannot pay again. "They removed everything," Tracy Schermer, the college physician, tells me. "They chose to save his ear, so they took out his right eye and the bone around it and left behind radiation seeds and filings, to deter new growth."

Schermer was in the operating room. "I wanted to keep these people aware that this was a unique, great, wonderful super kid. There were negative comments during surgery. 'Why's he doing this? He's going to be dead in a little while.' I wanted them to know, 'Hey, this is Mike.'"

The prognosis is poor, a matter of waiting for the cancer to return.

Stone chooses to spend his last reprieve at Kenyon, a place he knows and loves, even though he's been forced to withdraw from classes. He lives in a college-owned apartment, with his mother. I'd been thinking about him as the class he was supposed to be part of drew to a close without him, so I drop by.

He looks terribly beaten up, mugged and mugged again: the socket where his eye used to be is swollen and closed, scars slash across his chin and forehead. Still, he contains more life than death. No false bravado. We talk about Kenyon: how he chose it, what he made of it. Moving with surprising briskness, he leads me into the basement, sits down at a computer, fishes around for the essay that accompanied his admissions application. He has to put his face right up against the screen, reading inch-high letters. "Upon my first visit to your campus, I was immediately impressed with the unity and closeness of the students, faculty and community." Back upstairs, I ask him about leaving his cane behind in church, along with a handwritten prayer, before going in for surgery. That was impressive, I say, sounding fatuous. "I don't think it's impressive," he quickly counters. "I'd say it's the move of someone who has one card left to play."

🌿

TOWARD THE END of our visit, Tom Edwards drops by. He and Stone had planned a walk. Edwards retired as dean of students a couple years ago, but it nonetheless makes sense that he'd show up like this. For years he was the one who always got called by the cops, and he was the one who picked up the phone in the middle of the night to give parents the worst possible news. You think of colleges as privileged places, protected and safe, but Edwards knows different. Another time, I ask him about death at Kenyon.

Two students went flying in a small plane, in 1956, when Kenyon still had a flying club, a grass landing strip with a tattered windsock, a dirt-floored hangar. They died in a crash near Denison. Soft-voiced, thoughtful, Edwards begins the college necrology, and, after a while, I sense a rough pattern, death making its way here every few years, enough of a pattern so that, if some years pass by harmlessly, you wonder if we're due. A married Kenyon student who lived with his pregnant wife in an apartment over the Village Inn accompanied an English professor home to Mount Vernon after a party. The next morning they were found, accidentally asphyxiated by leaking gas. Autumn

1960, my freshman year, a Kenyon senior returning from Denison didn't make a turn on Route 229, crashed into a pillar. "I'll never forget that phone call," Edwards says. There's more: a motorcycle accident on Route 308, an automobile accident on Route 36, a woman student found dead in Farr Hall: she'd stopped taking medicine she needed to take, it seemed. Then a bizarre death—"the most tragic of all," Edwards says—occurred when a fraternity pledge attended an illegal bring-your-own-bottle party. Drunk, he veered right outside of Old Kenyon, staggered downhill, disoriented, past the old swimming pool, the tennis courts. At the bottom stood a decrepit old house used for equipment storage. "That's where they found him," Edwards says. "The sheriff came and got me. He was attempting to defecate, squatting, with his pants down. He fell over and froze. You could trace his steps in the snow." Edwards stops talking for a moment. In my time, he had a pro-fraternity reputation. He ended his career convinced that the college would be a better place without them. "Jesus, try to explain that to a parent," he resumes. "They send their kid to a college that's supposed to look after him. Another set of parents could have sued. I racked my brain, asking myself what could be done to relieve their suffering. But how needless it was, kids drinking themselves into oblivion in the dorm."

We continue. The college built Gambier's first high-rise, a nine-story dormitory, tucked among trees that are almost as tall. Kidding around in the elevator, a student plunged seven stories to the bottom of the shaft. A bicycling student streaked down the college hill and broadsided a truck. A student who'd withdrawn from Kenyon, then been readmitted, returned to Gambier and disappeared. "His roommate said he hadn't seen him since the previous day. I called his home, and his mother got worried right away. You could tell there was something wrong." Farmers, students, sheriffs formed search parties, combed the countryside. After a week, someone found a body hanging from a tree. "The parents knew he had suicidal tendencies," Edwards says. "They never told us."

❧

LENTZ IS TIED UP a lot lately, and my more frequent running companion is Ted Mason, another English professor, who sets a somewhat faster pace. He doesn't do things nonchalantly. The first time I ran with him, he talked on the physics of running, on how to take hills, on that certain point of speed at which an airplane ceases to fly and starts to fall. The second time we went out on the same course he looked at his watch, announced that we'd just done an 8:30 mile, a 9:30, whatever, and I realized that, in between runs, the man had been out along this road in his truck, measuring the route.

Mason's talk, too, is that of a professor who is keeping up with his field, keeping options open, staying light on his feet. He uses words like *dipolarity, alterity, valorize, disjuncture,* the language of the scholarly pack. Sometimes I press for clarification, sometimes I bluff. Also, though he's trying to break himself of the habit, he's attached to one of the most overused words on campus, right up there with *gendered* and *empowered.* That word is *cutting-edge,* which is okay if you're describing advances in pollution or birth control, but it feels wrong when applied to the kind of work that gets done at a small liberal arts college, where so much effort is spent in protecting and defending. What this means, I guess, is that Mason believes in progress.

Today's topic is complacency. No argument about that, about the feeling that we spoil our students, who think that a Kenyon diploma gets them into graduate schools, gets them a job, entitles them to success. Here's where they pay for grade inflation: the word is out about Bs. Only As impress anymore. Mason says that when the Rhodes scholarships are announced after Christmas, he plans to read the list aloud in class. If it's like every other year, there'll be lots of students from the Ivy League schools and from the top tier of liberal arts colleges, Amherst, Haverford, Swarthmore. Then there'll be a sprinkling of students from places no one's ever heard of, places with names like . . . oh . . . Roger Williams or Houston Dixon or something, Cinderella stories from out of nowhere. Kenyon falls between the regularly entitled and the regularly obscure. We deceive ourselves if we think that the world waits breathlessly to be resupplied with students who have pretty good grades from a pretty good school. Someone has to tell them.

❧

I CAME HERE thinking of this college as an island, of myself as a traveler, of what I'm writing as a travel book. If I'm right in holding to this island image, I'd say that our students are visitors to the island: their term here is closed-ended. Whatever else they do here, they cannot stay. The faculty are natives, an anthropologically diverse collection of tribes and individuals who live here in a variety of ways: there are some rarely seen aboriginals who hug the interior, cling to ancient folkways, worship old gods, and are rumored to take heads, others who hang close to the shoreline, trade handicraft, dive for coins tossed by passengers off cruise ships, and wistfully gaze out to sea, dreaming of escape.

The admissions people, John Anderson and his crew, are fishermen, practitioners of bait, nets, and hooks, students of wrecks and shoals, tides and currents. They worry about overfishing and pollution, the red tides of drugs and dyslexia. And what they bring in, from tuna to squid to sea robin, what spills out of their hold, trophy-class or undersize, fresh caught or starting to stink, is what the college eats: applications, "apps," for short.

The fishing season began months ago, back in April, when Kenyon anglers went chumming, casting about 100,000 brochures over likely fishing grounds. If they got a nibble, they responded with one of twelve different letters designed to keep the fish on the line. They started reeling in during the summer months: 200 campus interviews in July, 300 in August. And today they sort through the first catch of the season: a group of early decision ("ED") applications.

Dean John Anderson presides. A trim, athletic Californian with the lifelong youthfulness of a George Hamilton or Dick Clark, Anderson came to Kenyon from Earlham College nine years ago, attracted by an "institution that wasn't content with where it was, wanted to reshape itself, yet had a very clear sense of where and what it was." The dean of admissions in those days—Anderson came in as his assistant—was a local hero, John Kushan, a suave, solitary man, not without a streak of cynicism. An old Kenyon hand, Kushan was uncomfortable with what he perceived as the trendy, fashionable, politically correct changes that overtook the place in the seventies and early eighties. He didn't like Kenyon to emulate other places; he relished it as it was.

"Once," Anderson recalls, "when a student insisted on knowing what there was to *do* in Gambier, Kushan told him, 'There's absolutely nothing to do, and I don't think you should come.' He never went out of his way to make it sound more attractive than it was. 'If you want to spend a lot of time at malls,' he'd say, 'here's a list of colleges with malls.'"

Kushan is dead now, but some of Kushan's lessons, tricks of the trade, still apply. Some schools get in the habit of sending less than their best Kenyon's way. The answer to that, Anderson learned from Kushan, was the "bazooka blast." Turn down all that school's applicants. That gets their attention.

It's a tricky business. Some private schools regularly kite their grades.

California grades tend to be inflated, too: schools want to get their graduates into that state's university system. "It's rare," says Anderson, "to see less than a B from California." There's more. There's the relationship between a college admissions officer and dozens of high school and prep school guidance counselors. Some you trust absolutely. Others you loathe. For all the tests and transcripts and statistical tracks, there's the matter of taking someone's word.

"Our ultimate goal is a class with 420 to 425 students," Anderson tells his crew this morning. There are six others around the table, fussing with folders and computer readouts. The files include test scores, grade point averages, advanced placement courses, work in foreign languages and sciences. They indicate whether the student is first-generation to go to college, whether he or she intends to apply for scholarship aid. Doughnuts and coffee signal a long day coming. "We hope to end up with an interesting, well qualified, talented, diverse, wealthy . . ." He pauses. "Scratch that." That was a joke. "In picking through these applications, there's a tension between the desire for perfect students and the need to have a class."

At first, I suspect this facts-of-life lecture is for my benefit. Soon, I know better. Anderson is reminding his crew, and himself, of some things that are easy to forget once you start wading through applications: that the ability to be selective this morning is a function of the recruiting that was done months ago, when some students were convinced to apply and others walked away, unimpressed; that there's a need for balance of gender, race, interests, nonacademic talents; that somebody has to live in Lewis Hall—the all-male freshman dorm where I reside—and somebody has to major in things other than English; that "there's no formula in admissions, so one student may not be admitted because he or she wrote a terrible essay, while another will be admitted *despite* a terrible essay."

He mentions one more thing, before they start putting together the class of '96. Kenyon needs a class of 420 or so. The students who apply for early decision are willing to commit to Kenyon now and to withdraw applications elsewhere. Got that? *These fish are jumping into the boat.* Admitting one of these kids now is like admitting three, three and a half kids later on. Normal admissions will produce a yield of 30 percent or so, down from 37 percent nine years ago, down from 50 percent or more in my time, when students lost sleep about getting into the college of their choice. There are 78 applicants for early decision today. Last year there were 75, of whom 58 were admitted. This year, says Anderson, it would be "nice" if we could get 62, 63, maybe, "if we're lucky," 64. Granted, not many ED apps come from superstars. There are some good kids who've fallen in love with Kenyon and are ready to settle things right now. And quite a few marginal types, hoping to increase their chances by applying early.

The first thing I notice, in what follows, is the language of the trade, brusque, informal, even flippant. Cs are "cats," Ds are "dogs," Fs are "frogs." "Her essay is just garbage." "A pretty piss-poor test score." "She's mediocre—no need to fill up the class with modest English major women." "A tall lanky kid who opens up as he goes along, but I didn't feel any oomph."

Usually, the admissions officer who had personal contact with the applicant speaks first: impressions of the student, quality of his or her school, how other students from that school have fared at Kenyon. Then they go around the table and each member of the admissions staff gives the student two ratings, one for academic qualities, one for personal, ranging from a high of 5 to a low of 1.

"A hilarious writer." "He's gonna take off here!" "A band geek." "Gag scores." "Lotta cats and dogs." "A closet novelist." "A Renaissance man." "Kind of a geek but not a geek in a negative sense just . . . a geek." "Low scores, low rigor, low everything." "I hate rejecting kids. These letters come a few days before Christmas." "I like his interest in Chinese." "This kid is certainly no stranger to the concept of praising himself." "Service ace!"

It sounds flippant, but it's not. It's a room full of people making thoughtful decisions, one after the other, during a long, bladder-splitting morning. By lunchtime 23 applicants have been admitted, 12 deferred. No one's been rejected yet. That's the rub, I guess. The college feels like an island without a reef. All beach. Easily eroded.

After lunch, rolling through the middle of the alphabet, they come upon the first applicant Kenyon cannot accept or defer, someone it rejects. Applicant number 41. Rated 2 academically, 4 personally. Verbal score of 490, 370 science. "Problematic," says one admissions officer. "Tough," agrees another, "obviously not qualified." "No one wants to come here more than she does," someone offers. "If I thought we could slide her in I would," Anderson responds, "but I can't support her. She's just not very bright." They soldier on. Applicant 42, a student with upward-trending stats at Lawrenceville. Applicant 43, a student with inflated California grades but a lively essay. Applicant 45, a terrible essay, "dry as a biscuit," but improving grades. All admitted. The roll they're on ends at applicant 46.

"Here comes a toughie, maybe," John Anderson warns. Good grades, high class rank, but low scores. Verbal is 390, math 410. "Scary scores." And a bad essay. "One humdrum declarative sentence after another." The admissions officer who met the student speaks up dutifully. "She loves Kenyon. She visited twice. Once by herself, and then she brought her parents back." "But these scores," someone persists, "this is beyond low." Someone else agrees. "There's a limit, a point at which you have to say, maybe this kid can't read very well." They flirt with deferring the applicant till spring. But why bother? "There are schools she'd be much better suited for, and I don't think this is one of them." They've made their second reject and, right away, come up against an applicant who could easily be their third.

"Oh my God," an admissions officer sighs, looking over the problem file. "I can't put up much of a fight for my man." A student with a so-so record and no discernible personality. "No way," someone says. But there's a connection with someone powerful, someone who's played a role in the life of the college. This person isn't shoving the kid down the college's throat, it's not like that. But an interest has been expressed. Let's put it that way. "He may be a kid we have to swallow," Anderson says. "I don't think he's an *awful* swallow." They decide to defer: the kid is "full fare." Paying customers cannot be summarily dismissed. "We may come back to him in the springtime and his record will be no better and we'll say, 'Hey, we'd like to get paid.'"

By early afternoon, the discussion is just as careful as before, but the group is tired, starting to kid, indulging in a rough humor that protects them from the fact that, experienced and discriminating as they are, they don't operate from a position of great strength. So they roll their eyes, they joke a little. Confronting a horsey prep school applicant, someone does a nifty imitation of a clenched-mouthed town-and-country woman. Applicant 48 is a likable kid who seems okay, 49 "a nice admit out of Miss Porter's School," 50 "someone we'd like to claim as an alumna someday," 51 "a great kid with an awesome essay," 52 "a hard worker." All admits. Defer 53—a 2.3 GPA—admit 54, defer 55: "scores mediocre, grades mediocre, school mediocre, and if our pool's mediocre, maybe we'll admit her later on." After they admit 56, a personally appealing kid with a mediocre record, Anderson leans back and sighs. "That's the pattern of the day," he reflects, "a 2.7 GPA will get you into Kenyon College." That's not exactly true. They reject applicant 60, who has a 2.74 GPA but wrote a "simplistic, scattered essay" and ranks below the middle of her class. Their last reject has a 2.52, ranks 57th out of 170 at a public high school. At the end of it all, of 78 applicants, they've accepted 53, rejected 4, deferred 20 until spring, and saved one troubled case for later.

Later is now. The day's not over yet. It ought to be. Outside it's four o'clock, classes are ending, students headed back to dormitories along Middle Path. The faculty affairs committee appears. They're scheduled to use the room we've been sitting in for their weekly meeting. They're welcome to it: stale, funky locker-room air. The admissions crew moves to a table downstairs and works its way through the dregs, the 21 people deferred earlier in the day, like fishermen picking through the edible if less savory fish in order to increase the catch. It's wonderful what a few hours can do. Applicant 1, "not a particularly thrilling human being" in the morning, got better during lunch. And applicant 13, by God, has a 3.0 GPA and SATs that add up to 1,000. "He's batting 1.000!" someone exclaims.

By 6:00 P.M., it's 58 admits, 4 rejects, and 15 deferrals. Next year's freshman class starts coming together. The early decision kids are enthusiastic about Kenyon; thus the high rate of acceptance. Later on, both sides—applicants and college—will get a little more selective. How much more selective nobody knows.

"This is going to be a very nerve-wracking year," John Anderson predicts a few days later. No matter how much they worry about the quality of applicants, admissions officers know their non-negotiable goal, in a good year or a bad year, is to "make the class," to come up with the desired number of entering students. But sometimes, when John Anderson talks about the economy, about what's happening out *there,* then when he shifts to what's happening *here,* small mixed signals—campus visits up, telephone inquiries down—I sense that every admissions officer is dogged by a host's secret nightmare: what if *this* is the year we give a party and no one comes.

"We'll do well in terms of applications," Anderson suspects. "It'll be a good year, not a disaster. But, geez, I don't know what will happen when they have to make the decision about accepting. Whether we'll see waffling, extensions, people paying deposits and then backing out. It's not just people who lose jobs, it's the whole notion of uncertainty, of loss of confidence in the economy. *Twenty-five k per year for four years!* Yeah, it scares the hell out of me. Kenyon is more precarious than most places."

Right now, it seems to me Anderson probably has a better sense of Kenyon College than half of the people who teach there. Professors measure Kenyon against the college of their dreams. Admissions is what's happening now: today's marketplace, today's competition. Today's weakness. A certain shortage of bait on board the ship.

"We aid 35 percent of our students," Anderson says. "Oberlin probably aids 60 percent. There's no inherent virtue in that. But if push comes to shove, we have to substitute a less qualified full-pay kid for a better quality student who needs aid. I don't want to be cast as a whiner, but there are times when it does bug me."

THE SEMESTER WINDS DOWN, the academic year turns middle-aged. Last night in the dorm, students strolled the halls, raucously singing holiday songs, not sure whether they should sing seriously or play it for laughs. Upstairs, somebody played Christmas music on a trumpet, then shifted to "Deutschland Über Alles." A transfer-minded student looking for more challenge dropped by to ask for help in selecting a fifth course. I recommended Bill McCulloh's "Greek Literature in Translation." I always recommend McCulloh, confident the student will find him as good near the end of his career as I did at the beginning. A freshman slipped a paper on Raymond Carver under my door, asked me to look it over. "Favor time," he said. I obliged.

Christmas impends. Down in the basement of Ascension Hall, Cyrus Banning, ruddy and white-bearded, looks like Santa in his workshop, behind schedule on his list of toys for boys and girls who've been good. But Banning has just one toy to give—that tenure-track position in Philosophy—and about 175 stockings to stuff. So: lots of lumps of coal. He sifts through the application pile: letter, curriculum vita, three letters of recommendation, academic transcript, writing sample. They are all exemplary people, it seems, with glowing recommendations, superior transcripts, their commitment to cutting-edge philosophy matched only by their wish to enrich the classrooms at a small liberal arts college. How does one sort through all this excellence?

Banning considers the reputation of the graduate school, the importance of the references, the mix of courses taken and taught, the quality of the writing sample. It's a nuancey business. "All As is a commonplace among graduate students," he says. Some applicants submit course evaluation forms filled out by former students. These, too, report a good or excellent performance. "Students are not very hard on teachers."

The letters of recommendation turn out to be trickier than they appear at first. Some of the enthusiasm is a tad perfunctory; some smell of prewritten departmental boilerplate. "'Quiet, pleasant, cooperative,'" Banning reads from one letter. "That could be a euphemism for 'He's a hermit.'" Another recommendation gives him pause. "'He may not have the kind of flair that would make him a stunning performer in large lectures.'" And another letter appears to be damning with faint praise: "'I have had better teaching assistants, but I'd be pleased to have someone like him every semester.'"

There's not time for more than a glance at the scholarly writing samples. He just dips in to see if there's an interesting problem under consideration, if the candidate is using sophisticated ideas and treating them sensibly. One applicant finds Descartes getting tangled in his description of God's perfection. Okay. Another considers concepts of theory appraisal: how do you decide whether theories are good theories or not? Another tackles a philosophical puzzle about the relationship between knowledge and action: do you really know what you should do, if you don't do it? Interesting.

Some applicants are still in graduate school, coming onto the job market for the first time. Can they teach in a small college? Others have been around a while. These are the gypsies, the ones who move from one visiting position to another. Sad cases, sometimes. "They knock around for six or eight years in one-year positions," Banning remarks. "After a few years, the dossiers get stale."

Banning and two other members of the Philosophy Department will work their way through the applications and come up with a list of names. Then they'll make some phone calls—names becoming voices—and arrange for interviews in New York. In the week between Christmas and New Year's, voices will become people, and one of those people, one out of the hundreds, may become a professor of philosophy at Kenyon College.

"Truth tropic cognitive mechanisms."

The last rays of sunlight slant into Manhattan from out across the Hudson, catching the film of urban grit on the windows of Banning's room on the forty-fifth floor of the Marriot Marquis Hotel. Out west, the college hibernates through the holidays. Here, at the eastern division meeting of the American Philosophical Association, the job market is open and crowded. Banning and a candidate chat about "innate ethical beliefs," about "sensualism versus constructionism." Listening to talk of philosophy is like trying to read the chess column in the *New York Times:* I grasp the opening paragraphs, sort of, but after that I'm lost in a maze of numbers, letters, exclamation points, all describing coups and blunders I can't follow. When they turn to other things, though, my interest revives.

"What role does your philosophical work play in your professional life?" Banning asks.

"I do philosophy three ways," the candidate responds. He's a serious young man, hunched in his chair, leaning forward, fixed and intense. There's an inch of skin showing between the top of his socks and the bottom of his slacks. "I write it out for class. I teach it. And I write papers."

"How important is it to you to have courses you teach relate to your research interest?"

"Directly . . . no. It's not important. But there should be *some* relationship."

"I asked, and maybe you answered," Banning proceeds, "but there's not much room for private interest courses in our curriculum." He knows that his department is small, with lots of introductory courses and relatively few majors: between six and twelve a year. Of those, only a few go on to graduate school, which, in fact, is "not a good thing to encourage people to do. The ones who go are just the ones who can't stand not to go."

"I understand," the candidate says. "It's not a great sacrifice." He knows the sort of place he's marketing himself to. If he's also applying at a research-oriented university, he'll sing a different tune.

"It does turn out in almost every case," Banning cautions, "that research has to take a back seat to teaching, and there's just no way around this."

Another nod, another concession. Why does this remind me of breaking a horse to accept a saddle, a rider, and a lifetime of pulling wagonloads of students on hayrides? And why does it seem that the horses enter the room already broken, the bit firmly in mouth, trailing reins? When Banning asks what turns out to be his standard closing question—"Is there anything about you that I should know that I don't know yet?"—the response is dutiful.

"One thing I'd want to emphasize, I guess, is that I see my interest in philosophy intimately connected with the teaching and mentoring of undergraduates."

With that, he leaves, out the door, down the elevator, swallowed by the convention. No late-night poker games at this conclave, no market for hookers here. He probably thinks he's one of the lucky ones, and with reason. He had an interview with Kenyon College, which puts him up on the hundreds who come here with no prescheduled interview, hoping to snag the attention of a place that's still scheduling auditions. What's more, he did well in the interview, I sense. How well remains to be seen.

It's the shoes. The first candidate had black lace-ups. This next fellow has black, shined, tasseled loafers, filled with ample socks, and the polished, good-humored style of someone who might be at ease on "The David Letterman Show."

"From what I hear of Kenyon," he says, "it's a good, small liberal arts college, and that's the sort of place I see myself fitting in."

"What attracts you about a small college?"

"Small classes. Interested students. In a big place, they're just rows of heads. I like working with students in a small room, working with students who think philosophy's soft and mushy."

"And you disabuse them?"

"Sometimes I succeed and sometimes I fail."

I like this fellow. I don't have a moment's doubt he'd do fine at Kenyon. If it were up to me, we could call off the rest of the interviews and go out for Indian food. Kenyon gives its traveling agents thirty dollars a day for meals, and there are some places on Sixth Street you can eat at well for that. I'll spring for beer.

"My students hate Kant," the candidate is saying. "Well, I hate the way he writes, and they hate the effort it takes to read him, but some of them end up thinking he's neat."

"What constitutes success in an introductory philosophy course?"

"Keeping them awake," my man retorts. Maybe he's a little too glib. But then he gives a persuasive account of his teaching goals. "I want them to have a healthy respect for philosophy and issues in philosophy, to realize that these are issues worth expending effort over, that people aren't wasting their lives who spend time on these issues."

The shoes. The third candidate, a heavy older man who's been around, wears brown, oxblood walking shoes with sensible gum soles. Unlike his two predecessors, he trails the sense of someone who's been out of graduate school a while, teaching in temporary posts. In short: a gypsy, a utility player. By now, the dialogues are starting to sound like a catechism: the special quality of small colleges, the congeniality of small classes, the paramount importance of teaching that is enriched but never distracted by research.

"What should a student come away with from an introductory course?"

"It's like this," the candidate replies, with such enthusiasm that my heart goes out to him. "What I really love is when a student can look back, find that he took a position strongly contrary to the wisdom of the current day. I love it when students get deeply into something they never thought of and consider it seriously."

The moment passes, sympathy fades, the talk turns to Plato and Leo Strauss, and Banning asks if there's anything else he ought to know. "Teaching is very important to me, and I hope my record indicates that."

And the elevator takes him down.

"What would you do in a metaphysics course?"

"I'd develop three themes: time, causation, freedom and free will," the candidate replies. "I'd use Aristotle on time. Leibnitz on time and free will."

"Augustine on time?"

"A classic," the candidate declares.

"Wonderfully confused."

While Banning interviews candidates in one room, his Philosophy Department colleague, Ron McLaren, works next door. McLaren's got a suite, bedroom and sitting room, not for his sake but because current rules are that you don't interview a candidate of the opposite sex in a room that has a bed in it. And anyway, this particular candidate is nervous enough already. She has lots of hair—it covers much of her face—and a kind of downcast manner that seems to acknowledge her application is a long shot. "An independent scholar," she calls herself: unemployed. McLaren chats about the department, about courses she might teach, but I sense that it's not going anywhere.

"Behind that mass of hair and glasses, there's a scholar," he remarks after she leaves. "But I'm nervous about her."

A Kenyon graduate, McLaren was hired in the days of the old boy network. "I got a phone call one day. Did I want to come? I wasn't looking for a job. I'd have been content to stay in graduate school." His interview was nothing more than a chat, "just talking to other philosophers about philosophy."

The search resumes with three women candidates: one quite winning, one floundering and nervous, a third who seems shocked when Banning describes how small a place Kenyon is.

"Twenty students in a class?"

"Yes."

"That's wonderful! You know them personally by the end of the course!"

"Sometimes only too well," Banning replies.

The applicant I'll remember the most is one of the last, the last, that is, of the eight interviews I witness. McLaren and Banning have fifteen more at least, and then there'll be some callbacks, each checking out the other's likeliest prospects. This fellow I remember teaches at a large urban university. He's clearly head over heels in love with the idea of coming to Gambier, Ohio. He's earnest, interested, intense. Every question Banning asks he answers as though his life depended on it. I'll bet this is the only interview his applications have attracted, and, in the surrounding darkness, this glimmer of hope from Kenyon has become his lodestar.

"I live in a rough neighborhood," he confesses near the end of the interview. "I don't feel comfortable letting my kids ride up and down the sidewalk outside unless I'm out there watching them."

Banning listens and nods. It's just a coincidence that this job search closely followed my attendance at the Admissions Department meeting on early decision applications, but I can't help thinking of the college as a Jekyll and Hyde personality. In Admissions we ate most of what got put in front of us, sometimes wincing, feeling a little sick, knowing we might hate ourselves in the morning. And here, in the Philosophy search, what *feinschmeckers* we become, what utter gourmets, tasting, clearing our palates, sniffing, sipping, spitting out.

"A lot of people interview for four jobs, and it doesn't matter which one they get," the candidate says, pleadingly, "so long as they get a job."

It embarrasses me listening to this. The consolations of philosophy! No consolation prizes, though. The guy made the first cut—a couple dozen summoned for interviews out of nearly 175 applications. Now, though, there are more cuts to come: from 175 apps to 25 interviews to three invitations to campus to one who gets hired.

"This is a job I would take," the applicant continues. "Just so you know that. If I'm offered this position, I will take it."

Banning mercifully notes that there've been 175 applicants.

"It's tough," the candidate acknowledges. "I'm glad to have this interview."

"The job market is as bad now as it's ever been," Ron McLaren tells me. "I thought it was getting better, but it's not." He says the people he's interviewed so far are "mostly fine." Banning's been impressed, too. Of his eight interviewees, he reckons that two are standouts, two are better than average, and two are okay, i.e., "up to the job." Two are rejects. Put it another way: Banning predicts that six of the eight people I saw him interview would get tenure if they came to Kenyon College. Tenure. Lifetime employment. Sure, they'll grouse later on. They'll want a job for their spouse, less teaching load, smaller classes, more money, day care for the kids, you name it. This year's anxious rookie turns into tomorrow's trade-me-or-play-me prima donna. Never mind. First will come the offer, the tenure-track offer, the offer that turns you from a gypsy, a floater, a drifter, into an islander forever.

Six out of eight. Terrific from one point of view. From another: appalling. And as it turns out a few weeks later, none of today's top six will be invited to campus. The three candidates for campus visits turn up during the last two days of the convention, after I've left. No way of knowing what happened to all those others or what else they had going for them, in the week between Christmas and New Year's.

❧ *January*

P ART OF ME has always longed for what happened this afternoon, when I walked into a room in Ascension Hall for the first
meeting of English 68, section 2, "American Literature since
1945." I don't know whether I'm a Walter Mitty, dreaming of accomplishments in far arenas, or I'm someone far away, dreaming of becoming Walter Mitty. But there are others like me out there, I know, English
majors slugging out careers in business, journalism, advertising, dreaming of getting paid to talk about books. We're the ones who spend time
on planes, in bars, devising imaginary courses, doodling syllabi: lists of
baseball novels, of novels set in Hollywood, novels about journalism. A
course on the literature of World War I. A course of books on suburbia,
politics, marriage. The way other people read menus or work crossword
puzzles, we play with syllabi. Ethnic groups coming to America. "Bab-
bitt to Rabbit: Novels of American Business." Dream courses. It's a
game that appeals to nonprofessors. The people who make their living
teaching lack this playfulness. They look at your lists, sigh, tell you
they're way too long, no current student will read more than half the
material, so you should cut by two-thirds. Killjoys!

Okay. We'll start with *On the Road,* because it's in the American
grain, picking up on Whitman and Wolfe, and because it's no master-
piece. It should be interesting, sorting out the accomplishments from the
flaws, the fine, elegiac riffs from the pretentious and self-dramatizing
blather. Also, it's a book that's widely misread as a one-dimensional
hymn to friendship on the open highway when—though it is surely
that—it is also a devastating critique of unrealized friendship and point-
less travel. So the question arises: did Kerouac know what he was doing
or did it happen in spite of his original intentions?

I pair *On the Road* with another journey novel, Russell Banks's

Continental Drift, a long, ambitious tale of a blue-collar guy's effort to find a new life in—would you believe?—Florida. Where Kerouac-as-author disappears into his book, Banks hovers, summarizing, interpreting, Howard Coselling his characters. Two different narrative postures. After that, a lean, mean little book of travel *to* the United States, Bharati Mukherjee's *Jasmine:* Indian woman makes her way to Iowa and finds despair in the heartland, things not what they used to be in the fields of dreams. Then, since we've gotten into immigrant experience, the costs/benefits of becoming American, we go to *Portnoy's Complaint.* I wonder if the sex will annoy them. More minority experience, next, in David Bradley's *The Chaneysville Incident,* a mystery, a family drama, a meditation on black history and American character.

We'll be halfway done when we finish *Chaneysville.* Banks, Kerouac, Roth, Bradley, Mukherjee might enlarge the students' world, and that's fine. But I want something that will get to them where they live, and where they live, most of them, is in suburbia. Last time I taught Alice McDermott's *That Night.* This year I'll try Alice Hoffman's *Seventh Heaven.* Both novels are set in Long Island of the 1950s, when potato fields were turning into Levittowns. After that, *Rabbit, Run:* Updike bites off as large a piece of the time and place I live in as any writer I know. But how will the class take to Rabbit, a lazy mystic, a sensitive, sexist heel? The eighth novel is going to be problematic, dense, disorganized, self-indulgent, and magical: Fred Exley's *A Fan's Notes.* I want to show how the line between fiction and nonfiction is blurring, how novelistic techniques find their way into quasi-autobiography. Finally—it'll be April then—I want to teach a mystery. In April, good students get tired and bad ones get lazy. So I'll give an easy read but good, something to show that fine work can be done in genre fiction, Kem Nunn's *Tapping the Source:* surfers and motorcycle gangs at war in a tacky, nihilistic California beach town.

So much for my list. There's no point contemplating the good, maybe great, writers who aren't on it. This is like going through all your post-1945 music—jazz, classical, folk, rock, movies, and Broadway—and picking nine items to take with you on a trip. What I teach reflects what I know, what I like, and what I can put across to the students I get in the time that I have. Next year I'll have a different list.

We meet from 2:40 to 4:00 P.M., Tuesdays and Thursdays. I still have this damnable German-American habit of arriving everywhere early. I kill a few minutes outside, on the building steps, wondering which of the entering students is mine. The class is full and then some: I admitted a few hard-luck stories, including a woman who participated in the sit-in at fraternity tables in Peirce Hall. She's thinking of transferring, unhappy at what she considers a sexist campus—"You date a Psi U and you're a Psi Uterus"—so I let her in, hoping that neither of us regrets it.

Pumped up, charged, psyched—nervous—I enter the classroom and, damn, it's still early. I take an instant snapshot of the students, twenty-eight of them, place hat and coat on table, pace a little, glance at the clock again. I check them out: the laid-back, the earnest, the show-mes, the anxious smilers. They stare at me, head-on: *So that's the guy, oh yeah, seen him around, is he the one who lives in a dorm or something?* I'm conscious of being onstage, and, though it's still early, I want to get things started. I want whatever will happen to start happening now. Checking myself, I announce maybe we'll wait a little bit, for any latecomers. So I wait a bit. Thirty seconds, at the most. What was it Bill Klein said to me about teaching? "It's the only thing I know, except for maybe golf, that you don't get better at by trying harder." I tell myself not to hope for universal success. Lentz is good, but there are some kids I've met who think he's a "dickhead." Remember that. And I begin.

Housekeeping first: attendance, office hours, that stuff. I tell them all the things the course is not. It's not comprehensive: we don't do poetry and nonfiction. It's not a "best of" course. It's not a thematic course. I flirted with my topical lists but found them all too limiting. It's not a critical theory course: i.e., it's not going to help them get into graduate school. And last, it's not a canon course. The jury's still out on books written since 1945. We are the jury. That's what this is about, that's the challenge of it, and the fun, confronting books that may or may not endure, contending with hype, word of mouth, claims and counter-claims, a course where critical opinion hasn't accreted to much more than book reviews, which I often use in class.

I glance up at the clock. About fifty minutes down, thirty minutes to go, if I keep them for the full eighty minutes. Some professors, I know, walk in, distribute a syllabus, and leave after ten minutes: easy to blow off the first session that way. Any questions so far? I ask. Comments? criticism? observations? I notice I'm sweating some. I wonder if silence spells unquestioning acceptance or sullen acquiescence. Are they in awe of me? Or appalled? Never mind. Their problem. Not mine. Not yet. I press on. Why do we read novels? How do we read novels? We read them as literary performances, a series of authorial decisions, right and wrong. But we also read them as comments on America, indirect and oblique, layered and contradictory as they may be, and, no, it's not like reading captions under pictures but there is something about life in all these books, and if, ten years from now, they find themselves reading a novel it won't be because they care about the author and it won't be because they've been wondering about the fate of the novel but because these books tell us something—sometimes several different things— about the world we're in. So that's the idea. Old-fashioned, unfashion- able, and non-cutting-edge. These books are cars. First we crawl around underneath, poke under the hood, check out how they're put together. Kick the tires. Then we take the road, see how they drive. And where they take us.

Time, everyone.

As soon as it's over, and afterwards, I replay the class, guessing where I scored and where I blundered. Not since high school dates have I pondered strategy so thoroughly. I told them to call me Professor Kluge, till they graduate. Was that a mistake? Should I have gone with "P. F." or "Fred"? Gratuitous macho toughness? "Yo! KLUGSTER": I don't want to hear that coming at me down Middle Path! But what about that little aside, when I told them to cut me a little slack on gender-neutral language, that when I say "you guys" I mean students of both— whoops, should I have said *all?*—sexes. Or when I warned them that, if they blew off too many classes or missed too many pop quizzes, I'd mark them down. Did it really help for me to add: "You won't need a nightlight by your bed table, your transcript will glow in the dark"? Said with a smile, but you never know.

A secret of academe: we want our students to love us. In a small college, we want them to love us a lot, and we want the word of their love to travel to other students and to people in the department and to the provost and president as well. That's how local heroes are made. That's the game. Not writing books, not reading books, but putting them over, teaching them, a live performance in front of a live—albeit captive—audience. Love is the currency of small colleges. There's no bottom line here, no way of measuring profit or product. We live by our reputations. And our students know it. They become connoisseurs of performances—would that they judged books as acutely—Siskels and Eberts, whole classes of them.

Sure, any one student can be discounted as a flake, a crank. Con- versely, though, any three highly regarded honors students could put a serious dent in someone's bid for tenure or promotion. Sometimes, it's accepted, whole classes go off track: every old-timer has stories of a class from hell, a bad season that was or wasn't their fault. The year after a professor comes back from sabbatical leave is often dicey. "It's hard to get in stride," says an English Department old-timer. "You feel you're teaching poorly. You're out of synch. Your mind's still in Provence. It was important to recharge your batteries, but it's hard to get started again. It's like baseball. *Why can't I hit the curve? I can see it.* The students don't come by the office as much. You come out of class and say, *Hey, I didn't do much, I went 0 for 4.*"

Bad individuals, bad classes, bad seasons: those things happen. But there's more. Sometimes—at least in the humanities—it comes to . . . bad culture. A culture producing people who don't read, can't write, don't care. Those are the talks we have on slow afternoons, when students don't show up for office hours, or after we've graded a pile of student papers, or after we've had one of those class discussions that make you feel like an eighth-grade teacher trying to get students up out of their chairs at a grammar school dance where they just sit against the walls while you're out there saying, *Hey, tango! Waltz! Foxtrot! Check it out!* Anything to get them dancing, and they stay where they are. You can tell yourself the times are bad. But not for long. You can't stay at a place like Kenyon and not care about your teaching reputation.

Love. It takes different forms. There's tough love: pop quizzes, attendance taken, relatively harsh grading. Soft love: sit in a circle, use first names, and nobody gets less than a B. Carrot and stick versus carrot cake. We don't cure cancer at small colleges. Nobody gets a call to Washington when there's a new president or shows up on "Nightline" to discuss a crisis with Ted Koppel. And—though I know of five members of the English Department who are at work on novels—we're not celebrated for our publications. We measure ourselves in students. That's as true in Political Science, where Harry Clor and conservative company trade in eternal truths, they say, as in History, where Peter Rutkoff thinks it's only fair—"truth in advertising," he calls it—to announce he's a 1960s liberal, that's his perspective, take it or leave it. It's as true in crowded lecture halls as in the touchiest-feeliest little seminar; as true in the Music Department, which has the easiest grading reputation on campus, as in Economics, which has the toughest; as true of the teachers who seek universal approbation—aiming to bat 1.000— as in the grouchy sluggers who live for home runs. It's true of me—I always want to know what people are saying about me—and I suspect it's true of Kathryn "Ryn" Edwards, the biology professor who's teaching her controversial course in female sexuality again this year.

❧

THERE'S NO SUCH THING as an uneventful year in academe. Consider, for instance, the case of the indiscreet postcard. A couple Kenyon coaches were in New Orleans at a convention, and they decided to drop a line to a high school athlete they were hoping would come to Gambier. I know this sounds like small change; it's not like they were steering him through fleshpots in the French Quarter. "Thinking of you in New Orleans," the postcard caption read. Trouble is, the postcard depicted a woman, prone, lightly dressed, playing a clarinet. The student's parents protested this sexist message. Campus women's groups perked up. There was an outcry, there were meetings, reprimands, and the Athletic Department got branded as sexist.

Another time, it was a racial incident. Two years back, the brothers of Delta Kappa Epsilon fraternity gave a party, and, like many fraternity parties, it was attended by all sorts of people who'd never dream of pledging. There were the Dekes, there were independent students, there were women, some of whom went out with Dekes—Dekettes, they're called. (Go out with a member of Beta Theta Pi, you're a Beta Bunny; a liaison with a Delta Tau Delta brother turns you into a Delta Lady.) There were other students, too—including a former student of mine, a black woman—who were just out to party. Up from Virginia came a bunch of Dekes, visiting their Ohio kinfolk. During the party, the Virginians made a point of approaching and asking to be photographed with the black woman. Soon it turned ugly: it was some sort of dumb pledge stunt. They were supposed to return to Virginia with such a picture. People rapidly got pissed off, threats and shouting followed. The interlopers were escorted off campus. The Dekes depledged from their national organization, and, shortly after, claiming that the lesson had been learned, they rejoined. The last time I saw the black woman who was the innocent center of the controversy, she was at another Deke party, dancing.

What these two episodes have in common is that something minor was pounced upon and—though only marginally relevant—turned into irresistible ammunition in a war revolving around larger issues: fraternities, athletics, men. That's the usual pattern. Last year, the added attraction was Prof. Ryn Edwards's class in female sexuality. The gist of the story was this: a radical lesbian feminist was teaching a course in female sexuality at Kenyon College, used lesbian, countercultural texts, and—get this!—admonished the men in class to say little or nothing while the women talked.

The conservative *Kenyon Observer* attacked the course, the *National Review* picked up the story, and from there it spread to the foreign press. Newspapers in Italy informed their readers of odd doings in Gambier, Ohio. When Midwest college administrators met, they buzzed with talk of Edwards's course. When trustees came to town, they wanted to know what was going on here and why they hadn't been told about it before.

"The president and provost backed me up all the way," Ryn Edwards tells me. Privately, I know, the administration wasn't tickled. Edwards's course hadn't made life easier, they confided. But in public, they defended her. They arranged for her to give a couple lectures to alumni over reunion weekend last May. I attended one and found her impressive. That business about shutting up the men in class was readily explained. The course was about women, Edwards reasoned. Every woman in class had a female body, a history of growth, puberty, menstruation. Many had a history of sexual relations, some had had abortions and diseases. Men in class weren't similarly qualified. It might follow, therefore, that they'd have less to say and more to learn by listening.

It's the old guard that objected most to her course, Edwards thinks, "people who have a staunch commitment to what was. Anything new that creeps in—it may be okay, but it's not what Kenyon is about." At least one old-timer bears her out. Economics professor Carl Brehm doesn't support Edwards's offerings. "When Edwards proposed her course on women and what not," he tells me, "nobody said the woman's not qualified, the course serves no useful purpose, we ought to drop it. That should have happened, but we don't want to break each other's rice bowls."

Brehm's not alone. More than one faculty member thinks that the course should have been smothered at birth, in the Biology Department, or further up the line, by the faculty-run curricular policy committee, or even further, by the provost. But departments act collegially these days, and no one can remember the last time the curricular policy committee squashed a proposed course. "The faculty are by and large laissez-faire," Provost Reed Browning declares. Intervention from him, he seems to feel, would lead to mutiny. Couple all this with the college's notion that its faculty should be given a certain latitude in developing courses—even if it entails the risk of a bad course here and there—and you have a situation in which, for better or worse, there's been a collective loss of the ability to say no.

I'm sitting to the right, here in the Biology auditorium, the same place we have faculty meetings. It's the sort of no-nonsense modern room you picture John Demjanjuk being tried in. The first meeting, I sat in the back, as did some of the other males, five or six of us in a class of more than eighty. Ryn Edwards took care of that right away, moving everyone from back to front and stipulating that no males sit in the last row. Last year, evidently, some women students felt uncomfortable, sensing the men looking down upon them from above.

"This is a feminist course," she declares. A heavy, vigorous woman of forty-five, she enters the auditorium from a side door down below, pushing a cart, something like a hospital cart, loaded with books and syllabi instead of medical equipment. She wears a blue blouse and black slacks. Cheerful and forthright as she is—the same way she was when she gave me permission to sit in—I sense emotions and commitments beneath, not very far beneath, the professional surface.

"I call it a feminist course because that's what motivates my thinking," she continues. "I structured the course. We didn't all get together and sit down and talk about the structure of the course. I did it, and I take responsibility." Edwards' "Female Sexuality" is a feminist course, moving from anatomical and physiological subjects to discussion of health, health care, health care politics. Considerations of race, culture, class, age, and sexual orientation are taken into account.

She'll give grades in the course, she says, signaling that she does so with reluctance. "Evaluation is mythical for most students," she says, "mythical for most faculty, even though they might not admit it. But since this is a traditional institution . . ." There will be no exams, she continues. "If you're learning about your body, you shouldn't be graded on it." Grades will be based on discussion, on journals, on projects. The first three readings are by lesbians, Edwards notes. "Where you see lesbian, let it read *person,*" she suggests. "I think it works."

One of the readings offers four rules that will govern the class: (1) I speak for myself, and only I can; (2) there is no "given"; (3) I do not intend to persuade; (4) I attempt to recognize my privilege. Applying the fourth rule to herself, Edwards characterizes herself as "a white, middle-class, overweight, lesbian radical." The class laughs, won over. Edwards communicates a sense of purpose that the students welcome and a calm forbearance I suspect may come under strain before things end. Now she assigns the herstory. A *herstory*, Ryn Edwards tells the class, is to be the first assignment: a health and sexual autobiography from the women, to be completed and submitted in a sealed envelope. The women will be writing about themselves, of course. The handful of men will find a woman—a friend, sister, mother—they can interview. And, to show what she means, she once again gamely makes an example of herself. Edwards's herstory, from my notes: Birth, 1947, Washington, Pa., ill at birth; age 3–5, vaccinated against smallpox, measles, polio, "It took two nurses to hold me down," dentist visit—cavities; age 6–8, sick child, smallpox, chicken pox, mumps, participates in medical experiment re. tonsils, part of a group whose tonsils are not removed; age 10, first bra, "I didn't need it. I wanted it!"; age 11, oral polio shot, contact lenses, "They were huge. They hurt like hell!"; age 12, teeth treated with fluoride, molested by grandfather; age 13, kicked in head by a horse; age 15, first menstrual period, continues with regularity until age 42, never had cramps; age 16, intensely sexual "in my mind" with a girl-friend; age 18, surgery on dislocated shoulder; age 21, first gynecological examination, birth control pills, intercourse with boyfriend, "It was . . . okay," a lot of bleeding, very bruised and swollen; age 24, Dalkon shield—"a little spider thing"—cramps, last intercourse; age 29, stopped contact lenses; age 30, first lesbian sexual experience, first case vaginitis; age 31, shield removed, no birth control since then, though fitted with diaphragm; age 35, yearly pap test, mammograms every three years; age 36, new contact lenses, first longtime lesbian relationship, chronic nasal drip, allergy reaction; age 42, severe case vaginitis, cholesterol low; age 43–44, keeping track of menstrual cycle, hot flashes, menopause. "I'm looking forward, not to menopause, but to having it be over. Not to have periods anymore. What a relief!"

It's a startling performance. The professors I remember traded in distance that was based on education, reading, experience, age, and rank. Though we might sit around the same campfire, they were counselors, we were campers. Like boxers, they would sometimes land from outside, sometimes move in close for intimate exchanges along the ropes. Distance was for them to decide, class by class, student by student. That distance, it seems, is what Ryn Edwards seeks to abolish. The class should be interesting. So is the part of her herstory she didn't tell in class.

"This was a place that needed me." That, Ryn Edwards says, was her first reaction when she came to Kenyon in 1978. While attending Oberlin College she'd heard a little about Kenyon and hadn't liked it. "A terrible reputation." Kenyon was all-male, didn't interact with other colleges, wasn't activist. "They were only interested in importing women for weekends." The place had changed since then, of course, but not as much as it needed to. "Here I could make a difference. I was the third or fourth woman on the faculty. That was a challenge. The place was in the dark ages. It was not in contact with the real world. It was like going back in time. They were just starting on issues and struggles that had been decided elsewhere."

The first years were exciting. Women were organizing, and that, in itself, was heady stuff. And they were winning some early victories. Helping get rid of the ten-mile rule was one of the first wins. "It made me feel like I had a curfew," Edwards says. "It was like locking me in." Expanding the language in Kenyon's nondiscriminatory hiring policy so that it included sexual preference was another triumph. Adopting gender-neutral language. Raising women's salaries. Bringing women into tenure-track positions.

Resistance stiffened when women's studies was proposed. The faculty voted it down the first time, after prolonged debate. "I was there," Edwards says, "but the strategy was I wouldn't speak. That would get people's hackles up. Rita Kipp made some beautiful speeches. You should look them up in the minutes. But we lost. They asked, was women's studies an academic subject? It bothered the heck out of me. I was really angry. Was feminist scholarship real scholarship? We had to start right at the bottom. That's where the debate got hung up."

The defeat was only temporary. Women's studies supporters "regrouped, restrategized, resubmitted." The second time around they won, but their victory—at least in Edwards's eyes—was undermined when the college turned women's studies into "women's and gender studies" and hired a man, Harry Brod, as interim director. "In my mind, everything fell apart," Edwards says. "They approved a national search, and then they hired Harry Brod above some very good women who applied." Edwards thinks the presence of men on the search committee tilted things in Brod's direction. "As soon as you let men on the committee, their ideas become predominant and women go along with it. I've seen it happen again and again. Brod had an impressive curriculum vita and they selected him because a man would be able to convince and defuse the men who were out there stamping and kicking dust in our faces."

Edwards sees women's studies as a collective, activist, community-based endeavor, part of the feminist movement. Brod, she charges, turned women's studies into "just a purist academic thing." And, while women's studies was going the wrong way, other changes were overtaking the women's movement at Kenyon. More women showed up on the Kenyon faculty—that had been the goal, after all—but not all of them agreed with Edwards. Some were conservative. Some thought she was a bit much. "More and more women didn't like to rock the boat," she charges.

Soon her conflict with Brod took on a personal edge. A course she taught to thirty students one year, "Wimmin, Language, and Reality," attracted only two students the following year. She blamed Brod for diverting students from her course and into his own. Undeterred, she developed a new course: "Biology 14: Female Sexuality." Edwards is a plant biologist, but she believed her undergraduate experience in animal biology, her knowledge of cats—which she dissects with the best of them—and of dogs—she had ten boxers and terriers at home—prepared her for the course; that, and her experience of life. After the Biology Department approved the course, she spent a summer getting ready. Now she begins teaching it for the second time. The kinds of changes she seeks are happening at Kenyon, although slowly. "We're moving on," she says, "from focusing just on what white men have done, white men and some white women. We're looking at a diversity of opinions and perspectives, moving—the faculty will hate this word—to more *praxis,* a connection between what is learned and what is done in society."

She pauses, drinks from a can of Diet Coke that's seldom out of reach. "I don't cry every day I come in to work," she tells me. "I used to do that. The idea of facing another class of white elitist kids who weren't going to do anything to change the world got to me. It still does, usually in the second semester. Every March, I'm ready to leave for another job."

❦

THE MOOD OF THE COLLEGE is cheerful, as far as I can tell. It's a carryover from the holidays and—more than that—it's a reflection of attendance at professional conferences like the one I saw in New York. There are cutbacks all over the place, canceled job interviews, withdrawn positions, minuscule pay raises. People get a taste of that, return here, and Gambier's not such a bad place after all. It's a secure and pretty roost. Then, snow comes, our first serious snow, and the place takes on a winter carnival feeling. The bookstore—usually open till eleven, every night—closes early, because of the weather. My freshmen are out on the quad, rampaging like teenagers. There's austere beauty all around campus tonight, a sense of the place finding its true nature. The green surge of spring, carrying forward into summer and autumn, connects this island to other places. In winter, it is by itself. It stands alone.

At night, sometimes, I borrow a car and take off on the net of lonely roads that surrounds Kenyon. There's a mood that can catch you at night around here, when writing flags and reading palls, a mood that propels you, not to New York or Columbus—this isn't the need for a meal or a movie—but into oblivion, the way a swimmer rushes down a beach, plunges into the waves. In the old days, when the college was smaller and nights were darker, there were a handful of professors who took off on voyages in the small hours. "The night riders," they were called. Was it the fullness of their lives or the emptiness that propelled them? Was it despair at passing year after year in an obscure corner, or was it the sheer overflow of energy and joy? I feel it myself, some nights. There's no destination beyond the country itself, where headlights pick out the sides of barns, bridge girders over the Kokosing, illegible markers in a small cemetery, oil rigs stopped in midstroke, and lights outside of solitary farms, kept lit all night, for what? The way the land rolls around here, brooks running in creases, sudden ridges lifting you upward, you look back and spy the lights and towers of the college, of Peirce Hall and the Church of the Holy Spirit, breaking out of the line of oaks and pines and, heading back in, it feels like coming home, at least until you get there.

Returning to the dormitory, I sit in my room, lights out, sighting across the snow-covered quad. It's a month of birthdays. There was Plato's birthday party, a $21-per-head dinner at which Harry Brod, the featured speaker, mulled over "canons of masculinity in Plato." Martin Luther King's birthday was next: a small, candle-bearing procession down Middle Path, a "We Shall Overcome" so wavering it felt as though the seventy or so marchers were trying to get out of town without attracting notice. We stopped in front of Old Kenyon and, shivering in the cold, shifting weight from foot to foot, heard Peter Rutkoff deliver a short, bitter speech. "Let's not crap around," he said. "Why are we marching? I haven't earned the right to be here this year. I haven't done shit to advance the ideals of Martin Luther King."

A third birthday is coming up. Mine. My fiftieth. I'd never have guessed I'd be spending it back here, living in my old freshman dormitory. Or that my adult thoughts about this college would be as mixed and conflicted as my student feelings were. Confronting Kenyon's past, its traditionalists, I nod my head and have no problem with the view of the college as a defensive and conservative place. You need to learn the rules before you break them, master the traditions that you add to, or subvert. And yet—though I wince at Ryn Edwards's description of Kenyon before her arrival as being in the dark ages—I also sympathize with the people who want to shake the place up, change it, turn it inside out. So the divisions in the college have become divisions in me. I endorse tough, standard courses, fine as wine, and I abhor the stampede of hobbyhorses that the curriculum's become. Then again, I like new energy and angles, new subjects and voices, and abhor complacency on both sides of the argument. I like people more than they like each other and less than they like themselves. Part of me wants the college not to change; another part thinks it could use some shaking up. There are days when this place feels important. Other days, it's amazingly dispensable. These are island feelings, I recognize. One day, you're home forever. The next, you're looking for a ship.

"I WAS TALKING to a friend of mine about what happened to me here," Harry Brod begins. "'If Saul Bellow were a feminist,' this friend of mine says, 'you'd be a character in a novel. A small liberal arts college, WASP, finally decides to do something about women's studies and hires a New York Jewish intellectual man who in a desperate attempt to be politically correct makes the radical lesbian separatist feminist his chair, but she refuses to talk to him.' In a nutshell, my friend got it right."

I'd seen Harry Brod around campus but hesitated to approach him. The man had troubles that I didn't want to add to, and, besides, I doubted he'd agree to sit down with a writer, at least until his applications in two current hiring searches had been decided. So I talked to other people about the man Kenyon hired as acting director of its Women's and Gender Studies Department.

Harry Brod is a first-rate scholar, his supporters insist, one of a handful of people at Kenyon who transcend the local hero category and could be said to have a national reputation. He is a solid, impressive teacher, a busy writer, and, what's more, he is the kind of urban Jewish intellectual Gambier, Ohio, needs more of: ready to schmooze, happy to argue. Maybe that is part of the problem. "Since he's willing to talk to everybody," speculates one Brod backer, "he's trusted by nobody." He is distrusted because he is an outsider, envied because he is a scholar, resented because he is a man. "The trouble with Harry," cracks one professor, "is he has a dick. It's a tragic situation."

Harry's dominating and self-centered, his detractors counter, a male academic in a department that requires a female activist. "He lacks self-awareness, comes off as a classic patriarch," says one professor. "When he goes into a discussion he tends to take over." A woman administrator adds another complaint: "He doesn't talk to you unless he thinks you're important, and that irritates people."

I had spotted Brod coming out of an elevator at the American Philosophical Association in New York last month. "Harry Brod from Kenyon College!" I shouted. It was the first time we'd spoken. Somehow, it was easier to hail him in a New York hotel than to approach him on the streets of Gambier. To my surprise, he suggested we might get together and talk sometime, back in Ohio. A few days ago, I caught him in performance at Plato's birthday party. He's a big, bearded man, an ursine presence at the lectern; a passable Tevye, if Kenyon attempted *Fiddler on the Roof.* I wondered if he knew what he was getting into, coming to Ohio, how he'd be buffeted from all sides. I've seen a letter an angry alumnus wrote the college, his anger cloaked with humor. He was hoping, the alumnus said, that all this women's studies stuff was a put-on, that Harry Brod was a misprint for "Hairy Broad." Those attacks he could withstand: rumblings from out of Kenyon's past. Local antagonisms proved harder to endure.

"I knew nothing about a small liberal arts college setting," he tells me when I ask what—what on earth, I almost added—brought him here from USC. "I wanted to be at a liberal arts college. The longer I've been here, I've come to see I made a fundamental mistake. I thought this was a college that happened to be in a village. The more I'm here, I see it's a village that happens to be in a college."

When he applied for the job, four years ago, he proceeded carefully, Brod says, sensing that the appointment was controversial. The search committee assured him—unanimously—that his sex was not a problem. "They said it was fine," he says. "It turned out it wasn't fine."

His troubles began before he arrived. "When I came to look for a house I started to hear that some women were very upset. Ryn Edwards had been on leave when I was appointed. My interpretation, in retrospect, is that Ryn never dreamed they'd hire a man. That was beyond the pale for her. As for me, I had been led to believe a conversation had happened that hadn't happened."

Edwards headed the advisory committee that oversaw Brod's efforts, but the two of them couldn't work together. "There are different versions about what went on," Brod says. "My version is I was waiting for direction I never got. Ryn felt what I was doing was so irrelevant to what needed to be done."

These days, Brod has the air of a man playing a part in a drama that astonishes him. It's as if he can't believe what's happening to him, one unbelievable thing after another. His original appointment in Women's and Gender Studies was accompanied by a visiting appointment to the Philosophy Department. Two years ago he applied for a tenure-track job there. The search ended in no appointment. "The Philosophy Department wouldn't recognize a good philosopher if it tripped over one," he snaps.

This year, the stakes are doubled: he's applied for tenure-track directorships in Women's and Gender Studies and IPHS. Obviously, he hopes something will come through, but I can sense that he's prepared for more disappointment. He's gotten wary of Kenyon, of what he's gone through, of what is yet to come. And he's starting to mull over what it takes to fit here and why he doesn't. Gambier is starting to feel like a party where you might not be welcome or a neighborhood you've moved into where you sense—is it you? is it them?—you'll never quite be at home. You sense diffidence, resistance, fields of force that keep you out.

"I come from a tradition where people argue about ideas," Brod says. "In faculty meetings here, whenever someone says something of substance, the next two speakers arise to say, 'Let's not be divisive.' That's the village mentality. There's a deep conservatism about Kenyon, about the way we do things here."

He pauses, noshes on the chips that accompany his club sandwich. I contemplate ordering coffee. But the Kenyon Inn serves the most anemic brew in town. Suddenly, looking over at Harry Brod, I recall someone quoting an old saying about this place. "In Gambier, everyone feels left out." Who was it? Then it comes to me: the president said that. Phil Jordan himself.

"The fact that I survived at all is a miracle," Brod says. He had a heart attack early in his stay here. "As a man of the left, I've been attacked from the right. Here, also, I've been attacked from the left, as a male. Completely isolated, no structure, no connection. Under fire. Incredible."

❧

IN MY CLASS, there's still a sense of acquaintance-making, of feeling each other out. A few students announce themselves, raising their hands, but the bulk hang back. Kenyon students' attitude toward class discussion resembles Americans' feeling about voting rights. They insist on having it. They resent losing it. They don't necessarily want to use it. So, mostly, it's up to me. Like a host checking a party, I sense most guests having a good time—too good a time maybe—and others, lurking in corners, clock-watching, wishing they were someplace else. One thing that drives me crazy, even on the best of days, is how they yawn. I can understand people coming in tired, sometimes, and feeling a yawn coming on. That's no insult. But whatever happened to stifling a yawn, to putting a hand over your mouth? These guys—men and women, this is gender-neutral—open wide right in front of me, tongue, teeth, and throat. At first I felt insulted. It was bad manners. Then I consulted with Lentz. His pet thesis is that we live in an age of solipsism, people aware only of themselves. The students who look at us perform, he thinks, never consider that a fellow human being is looking back at them. It's as if we were figures on a television screen, a show they've been forced to watch. They can't change channels. So they yawn.

I started with a survey of Kerouac's life, announcing that we'd be talking about the James Dean of American literature. Then I realized that they might not recognize the reference, or maybe they'd confuse James Dean with Jimmy Dean, country-western singer and TV pitchman for his brand of breakfast pork sausage. It's hard to know what you can count on students to know, what their generation retains, what slips away. Hemingway is as far back for them as William Dean Howells was for me, and Vietnam is as remote as World War II. I cite Kerouac's early work as in the tradition of Thomas Wolfe. No, *not* the author of *Bonfire of the Vanities*. The other guy. And I ask someone to describe what Wolfe's novels are like. No one does. Okay. Scratch another dead white male. It's not as if we're building an edifice around here, each course a new stone that's added to an ancient wall. There is no wall. There are various rocks.

❧

SOMETIMES, when colleagues drop me off at the end of the evening, I invite them in for a tour of Lewis Hall. Attracted and repelled, they hesitate. Isn't there some sort of rule against this kind of thing? Something about sex or privacy? No, no, come on in, I say, it'll be all right. In they come, into a new world: you can spend a lot of years at this small liberal arts college and not set foot in a dormitory, especially this most ornery, horny, and reprobate of dorms, the last all-male dorm on campus. I show the guests my apartment, bare walls and burned orange carpet and the floor fan I borrowed from Jane Lentz and run, all night long, to screen out the animal madness beyond these thin, bare walls. People have a hard time picturing me here, a harder time imagining I'm happy. Soon, they're ready to leave, but first I insist they stroll down the hall with me, down to the east wing, ground floor, where I lived twenty-two years ago. Come, I urge, and let all your senses be engaged: the smell of pizza and unwashed laundry and spilled beer, the pounding sound of rap music—Public Enemy hurling "fuck you"s while prospective students and their parents visit the place—and the sight of a salami, stuck phallically to a door, the graffiti artistry of defaced college announcements about drinking and date rape, of notes from one young scholar to another:

*Greg, if you ever fucking touch my stereo or my Velvet Underground c.d.
again, I'm going to pound your little fucking vegetarian body so hard that
it wouldn't be suitable for gerbil fodder. Get it? Love, George*

So much for the hall. Now the cages. There's room 1, my old room, off-the-charts squalid, home of Mark, consensus choice for master procrastinator. "It's a skill," he confided when I asked him about his reputation. "You realize you have work to do, and you have a motivation not to do the work because you know it's going to be hard. You have to do the work, but you don't want to, so you have to be busy. I wander around, I go from one place to another. I sometimes try to pick intellectual fights. Or I pick fights with girls, or they pick fights with me, and that takes up a lot of time. Or I get insanely sick and lock myself in the room and read dumb things like Beat Generation short stories. Anything too intellectual defeats the purpose. Sometimes you just kind of sit in rooms and talk. That's good procrastination. Master plans about how you would run the world, or solving Kenyon's problems. Talk about Kenyon's problems counts as studying." Across the hall there's Greg, another Kerouac fan, and Grant, a fledgling writer who's given me a tone poem to read, a day in the life of a suburban shopping mall, a kind of franchise-era *Our Town*. Then there's a room with bong pipes and beer cans and a piranha named Bucky. One afternoon, Bucky took the head right off a goldfish. A student scarfed the bottom half of the goldfish. One of the guys in this room is said to have run through $4,000 pocket money in just one semester. Then there's the room that Alex and Ryan share. Ryan seems thoughtful and—dare I say it?—serious, making his version of "Why Do Fools Fall in Love" at a Kokosingers concert all the more striking. His roommate Alex is another story, talkative and outgoing. If he's read something he likes—Emily Dickinson or Max Weber—it fills him up, he gets excited, he wants to talk about it. He takes a holistic view of college experience. Alex came to Kenyon expecting to play soccer. Instead, he's gotten hooked on dance. "It was totally unexpected," he says. "In the fall dance concert, there was a big piece, a really sexual piece, and I would never in my life have imagined myself dancing onstage in just a loincloth, in front of hundreds of people, including my hallmates."

Another room is schizophrenic, one neat resident, one less so, with a kind of Mason-Dixon Line down the middle. The neat half belongs to Matt, a guy from Millersburg, one county north of here, close enough so that he thought of Kenyon as "a big, hippie, druggy school" and visited it as an afterthought one April, having been all set to go to Wake Forest. "I came home and said to my mother, 'This is bad . . . I like it.'" He worried about flunking out, though his apprehension only lasted a few days. "If you go to class and you're there, you're not going to flunk out," he's found, "and with the kind of faculty you have here, you're going to learn something." Matt is in Lentz's class, as is George, who lives across the hall, in a room that's become kind of the lounge-party room, since the absence of a carpet means there's less of a problem with spilled beer. George is another guy who showed up here uncertain about Kenyon. During orientation, the place struck him as "the most expensive day care center on the planet." Now he's gotten attached. "I came to this school because I got in," he says. "I didn't fall in love. Not yet. I will when I graduate because that's the way it works. Things grow on me."

Like everybody else, I gravitate toward the room George shares with Andy, park myself on a chair, question their taste in music, and get ridiculed: they jeered when I said I liked a group called the Platters. They mull over what Lentz was up to that day. Now the fraternity rush season is beginning, and they've got to decide whether or not to join:

fewer than half of Kenyon's males belong to fraternities these days. Rush rules prescribe that courtships begin in the second semester, and that it be a "dry rush": no alcohol served. This means that fraternities take freshmen to Columbus, drink in Ohio State bars, take in a Columbus Chill hockey game, and head back to Gambier. Local entertainments include spaghetti dinners, parties, and not necessarily G-rated movies. Lately, there's been a lot of talk about fraternity initiations and stunts, hell-week stuff. One fraternity leads a blindfolded pledge to a toilet, obliges him to reach in the bowl for what he can only assume is a turd, makes him eat what turns out to be a banana. And this is one of the milder initiations I've heard about.

On tours, I always save Pete's room for last. Pete's a junior from Lancaster, Pennsylvania, a Beta, a football player, a political science major, and, in Lewis Hall, an RA, "resident adviser." The message board on the door lists where he can be found—class, library, football practice, etc.—and a pin stuck in the corkboard is supposed to point anyone who's looking for him in the right direction. To the official list, his irreverent wards have added "Nintendo." I can vouch for the Nintendo.

When you open the door, it's as though you've been swimming in a polluted harbor and have rescued yourself, lifted yourself up onto the stern of a passing ship, only the ship turns out to be a garbage scow, fouler than the waters it traverses, an Exxon Valdez of Pringles cans, comic books, mulching, unwashed laundry piled willy-nilly on an un-made sheetless bed, surrounded by books, papers, soft drink cans, and chewing tobacco spit cups. And across this ruined vista, back to the door, Pete reposes in front of a video screen, riveted, as though piloting this garbage scow into a treacherous harbor. On the screen, figures move and clash, cheer and grunt.

The first semester, it was Nintendo, Pete explains. Now he's graduated to Sega-genesis. "I play twice a day for twenty minutes," Pete insists, "and more on weekends, two or three hours maybe." My doubts about this are huge, and I am not alone. "He gets a new game and gets his ass kicked," one of the freshmen tells me. "Then he plays it for three weeks by himself till he's unbeatable, and then he sits around and gloats."

"My room is a collage," Pete says. There's a book by John Locke next to a comic book by Stan Lee. "Comic books are huge on this campus," he reports. On the decaying food around the room—Cheez Whiz, wheat crackers, Pringles when he wants to splurge—"Well, food *will* sit around." Dirty clothes there are, he grants: "I do laundry in small amounts to get me through." I ask him where he sleeps, for the mattress is bare of sheets and piled high with debris. "For the last four years," he says, "the most I've ever had is a bedspread and a sleeping bag." Looking on the sunny side of things, he tells me he cleaned up his spit cans—"two or three spitters"—just the other day.

❦

MY WIFE COMES DOWN for my fiftieth birthday. The bookstore had a sign in the window this morning, a huge sign, so the whole town knows about it. And Barb, the English Department secretary, put out an all-points E-mail message that's generated condolences from all over campus. It turns out that my birthday is close to that of Helen Forman, John Crowe Ransom's daughter, who works in the bookstore, reads everything, smokes cigarettes, cannot be relied upon to keep a secret, and makes Gambier a place that's not like other places. Liz Forman, her daughter, is throwing a party for both of us. It'll be good food—great food, by local standards—and a lot to drink and killer word-games afterwards. Guests have been invited to bring celebratory limericks. On the way out the door, a voice hails us from behind.

"Hey, Kluge . . ." I turn, half-ready to brace someone with "Professor Kluge, till you graduate." But this one isn't going to graduate. It's a freshman who loved poetry, or at least the idea of being a poet, or the idea of drinking as a preface to poetry. He was suspended part of last semester for pissing on a tree. There've been more incidents: identifying himself as "Calvin Coolidge" to the local sheriff, breaking a window someplace. Now he stands there holding a bag of laundry. "I got kicked out," he says. "If I don't see you again . . ." He wears a navy pea jacket, and I picture him in the Coast Guard, knocking around. Instead, he'll probably wind up at another school. Or, maybe, back at this one. Later, I find, he's left a note to the campus cops taped on his door. "Dear Security: Thanks for the memories."

❦

"YOU MAY BE A FIGMENT of my crazed imagination," Lentz tells his freshmen. "Something I have concocted to plague me with papers to grade. Why I have done this beats the hell out of me."

He's teeing up *Richard II* and, to get things started, has asked every-one to look up and write down a dictionary definition of *solipsism:* "the theory that the self is the only thing that can be known and verified." His point, it develops, is that solipsism may be part of Richard's problem, underlying his famous "I have wasted time and now time doth waste me." Then he segues into some Gambier solipsism. He recalls a student who came late to an exam he was giving in Philomathesian Hall. She came clomping across the hall, boards creaking underfoot, distracting the test-takers. Afterwards, handing in her blue book, she complained that she had less time than the other students. Lentz countered that she'd done all right on an earlier exam she'd come late for. "Oh," she responded, "I haven't read your comments yet." Thus, a triple solipsism. She wasn't mindful of her fellow students, whom she disturbed, of the passage of time, which she neglected, or of her professor, whom she ignored. After class, Lentz tells me this was a student he had five years ago. It's interesting, in teaching, how our failures haunt us.

Right after Lentz's class, I step into Ryn Edwards's. It's Martin Luther King's birthday. "Kenyon, unlike most of the nation, doesn't take the day off," she notes. She offers a moment of silence, then proceeds to lecture on the characteristics of cancer cells, which divide, invade, elude. Two kinds of professors, two different personal styles. After class, I told Lentz of Edwards's comment that Kenyon was in the dark ages when she came, the Kenyon of Ransom, Jarrell, Lowell, Doctorow. Our Kenyon, too. Something brought it to mind. Something about solipsism, maybe.

"Could have fooled me," he said, and left it at that.

🌿

THE PHILOSOPHY DEPARTMENT invited three candidates to Gambier, three out of 175 who applied, and, even now, at the end of the race, two will lose and one will win. Two will be housed and fed, chat with potential colleagues and bosses. They'll stroll the campus, glance at houses they might live in—it's like trying on a life, they're that close—and in the end, not be heard from again. The winner, however, will be on the edge of a lifetime contract.

What starts as a tough competition turns tougher at the end. The first thing a candidate must do is teach a sample class. Observers, members of the search committee, possibly the provost, sit in back. "It's a hard thing to bring off well," Ron McLaren says. "A single class with strange students. It's hard to decide whether to make your pitch to students or observers. You're always aware of being watched, and that gets in the way of carrying it off." One class, one hour: it's like hauling a comedian onstage, sitting back, and saying, "Okay, be funny."

The second hurdle is an open lecture that is supposed to reflect the candidate's philosophical interests. Compared to the sample class, this ought to be a snap. Instead of contending with a bunch of unknown students, you deliver a gloss on your graduate school thesis. There are hazards here, too, and more than one candidate who's delivered a winning class has delivered a lecture that seemed problematically impenetrable. Or, maybe, problematically *penetrable*, facile and derivative. Once again, the audience is mixed: students, faculty, administration.

It's not over yet. There are interviews with the president and the provost and the academic dean, dinners with the search committee, lunch with students. It's not a question of spilling wine or using the wrong fork, but it's still a trial. People who dazzle on paper can disappoint in person.

Candidate A, a woman, was likable and personable, maybe a little soft. Her class explored definitions of love and ended, cutely, with a consideration of Erich Segal's definition: never having to say you're sorry. Her paper came off as more literary and historical than philosophical. "Not persuasive, not convincing," one committee member said. Candidate B was a thorny, complicated-seeming chap who taught a playful, quizzical class. Riddles of identity were his topic. If there's someone you love and that person's brain is placed into the body of a cockroach, is this still the person you love? What if someone else's brain is transplanted into your lover's body? Then again, what if some "Star Trek"–type machine annihilates your lover and then proceeds to create an exact duplicate? The class was fun. Candidate B's lecture was a tour de force, delivered from memory, and hard for me to follow. The man struck me as hard to connect with, possibly brilliant, but who can tell? I couldn't. Neither could Phil Jordan, it turns out. Kenyon's president was a philosophy major at Princeton. He figures that someone who proposes to teach philosophy here ought to be able to connect with him. "I just thought him odd," Jordan tells me. "I was more mystified at the end than at the beginning. I like to have someone who, with a good deal of effort on my part, can make me understand things, and we had a lot of trouble getting on the same wavelength."

Candidate C was lively and personable. "Philosophy," he told the class, "is the study of all the things we don't want to think about." He confronted them with the kind of thorny ethical choice philosophers love: two kidneys are available for transplant and a couple dozen patients need them. The life-or-death decision is up to you. You must choose, and have reasons for choosing, between a Good Samaritan doctor with a drinking problem, a millionaire who's mentioned the hospital in her will, a welfare mother pregnant with a crack-addicted infant, and so forth. How to decide. "No one rules guiltlessly," Candidate C warned the class. Later, his lecture—on the relationship between beliefs and perception—was something I could almost follow. Halfway through, Adele Davidson, an English Department professor who's serving as an outside member on the search committee, slid me a note: "I think this is the one."

Now, the search committee's final meeting begins with Banning writing a summary of returns from other precincts on the blackboard. Ron McLaren and Ulf Nilsson, the other Philosophy Department members of the search committee, and Adele Davidson study the results, which look pretty clear to me. The president, the provost, the academic dean, and five students who worked with the search committee have all rated the candidates 1, 2, or 3. Combining and adding the scores, Candidate C—my favorite—is in the lead. Candidate A is second, well behind, and Candidate B is a very distant third.

"The next question," Banning says, after scrutinizing the numbers, "is, what do we do?" The early discussion amplifies what the numbers suggest: Candidate C was impressive. He's everybody's first or second choice. Candidate A was good, not great, and it's not clear whether she'd get the offer if Candidate C withdrew. Candidate B is unacceptable, more or less. This means that if the other two got assassinated and he alone were left, it's likely they'd call in more candidates.

You'd expect that the search committee would spend time comparing their first and second choices, C and A, but professors are like bright students who do poorly on multiple-choice tests because, shunning the obvious pick, they linger over the plausible second choice and go way out of their way to accommodate the third. That's what happens now. One member of the committee saw something promising and remarkable in Candidate B. It's not that he doesn't like Candidate C—"he's obviously one tough cookie and he's smart and he knows a lot and everything"—it's just that this other guy, the one that ranked lowest, might, in fact, be someone special. There's something about him. Maybe it's the very same quality that made him so hard to grasp, so off-putting, so difficult to chat with.

"You have to weigh the possibility of having a top-ranked philosopher at Kenyon against all that other business, which is teaching-related," the committee member says. "I talked about Kenyon with my wife last night. We get a lot of students at Kenyon who think they know a lot. They go through, and no one ever pulls them up short and tests them. This candidate would do that. And that would be a good thing."

For a while—a long while—the committee ponders possible strengths of the fellow who'd started out the meeting as consensus third-choice. They contemplate his possible brilliance, difficulty, depth. There are a lot of professors around who, lacking these qualities, put on user-friendly classes, "dog-and-pony shows." Maybe it's time to have someone who wouldn't do that. But—here's the question—will this man connect with students at all? "I'm concerned about having people around who are thinking," someone says, "but it's no good if there's no one around to talk to."

Eventually they decide to offer the job to Candidate C, and everyone feels good about this choice, for a minute. But it doesn't take long for the mood to change. Anybody who likes poetic justice would appreciate what happens next. From the very beginning of this search, Kenyon College has held all the cards. Kenyon chose from nearly 200 applicants, Kenyon chose from dozens of people interviewed, Kenyon chose from three who appeared on campus. But while Kenyon was weighing and measuring, the candidates were making judgments, too. They had their eyes wide open while they were jumping through hoops. And we are now in that delicious and uncertain phase in which the college must wait for someone else's decision. It could last a week or a month, it could end in an offer to a second- or third-choice candidate, in a renewed or aborted search, in triumph or despair. And like any of life's rejections, it might in the end have little to do with Kenyon. Or—then again— everything. So we shouldn't take things personally, we professionals, and yet we do. Boy, do we!

"I'm not sure we can get him," one member of the search committee says. "This may be too constrained a community. He may not say yes."

"We haven't decided what to do after he turns us down," someone else frets.

"How long do we give him to answer? Two weeks, is it?"

The worries begin. Last summer, I talked to John Ward, former English Department chair, about what this phase of searches feels like. Because it competes at a higher level, possibly, in a tougher field, the English Department has faced rejection more than once.

"That's when you get defensive and anxious about Gambier and its limitations," Ward says. "You become aware of the things you're repressing or ignoring or accepting. We get defensive. Or we get insightful about our candidates' immaturity and inadequacies. It's always a matter of defending Gambier, during the MLA convention, during the visit. It's a debilitating dialogue. It's like a catechism. *I believe, I believe, I believe . . .*"

You can feel helpless, isolated, small, and small-time during this phase of the search. Getting the first choice, Ward says, is wonderful. "It's a double hit. You get number one, and you're done with the search in January. You're deliriously happy. If not, you get tired. The sniping starts. Maybe you make an appointment, out of exhaustion, that you don't want to make."

Why does Kenyon get spurned? It could be because there's a spouse with not much chance of employment in Knox County, Ohio. It could be money. Usually, though, it's not. "The big one," Ward says, "is someone who says, 'I want to go to a research institution. I want to be able to write. I don't *care* what I said at the MLA. Writing and research are what I've been doing, and that's what I want, rather than this idyllic situation where you're teaching your brains out. I get a 2–2 teaching load at Michigan, with time to write, and one of those two courses is a specialized seminar that plugs right into my half-done book.'"

Banning makes the call. And waits for the reply.

❧ February

N OW, FEBRUARY, "that gray, wet, muddy, black season," as Kenyon's president calls it. Bleak, truncated days, long, inhospitable nights, a month without vacation, a dark passage between Christmas and far-off springtime. If the academic year were World War II, this would be November 1942, our Murmansk run. "As I get older," Phil Jordan tells me, "I like the dark seasons less."

We muddle through. A few years ago a trustee gave the college money to throw a campuswide party to relieve the February gloom. "Philander's Phling" is the result. A stretch limousine shunts students from dorms to Peirce Hall. Entering, they find poker tables, craps, blackjack, other games of chance; an artist doing caricatures; a big band playing nearby. No alcohol, but students imbibe beforehand—"frontloading," it's called—and show up in a festive mood, most of the men in tuxes, the women—who dress like vagabonds most of the time—in killer dresses. Professors and administrators serve as croupiers. Las Vegas comes to Gambier, Ohio. And the supply of money—play money—is infinite. Students walk around with wads of hundred, five-hundred, thousand-dollar bills that they're issued on entering. There's always more for the asking.

Philander's Phling is one night only, however, and as the month comes in, gray and lumbering, I sense inevitable confrontation with the issues I predicted might arise this year—hiring searches, residentiality, tenure and promotion. And one other: the Greek alumni—the aggrieved fraternity men—are back at Kenyon. Each visit gets a little angrier.

❧

"WE WANT HEALTHY and constructive dialogue," says one irate alumnus. "The administration says they support the fraternity system, and I can tell you it's not true," a current student declares. "They don't let sophomore members live with us, they've taken our lounges, and they don't give us adequate housing," he adds. What's more, fraternities are compelled to "dry rush": "The security guys count the cans in our recycling bins," a student complains.

Once again, they meet in Philomathesian Hall, yesterday's fraternity members and today's, reprising complaints that add up to this: whatever it says, the college is out to get fraternities. When someone says that the administration expects to review its housing policy in three years, Ray Grebey flares up. Three years from now a couple of the shakier fraternities could be dead. "The administration's policy is arbitrary and unacceptable," he declares. "There are elements that want to sue the college. I personally don't. We have a noble history and tradition, and we don't want division. But we would pursue it if there's a failure to negotiate."

A lawsuit against the college seems more and more likely. Some people I've spoken to are appalled by the prospect. They compare it to regicide, parricide, infanticide, you name it. They call it treason. But— it's only fair to say—the fraternity guys are the ones who feel betrayed.

"We're tired of not being included and not being communicated with and misinformed in meetings with the president," Grebey charges. He says that some alumni have stopped giving to the college. Others have reduced their gifts. Bob Price reports that the law firm that looked over documents between the college and the fraternities thinks that the Greeks have a case. It would cost $125,000 to pursue. Price says he's already lined up some alumni who will finance the litigation.

In a last effort to stay out of court, the Greek alumni decide to go over Jordan's head. "We want to talk to the board of trustees about a decision made by their chief executive officer, the president of the college," Grebey reasons. He plans to make the request to the board through the alumni council. At a meeting of the alumni council, he repeats his case. "We got stiffed," he says, "and I don't like getting stiffed." He's not asking them to endorse his arguments, just to pass along the request for a sit-down.

❦

SHOULD KENYON COLLEGE'S FACULTY be advised? urged? required? to spend a certain amount of time at Kenyon College? The residentiality issue arose at an otherwise soporific faculty meeting last week, and, as usual in these venues, it came up obliquely. No one stood up and said that commuting-to-Columbus, punch in–punch out, two-day-a-week professors subvert Kenyon's traditions, violate its spirit, and contradict its advertising. What happened was that, during some talk about a new executive committee, Rita Kipp suggested that some positions on this committee be reserved for nontenured faculty. This was her way of bringing newcomers into the fold, socializing them, giving them a stake in the college, and making Gambier feel like home. If you wait six years, until people have tenure, before involving them in college government, it may be too late, she reasoned. The measure failed by a wide margin, defeated by a majority who evidently think that you shouldn't let committee work and intramural politics distract you, at least until you've got your green card. Ted Mason is one of those who think that, all talk of community values aside, untenured professors should mind their own business. If they immerse themselves in college committees, faculty affairs, all the rest of it, and then don't get tenured, they risk disaster in the job market.

"Here's what I'd say to Rita," Ted Mason remarked as we went running a couple afternoons back. "'Okay, Rita, you've made a choice. You've chosen to make your life here. You find it an affirmative place and that's fine. But, given the nature of the marketplace, the fact that other places have higher publishing standards, if not higher teaching standards, it would be irresponsible, not to say criminal, to tell untenured faculty members to involve themselves in college governance. An untenured professor's response to every request of that kind should be 'No, no, I don't want to do it, no.'"

This discussion at the faculty meeting was just a preliminary skirmish. I suspect Kipp knew her proposal wouldn't fly. But she also knew academics like to discuss long-shot notions. That's what happened in the Philosophy search, when they took a long look at the last-choice candidate. It's as though stillborn babies get more attention—autopsy, obituary, elegy, and burial—than the live, squalling, shit-making troublemakers of tomorrow. Anyway, the residentiality issue now belongs to the faculty affairs committee, which is spending Thursday afternoons deciding whether there's a problem and, if there's a problem, whether there's a solution that won't create more problems than it solved.

❧

WORD COMES EARLIER than expected. The Philosophy Department search is over. They got their first choice: Joel Richeimer, finishing up a Ph.D. at the University of Michigan, author of a thesis on "Perceptual

Expertise and the Poverty of the Input Thesis." He also has a master's in cognitive psychology.

🌿

I KEEP THE ENERGY LEVEL HIGH in "American Literature since 1945." I go in pumped up, and I leave drained, monosyllabic, nearly mute. I spend a lot of time—maybe too much—taking the class through the story, emphasizing the context of the book, the course of the plot, the development of character and situation, a lot of time, in short, *making sure they get it.* Whether or not they like what they get is hard to say. *On the Road* turns out to be a tricky text. I wanted to show the dark side of a book that is simplistically regarded as an exultant buddy story. I wanted to stress how the energies of the book run down, the traveling tires, the friendships disappoint, so that the whole enterprise is sadder and more equivocal than people realize. I did my job too well. The class barely nodded at the upbeat parts, the restless joy, the wondering, wandering sense of America. And they all too readily acceded to the negatives: Sal Paradise and Dean Moriarty as failed friends, macho womanizers, moral imbeciles. So we ended in a quizzical mood: *Yeah, so, why are we reading about these . . . losers?*

Then, though *Continental Drift* is different in so many interesting ways—style, structure, authorial control—it confronts them with another white, male, working-class loser, a New England furnace repairman who escapes with his family to Florida, a viciously, vividly described land of detritus and decay, where he fails and perishes. *Not this again,* I can hear them thinking. We are moving, though. Breaching protocol, I gave pop quizzes on consecutive days, to make sure they were doing the reading. I wanted us to be in this together. "I want to say more than 'Thanks, you've been a lovely audience,' when this is over," I told them. But they remain an audience, and I remain a performer. A salesman of books, a Crazy Eddie spokesman, a figure on a television screen, though I sometimes come crashing out of the tube and into the living room. We've told them for so long that literature is about life that a book's relevance to them must be instantly established or interest withers. It's as though the authors were on trial, or maybe the professor, but not the class. This might not happen in Shakespeare or Milton. Shakespeare is a fixed menu course, Milton is forced feeding. Recent literature is a smorgasbord, and consumers feel they have a right to be a little pickier about what they put, and leave, on their plates.

❧

WHAT LENTZ AND I DO sometimes on our runs is go through the English Department, one by one, deciding who can leave and who can't. It's an island-type conversation, and it goes right to the heart of a place like this. It relates to happiness and unhappiness, fame and obscurity, coming and going. If you grasp this, I think, you've gotten close to something important.

Kenyon is a teaching college. Forget John Crowe Ransom. He was a fine, misleading exception. The place was made by local heroes, professors who performed in classrooms year in and year out, people whose ambitions were defined—confined, maybe—by the college. Teaching is the primary requirement for job candidates. It's the sine qua non for promotion: it counts for 55 percent, scholarship for 35 percent, community service for 10 percent. Teaching is what brings you to the island and keeps you here.

"I always told candidates that we tenure people at Kenyon," former Kenyon English Department chair John Ward said to me last summer. "We're not an institution that offers a tenure-track job we have no notion of filling. If you do as well as your record suggests, you will be tenured. That was the first thing. And the second was that if you're a good teacher you'll make it at Kenyon, no matter what scholarship you're producing. And if you don't manage the teaching, you're going to be miserable."

Come, teach, be happy, and stay forever. It sounds simple, but it's not. New recruits come out of graduate school, where research is emphasized. They've got scholarly ambitions. Should they beat their scholarly cutting edges—tweezers though they might be—into pedagogical plowshares? What's more, the college expects its professors to stay sharp. No, they don't expect anyone to fight for a title. But they do want them to stop by the gym between classes, skip rope, work on the heavy bag, maybe spar a few rounds just to stay in shape. This isn't publish or perish. Nobody will get fired if they don't get stuff into print. But they might not get promoted. This is the flip side of John Ward's counsel to newcomers. "If you're a good teacher," he'd say, "you're going to be tenured. If you're a good teacher for twenty years, in a small department, plugging away, not doing anything distinguished, you might not get promoted to full professor."

So research does come into play. It affects the way you're regarded— by the administration and by your colleagues—after you arrive, before tenure, after tenure. It affects the way you think of yourself. And it affects your ability to leave. It's the measure of your freedom. If you're a great teacher, you probably can't leave. You're a lifer, maybe you're a local hero. But you can't leave. To the extent that you've obeyed Kenyon's first commandment—teach your brains out—you've disabled yourself. As your scholarship dwindles, your marketplace value becomes nil. Playing by the institution's rules, you've become its hostage. You sink roots. That's fine. For a tree. But you can't move. You haven't got the publications. You've surrendered your passport.

The history of research at Kenyon is like the history of drinking in America. These days Kenyon encourages research in moderate, social amounts. Don't get drunk, God forbid, but a glass or two of wine with dinner, fine. That's today. But Ron Sharp arrived in what he perceives as the depths of prohibition, when the drys ran the campus. "When I came in 1970," he says, "there was no expectation about research. I decided, after a couple years, I wanted to write. That was new for me. A dilemma. I wanted to have my cake and eat it. I had a commitment to teaching, but I wanted to write. I agonized. The ambiance was not just no emphasis on writing. It was dramatically clear that writing and research was a major violation of your responsibilities. I'd set aside one morning a week, and I'd come in the next day. 'Where were you?' people would ask. 'What's the matter?' I started making up excuses about dentist appointments. Then one day I had a conversation with another English professor, Galbraith Crump, who said he set aside time for writing, just like you set aside time for class. 'Are you serious?' I asked. My jaw dropped. 'You're doing this regularly?' It was a gigantic revelation. It was almost like coming out of the closet."

I'm not sure how accurate Sharp's account is. There may be something of a young professor's angst in it. Other professors—Lentz is one—give a more moderate account of things. And Bruce Haywood, provost during the years Sharp describes, sums up the attitude toward research: "A full professor should do a book or two but there was no requirement to publish little articles regularly and routinely. When push came to shove, it was the college's interests that ruled the faculty." Still, I suspect there's something to Sharp's story. Research made people nervous. It made the college nervous, too.

Things changed, everyone agrees, in the seventies and the eighties. The college made clear it wanted faculty to do research, to stake a claim in their fields, to be known by their counterparts at other places. "The real sea change since the sixties and what we all think we remember as the golden age is what happened to how we conduct our professional lives," Phil Jordan says. "We were bringing faculty who were really ambitious to be people who wrote, who presented work, who lived scholarly lives elsewhere and here."

If a professor didn't keep his research active, if he didn't stay up, if he just taught, something in him died. Maybe not in every case, but usually. Maybe not right away, but in time. "I haven't seen many people who can sustain just teaching for very long," Ron Sharp says. "I've seen people make dazzling starts. They attract lots of students. There are students in the office, on the phone, over at the house. But after a few years go by, these fabulous, bright teachers with no commitment to scholarship burn out. There's bitterness and resentment. That's the pattern. *You just can't be feeding them the same shit.* People of real subtlety—with rare exceptions that I'm willing to grant—can't sustain a life in Gambier, Ohio, without some sort of intellectual stimulation. At first, you're smart, articulate, witty. You have students almost at will, and you wow them with four or five shticks that are winners. But after a few years it's too easy, you sense a little phoniness. So research isn't selfishness. You're a human being, you try to teach here, but there's a whole other life. Just teaching—it's not enough."

Moderate as it was, the emphasis on scholarship kicked off some grousing. It still does. "If they want to be university professors, they should get university appointments," one old-timer tells me. Some believed that, when you got right down to it, a small residential college had more in common with a preparatory school than with a university. Oh, granted, one "kept up" with things through reading. But what was the point of churning out a turgid article for some little journal? That wasn't Kenyon's game. Here, professors taught, lived, stayed close to campus. Those were the things that counted, the people who counted. You came back from sabbaticals with stories and carpets, not with manuscripts. But now these professors saw the values of the college being diluted by the values of the university: i.e., city slicker styles coming to a country town and creating something that wasn't country and wasn't city. Suburbia: boring, boxy houses on small, dull yards.

Still, even while it said it esteemed research along with teaching, Kenyon continued tenuring more than 90 percent of its tenure-track faculty. Thus, the policy that the college announced didn't result in particular rewards and punishments. In the end, like a campground that comfortably accommodates opposing armies, trailer hookups, hot showers, and all, Gambier had room for teachers who did little or no research as long as they were passable teachers, as well as for teachers who aspired to fame in their field. The two styles, the two types, coexisted, uneasily, both managing to feel underappreciated and ill used.

"People began saying we were moving towards publish or perish, there was too much emphasis on research, nobody cares about teaching," Ron Sharp says. "But look at tenure decisions. Everybody's still getting tenured. People who publish a single book review get tenured. It's not an issue. Go look at the figures. Once every four or five years, a total incompetent or someone who pisses everybody off doesn't get tenured. This is publish or perish?"

In the end, there's something permanently tricky and equivocal about faculty research in a small college. It's a tension everyone feels, a continuing drama in everyone's life, a drama played out in offices that are locked—are they home writing or raking leaves?—and in lights burning late—grading papers or updating résumés?—in mail that does or doesn't arrive, in phones that do or don't ring, those phone calls that you move a little faster for, the double-ring phone calls coming in from outside, not the single-ring calls from the intramural PBX. Research tones, sharpens, invigorates, in moderate amounts. But if research takes over your life, there's no telling where that might lead. You might get carried away . . .

🌿

OUTSIDE THE BOOKSTORE DELI, I meet Eugene Heath, a visiting professor of philosophy and one of the unsuccessful candidates in the just-concluded search. He suggests we should talk sometime, and I agree instantly, annoyed at the timidity that had kept me from approaching him on my own. I'd looked hard at the anxious candidates in New York and closely followed the three who auditioned here in Gambier. All the time, Heath and his colleague Steven Emmanuel were here, insiders on the way to becoming outsiders.

"I came up here for a one-year job," Eugene Heath tells me in my office one afternoon. "I understood that." He'd been teaching at the University of Charleston when word came that his friend Tom Short, conservative philosopher, bête noire of campus liberals, foe of gender-neutral language and political correctness, was going on a leave of absence from which he was not expected to return. At first, Heath resisted coming to Kenyon, but eventually he relented.

"I really liked the place," he says. Heath is a tall, thin man, soft-spoken and measured. He's thought through what he's saying to me, I guess, and this isn't just a rejected applicant sniping at a former employer. There's a whole stratum of visiting instructors and professors like Heath who have to tough it out here; it can be lonelier for them than for the loneliest of students. *Visiting* professor suggests that they have a home someplace else, a job they can go back to. Usually, that's not so. They come here on one- or two-year contracts and—unless they get lucky—they move on. These are the faces you don't recognize when you look back at your college yearbooks, the professors you don't find when you come back for reunions. Not for them the white clapboard houses and social porches of Gambier, the remodeled farmhouses on the outskirts of town. These are the ones who live in nondescript rentals in Mount Vernon, in duplexes and garden apartments, college-owned, in Gambier.

"Now I realize it's not the way a single person ought to be living," Heath says. "On Friday, you'd look up and say, *Gee, it's ten o'clock.* Or on Sunday, you'd ask, *What did I do this weekend?* It's pathetic, or—let's dignify it—it's existential loneliness. But I made my peace with the place. I thought we got along."

The search committee decided not to formally interview inside candidates, to treat them as "known quantities." That was a reasonable-sounding decision at the time, but now Heath sees it as part of a pattern that denied him a full, fair shot. He suspects that his friendship with the controversial Tom Short may have hurt him, he suspects that a research paper accompanying his application wasn't even read, and he suspects that the teaching he'd been doing was discounted.

"I think I'm a better teacher than a lot of people around here," he says. "I know it sounds arrogant, but I don't care. They should just go and talk to students and see what they say. Student opinions aren't all-important, but they have some role, and we're not just talking about students who want a dog-and-pony show . . ."

He stops a moment, weighing what to say next. A couple months of teaching here remain, but he's already talking about Kenyon in the past tense.

"Maybe I shouldn't have spent so much time teaching, putting comments on papers, going back to my office to meet a student. It doesn't count. What I should have been told was you can't take this teaching business too seriously, you shouldn't assign all these papers and have them rewritten. You should have assigned one long paper at the end of the semester and just graded it, with no comments. That's all they care about, the grades. Instead of that, you should have worked on your dissertation, sent it out for publication . . ."

I'd always thought that inside candidates had an edge over outsiders: contacts, networking, back channels. I still think that's so. But it must not have been easy, I sense, watching from the sidelines while the search committee ushered its top three candidates around campus. An awkward time all around, no doubt. "We lack the pastoral skills," Phil Jordan told me a while back: the thoughtful phone call, the caring question, the timely, stroking conversation.

"I probably wouldn't feel this way if someone had just talked to us," Heath says. "If we'd been treated with some decency. We weren't even introduced to the candidates. Maybe that's what I should do when I leave teaching. I should run an etiquette service."

❧

AT SUNSET COTTAGE the English Department copes with a resignation, coming from the member of the department I knew least well. He'd been up for tenure review earlier in the year. All of us were supposed to arrange to visit his class, then include impressions of his teaching in the letter we're each supposed to send to the provost. Meeting this tenure-track colleague at the department mailbox one morning, I asked, should I just drop in or did he need advance notice? My question angered him. The college was so wrongheaded in insisting people visit classes, he said. Visitors disturbed his class. That went for parents, prospective students, and—he seemed to indicate—it went for me. But it didn't apply to other, more senior members of the department, whose requests for permission to visit were more cordially fielded. We never spoke again. Now, it seems, he's gotten an offer from a big place down south, and what's interesting to see is what the rest of the department goes through when one of its members is about to bolt. It's like the stages people go through when facing terminal illness: denial, anger, rejection, acceptance. People get upset at first, very touchy about this loss to the department. Shouldn't Kenyon make an effort? And if Kenyon tries to retain this fellow—a little more money, a little less teaching—won't that set a precedent? So they watch: will Kenyon bid against another institution? Will the provost exert himself, sweeten the deal, for Pete's sake, *be a mensch*? It gets to be a ritual: how much do you love me? how much did you love me? could you love me more? Then, when the provost sweetens the deal, the fellow leaves anyway and the little drama ends.

A much larger drama follows.

🌿

"GOT A MINUTE?"

The way Ron Sharp tells it, he was sitting in his office at Sunset late one morning, and there stood his former student, Mike Stone, standing in the doorway. Sharp motions him inside.

"I wanted to tell you something," says Stone. "I didn't want you to hear it on the grapevine. I went back to the doctor last week . . ."

He stops a moment, seems to struggle to find his voice. Then he gets it back, and a grin with it.

"It won't be long before I'll be up there hanging out with Keats."

The cancer is back, on both sides of his brain. There's a possibility of more surgery in California, an experimental procedure that offers no real hope. Stone rejects it. This is it, and here is where it ends. And soon. Everything's been arranged. He'll stay here for a few weeks, and then he'll go home to suburban Chicago to die, and when that's done with—before the class I'm teaching has turned in its next set of papers—he'll be buried in the college graveyard in back of Rosse Hall.

After Stone leaves, Sharp—still flabbergasted by Stone's guts and humor—goes downstairs to the English Department office to talk things over with Barb Dupee. They have an idea. They call Phil Jordan. Stone doesn't know it, but he's bringing out the best in the college. Sharp proposes the college give Stone an honorary degree. Phil Jordan readily agrees. Sharp is on his way to tell Stone of the decision. Jordan asks to accompany him. The two men walk to Stone's apartment together.

"Jordan looked nervous," Mike Stone tells me later. "He was shifting his weight from side to side. Then, after he told me, I got a two-minute presidential hug."

I was okay, we were all okay, in the basement of the Church of the Holy Spirit: there's something fundamentally self-deprecatory about putting on caps and gowns. We marched upstairs, down the long aisle, most of the English Department and a handful of others. We filed into a pew and sat down. I looked around for Stone and couldn't see him. He wasn't at the pulpit, wasn't left or right of me. I wondered if he'd make a separate entrance. Then I saw him, right across from me, sitting next to his mother, and I knew that I was absolutely going to lose it, seeing him there, in graduation robe, one eye blind, the other sewn shut, all small, scarred, and swollen, all his senses—except his sense of humor—headed south, eyes, voice, ears, kaput, but on his face an amused, grateful smile. You'd think his body, slight and hunched, was overloaded with blessings. Everyone who spoke was at his best, Phil Jordan, the college physician Tracy Schermer, Ron Sharp. We were all at our best. And my tears felt non-negotiable. For a minute I tried thinking of other stuff. Taxes. I'll need an Ohio nonresident return. Or maybe I'm a resident. But as soon as I looked at him again, I was crying. Not just me. About half the department. They called him forward, awarded him the degree, the sash, and the scroll, and he stood there, smiling, while we all stood and applauded, a long ovation for a doomed student catching the late afternoon sun, streaming in through stained glass windows.

Local hero.

ON THE ROAD to *Continental Drift* to *Jasmine* and, now, to *Portnoy's Complaint*. The room feels awake and alive, but I've been warned against getting cocky. Lentz told me that what happens is you think you've been having a great conversation. Then, when the first papers come in, it's as though you've been teaching at Berlitz. I might have had a foretaste of this the other day when I threw a pop quiz on *Portnoy's Complaint*, asking how a minor character, Ronald Nimkin, commits suicide. He *hung* himself, more than half the class responded. And, come to think of it, I wish they'd asked me, instead of me asking them, about another reference—who was Eddie Waitkus? and that they had relied on themselves, not me, to translate any of the dozens of italicized Yiddish words Roth sprinkles through the text. These students convey a kind of nonchalance, a lack of urgency, that bothers me. That doesn't mean there's no progress. I'm trying to get them to engage the book that was written, rather than the book they might have written or preferred to read, to meet the authors halfway rather than sitting back and expecting them to cater to readers' predispositions. I'm trying to persuade them that what they *feel* about the book, whether they *like* it or not, is the last question to ask, not the first.

Maybe it's working, but you can't be sure. I might be mistaking relaxation, friendship, proximity, for something else. You get attached to each other, feel closer than you actually are. And then—every now and then—something happens that makes you shudder. During class, I referred to *U.S.A.* and *Lord Jim*, to Dos Passos's mixed bag of novelistic techniques and to the moral crisis—abandonment of a ship—underlying Conrad's novel. I sensed that the message wasn't getting through, and I asked a question that I'm sure annoyed them, the kind of question I ask too often. I asked how many of these twenty-eight students, mostly seniors, mostly English majors, had read these two books. None had read *U.S.A.,* one had read *Lord Jim.*

I've been thinking about this ever since, talking to people, maybe trying to rationalize it, since ragging on students gets to be a tiresome game. One person suggested that Dos Passos had gotten bumped for Zora Neale Hurston, Conrad for Virginia Woolf, and that if *Lord Jim* has slipped away, maybe *Heart of Darkness* sticks around. David Lynn, a Conrad scholar and admirer, made a plausible case that what we're doing here is teaching the enjoyment of literature and the beginnings of critical thought, and it's not what we cover per se, but how we cover it. I nodded but kept on wondering, and asking. I dropped in on another colleague, Bill Klein, and told him what was bothering me. Klein took a while to respond.

"I'm thinking what name to put to what I feel," Klein said. "I can't be upset because I'm not surprised. It reflects conditions that have been around for fifteen years." He suggested that Conrad and Dos Passos weren't the only victims, that Henry James was fading, too. "They haven't heard about him. They're not interested." Ditto Hemingway. After a while I suspect it's not just what we require students to read, it's what they want to read on their own, on summer vacations, say. I went to Lentz. Maybe I shouldn't have. His concerns with curriculum run long and deep, a series of rearguard losing battles that go back for years. He knows of an English major who graduated from Kenyon without having studied Chaucer, Spenser, or Milton. His daughter.

✣

BACK TO THE PHILOSOPHY SEARCH. I find Steven Emmanuel in his office one afternoon, studying a Hebrew text. Learning Hebrew is a project he's undertaken in his spare time here. His story parallels Eugene Heath's. He left Grinnell to take a one-year job at Kenyon, hoping that he'd be taken seriously as a candidate for this year's tenure-track position. All indications were that his chances were good; no promises, of course, but he was told he'd be "an extremely serious candidate." Coming in, he did everything he could to safeguard his chances. He even called the departing candidate, Tom Short, then on a leave of absence, to make sure he wouldn't be returning. When he came, he thought his prospects were good. Things fell apart immediately.

"There was a get-together in September," he recalls, "and I told someone I was here temporarily but hoping to get a tenure-track job. 'I'm sorry,' she said, 'I don't mean to deflate your hopes. I don't think there's any chance you can get this job.'" This ominous, puzzling warning was followed by confusion about whether there was even going to be a job search. After the search started, the job description was written far more broadly than Emmanuel had expected: what had seemed the perfect fit for him—"a bull's eye"—was something almost anyone could apply for. "Things didn't mesh," Emmanuel says, "what was said last year and what was happening now."

The search committee's decision to treat inside candidates as "known quantities" and not formally interview them "marginalized" him, he thinks. When he showed up as fifth on the committee's list of candidates, he felt he'd been treated in bad faith from the beginning, induced to take a short-term job, baited by the prospect of a long-term arrangement for which he was never seriously considered. "Being number five on the list is as good as not being on the list at all. Often enough, you don't get your first candidate. Often you do get your second, if you don't get your third you did something wrong, and if you don't get your fourth you mishandled the search. Number five is as good as no chance. And I felt I was never close. From the time I arrived, I felt something was wrong. In fact, I was never a serious candidate for the job."

He'll be all right, I'm happy to hear: there's a post at the University of Arkansas at Fayetteville. But Kenyon will be a bittersweet memory, and I guess there are a lot of other professors, at this and other colleges, he speaks for.

"They put you in an impossible situation," he says. "Every year they expect you to publish something, but if you move from year to year, state to state, job to job, it's harder to have continuity and get stuff out. It becomes a catch-22. It's odd. In other fields, experience counts, but not in academe. It's something about newness, about potential. You offer coverage, experience, teaching. You're a known quantity, but the department is eager to look at unknown quantities, what the provost calls 'promise.' That's the concept that's become so distressing. People are evaluated according to promise. We ought to be wiser. Promise is infinite. I can't compete with promise. I could have twelve books at the Oxford University Press and be at the top of my field, but I could still not compete with promise. The new guy could win the Nobel Prize . . ."

🌿

OTHER PEOPLE'S CLASSES.

Lentz, launching into Shakespeare's history plays, warns that "the distribution of justice in these plays is completely political." And another thing: "If you're going to deal with ambiguity, you'd better learn to write compound sentences, because the plays refuse to be reduced to simple equations." Across the lawn, Ryn Edwards begins to deal in politics and ambiguity as well. There was plenty of biology, detailed and painstaking, in her early lectures. Some of that remains, but I sense we are getting into touchier stuff. Today she dealt with the relationship between biological characteristics and social. Example: society traditionally keeps women at home, breeding and rearing, while men do the world's work. Those are supposed to be ordained roles, biologically sanctioned. But men's genitalia are exposed—vulnerable—and women's genitalia are concealed. Couldn't this be a biological argument that men should stay at home and women sally forth?

🌿

IF I'D HAD TO CHOOSE one faculty meeting to attend, just one, this month's would be it. This is when we're supposed to debate whether the Kenyon faculty should form a tenure and promotion committee that will review departmental letters and recommendations and, in turn, make its own recommendation to the president and provost, who make the final decision. The administration favors such a committee, as do many younger and/or more liberal faculty members. A faculty has to take a hand in important matters as tenure and promotion, they argue; they can't evade this responsibility. The opponents, many older and more conservative, fear that such a committee would become a politicized, left-leaning "committee of public safety" that would transform the current ideological sitzkrieg into open, bloody war. It may look like a petty spat from the outside, but whoever controls hiring—and, possibly, firing—controls the college. Everything follows from hiring: who teaches, how they teach, what gets taught. The debate about tenure and promotion is a debate about power.

The great debate begins awkwardly.

Political Science's Fred Baumann suggests that, to get things going, someone should make a statement in favor of the tenure-promotion proposal. The faculty chair, Bob Bennett, concurs. Then, there's a funny little silence while they wait for someone to offer such a statement. "I ain't gonna give it," Baumann jokes.

Peter Rutkoff raises his hand. Rutkoff of my History Department mornings, Bullshit 101, of the Martin Luther King march, of the heart attack. A divisive partisan to some, a near-saint to others. He's made a mark here, but in Gambier disappointments linger longer than victories.

"In the too many years I've been here this is the single most important thing we've considered," he begins. "First, we really need to learn how to trust each other. Second, it feels the last five to seven years we have lived in Czechoslovakia in 1969, in a state of partially self-imposed silence, in fear of speaking out, in fear of giving away too much. We have given away our ballgame."

Now Fred Baumann is ready. A stalwart in Political Science, a respected teacher. "My God, Baumann!" one student exclaims. "A teddy bear outside of class. Inside, a thunderbolt, a tornado. Frightening eye contact. The trick is not to look at him. Look at papers, tables, walls, other students."

"This is an idea that keeps coming back," Baumann tells the faculty. "In 1987 it was overwhelmingly defeated, even though most thought it would pass. It was a bad idea, and nothing has changed. It's still a bad idea."

Tenure decisions are overwhelmingly favorable at Kenyon, he notes. There might be a place for a tenure and promotion committee in big universities, but in a small college where everybody knows everybody and nothing is confidential, it would lead to horror stories, to "unshirted hell," for the people serving on the committee and the campus as a whole. It would threaten diversity, minority departments, minority views.

"We're asking for hell here, for a struggle of group against group, department versus department, that is going to be absolutely miserable," Baumann charges. "Ask yourself if you want to be judged by a committee like this, an elected committee. It would take wild horses to attract a fair-minded person to serve on such a committee. I think anybody who runs for that committee ought to be automatically disqualified!"

After Baumann finishes, Rita Kipp raises her hand. Instead of just speaking from her seat, or getting up in front of it, she asks permission to go down to the lectern at the front of the hall, to deliver what's obviously going to be a carefully prepared message on behalf of the tenure and promotion committee.

"There's no denying the costs of implementing this proposal," Kipp concedes. There'll be more work, more time, more difficult decisions, some of them "heart wrenching," she grants. She knows what she's talking about, I guess. As chair of the current Women's and Gender Studies search, she just called the first three candidates—Harry Brod among them—to tell them that they'd been rejected. "I decided I never wanted to be provost," she told me. "I hung up the phone . . . I didn't realize I was upset . . . but I hung up the phone and started crying."

The tenure and promotion committee would induce faculty members to talk, to persuade each other, Kipp says, and this would lead to "professional adulthood." That's one argument. Another is that people would learn to trust each other. Her third argument is practical—and controversial. "This committee would probably mean that there would be some reduction in the number of tenure-track people who receive tenure. Why have virtually 100 percent of tenure-track positions result in tenure? For one thing, we do a good job at the recruiting end of things. BUT NOT THAT GOOD!"

Now it gets interesting. Too many people are sailing through the place, Kipp implies, because one man—the provost—can't buck gemütlich departmental decisions. It's time to get tough, time for pain and gain. So we're talking about self-determination, which is fine, about communication and trust, also fine, and about axing people, which is . . . *wait a minute!* . . . maybe not so fine. I sense a ripple of doubt in the room.

There's scattered applause when Kipp finishes, but then Harry Clor gets up for the rebuttal. When we talked a while ago, Clor cast himself, and his department, Political Science, as lonely defenders against political encroachment. He lamented that so few other faculty had joined with them. "They're too genteel to get involved in curricular fights," he said. "If I am 90 percent on the courage meter at Kenyon, and I think I am, then this place is very cowardly." Now he's involved in a new battle. Or an old battle all over again.

"Judging from some of the arguments in favor of this committee," Clor says, "one would think that we have been living under an undemocratic system, that we've been children, failing to exercise our responsibilities." Clor doesn't buy Kipp's suggestion that setting up a tenure and promotion committee would be a sign of mature responsibility. What's actually going on now, he suggests, is that say-so about personnel decisions resides in departments. Grass-roots democracy! The provost goes along with what departments decide, and that, Clor suggests, is less risky than having a committee around. "Are we to ignore all that we read and see about a politicized faculty?" he asks. "The harsh reality is that, as I said five years ago, this faculty is rather factionalized. A further reality is that some among us are willing to say and write that all education is, and even should be, political and scholarship is governed by political, race, gender, or whatever other factors. . . . Do you want to be judged by faculty members believing that? And do the proponents want to be judged by me?"

After Clor, the debate rocks back and forth a while longer. "If this motion fails," Dean of Academic Affairs Anne Ponder glumly notes, "Kenyon will continue as virtually the only high-quality liberal arts college without such a committee." That prospect doesn't bother John Macionis, who declares the debate "incredibly political" and contends that "this motion is not something in the best interests of all of us."

As the meeting ends, I find it hard to picture an outcome that is not equivocal. There was something backwards and oblique about the whole discussion, an underlying issue that peeked out from time to time but never came into full view. There was a sense that the college has gone soft in its personnel decisions, that too many people are getting tenure. The every-kid-a-winner syndrome doesn't just describe our treatment of students; it describes their teachers also. The values of the community, small and collegial, have overtaken the interests of the college, which are not invariably the same. The primacy of the departments, which began late in Bruce Haywood's term as provost—against his wishes—has continued since then, and now, unless it can invoke poverty—unless it can say it can't afford to do something—the college has lost its ability to say no. Those are what Rita Kipp called the "agonizing decisions." If, whatever else they disputed, they could have agreed on the need to take charge, or the need for charge to be taken, they might have gotten somewhere, but all their other disagreements overwhelmed this one possible consensus. In the end, it sounded like they were talking about buying a knife without deciding what, or who, or how, to cut.

Outside, after the meeting, I hear people bracing themselves for defeat, or victory. "I don't care." "It really doesn't matter." "I don't give a shit." "Nothing will change." Walking home, it feels good to be out-of-doors, away from the arena, out in this odd nonseason that wavers between mild winter and false spring, a time of high rivers and flowers popping out of the ground way too early. Every year, they make the same dumb mistake. A gray, drained landscape and a faculty to match.

Back in the dorm, my faculty-free zone, I think about the meeting. The speeches were intelligent and well organized, if predictable, and the debate was lively, though I doubt anybody's mind was changed. There's no escaping the obvious conclusion that my colleagues are in many ways divided. But the opposite is also true. I sensed it, watching them walk out of the auditorium, across the grass toward offices, parking lots, Village Market. They live in the same small place. They shop in the same stores, send their kids to the same schools, teach the same students, browse in the same bookstore. They cash similar checks at the same bank, are covered by the same health and retirement plan. A few months ago, I compared them to an opera company. Now, a new image occurs to me. Pro wrestling. They file into a locker room in drab street clothes, change together into sneakers, capes, masks, and tights, and out of this undifferentiated mass there comes a Gorgeous George, a Hulk Hogan, a Sergeant Slaughter. Then, for a little while, they enact a nearly ritual combat. They carom off the ropes, bounce off ring posts, pound the canvas, play to the hooting crowd, scream of dirty tricks—a knee to the groin, a gouge to the eye, a pull of hair, a hidden nail, or a piece of sandpaper. They appeal in vain to the referee—the provost, that would be—who always misses the foulest offense. And then, when the show is over, they're back in the locker room, changing into civvies, walking out together, piling into fuel-efficient cars, dropping by the market before it closes at six, and driving home. And so, as February ends, I add another to my list of island rules. Not everyone who wants to come can come, not everyone who wants to stay can stay, not everyone who wants to leave can leave: those were the first three. Their truth is demonstrated daily. The trick is applying the right rule to the right person.

My fourth rule is across-the-board. "The rule of less," I call it. In a small academic environment, every reputation, whether for alleged virtue or vice, is inflated, as is every issue. A small college affirms its place in a larger world by way of local exaggeration. When you're an ark and you've got only two of each kind, you maximize the importance of the pair you've got on board. Mere specimens become exemplars, paragons, avatars. But when you come to know these people, when you talk to them, the enlarged reputations drop away: the brilliant are less brilliant than advertised, the stupid less stupid, the Machiavellian less subtle, the straightforward less ingenuous.

Taken on the whole, this is good news.

❧

"I LOVE THE WAY the semesters die here," my colleague Tim Shutt remarks. It's an odd thing to say in what's still the middle of winter, mild as this winter has been. But already you can sense the end of things. "First there's no more reading," Shutt says. "Then there's no more papers. Then there's no more classes. And then there's no more meetings! April, May, June, and the long slide into summer."

❧

DORMITORY NOTES from the last night before March vacation. "You have a good night, professor," one student says as I turn into my apartment. An oddly gentle greeting: am I showing my age? "What do you know about John Locke?" asks another who comes to my door. "Weren't you and he born about the same time?" A third, cranking out an essay on Joseph Conrad, comes by to ask me about "the significance of moonlight in literature." Another note slipped under the door invites me down the hall, to room 8, where some freshmen want me to autograph copies of my most recent book, *The Edge of Paradise,* which they're giving their parents for Christmas. Granted, these parents may end up paying for their own Christmas presents when they settle their sons' bookstore accounts. Never mind, I'm happy to oblige. There's only one copy left in the bookstore, someone says. I press Alex to buy it. He plays hard to get. Is the book any good? the tactful freshman wonders aloud. After I give him a money-back guarantee, an author's warranty, he heads for the bookstore.

❧ *March*

I'D BEEN WANTING to talk to Tim Shutt for some time. His classes—Renaissance, Chaucer, Dante—are hugely popular. I'd seen him at work, dressed in jeans and a flannel shirt, looking as if he'd just finished checking a line of muskrat traps. He perched on a table, holding an enormous beer stein full of coffee, fielding comments on Chaucer, even dumb, tentative comments, with energy and grace. "He's really something," one student tells me. "One minute he's talking about his favorite color M & Ms, he's talking about his favorite razor blades, and the next thing, you're deconstructing love in Chaucer."

Personable and peculiar, Shutt is just the sort of lively, winning teacher I'd figure would stay forever. The students like him, and he likes them. Though he's Ohio-born, he announces football games like a Monty Python reject: "It appears to be a three-yard gain, or there-abouts." He times swim meets, he judges lip-synch contests. More controversially, he serves as faculty adviser for Delta Kappa Epsilon fraternity, a group many of his colleagues wouldn't give the time of day. "I got tired of them being picked on," he says.

Still, I'd noticed tension, more than the normal academic angst, more even than what you'd expect in a faculty member up for tenure this year. As a Republican, a Catholic, and a conservative, he walks carefully around this sometimes testy college. There was that outburst at the Greek alumni meeting a couple months ago, when he said he felt at risk just being there. There've been moments at department meetings when it seemed he wanted to say more or regretted having said too much. He takes pains, it seems, to avoid arguments, dashing in and out of Sunset Cottage like Reagan jumping into a helicopter bound for Camp David, scrambling to get out of earshot of nosey reporters. I've wondered, then, how Tim Shutt felt about things. Last week, finally, I caught up with him, and something he told me has been nagging at me ever since.

"Kenyon is the best school I know at its chosen role," Shutt said. "If you want people who can think and who can play in at least the triple-A minors intellectually and are interested in you and are not self-serving careerists, you're more likely to find them at Kenyon than at any place I know. That's the distinctive thing about this place. That's what we sell."

Most of the students who come to Kenyon are good, often very good, not great, Shutt reasons, and here they find a school—often very good—that matches them, a college that flushes out strengths and forgives weaknesses, a college that knows what it's doing, a place that knows its place. So far, I follow him. I nod in agreement. Then I hear something startling.

"At Kenyon," Shutt continued, "elitism is moderated by a sense of fundamental second-rateness. Who else do you think's going to come here and pay twenty thousand dollars for something that, in principle, is of no immediate practical use? We know we're not Williams, and that's part of our identity. We're the best imitation of Williams west of the Alleghenies. There's always a market for the second-best Italian restaurant in town."

The second-best Italian restaurant in town . . . It dogs me for days, stays with me as I return home to Chicago for the first two weeks of March, on the misnamed spring vacation. I picture colleges as restaurants. Ohio State—55,000 students—would be a mass feeding operation, golden diploma replacing golden arch and a sign boasting so many million students graduated. Open all night, open all year. Eat in or carry out, it's up to you. And Williams College—the best Italian restaurant, in Shutt's metaphor—would be coat-and-tie required, reservation recommended, and it helps to know the maître d'. It's got carpets, tablecloths, hovering waiters—those would be teachers—and all sorts of daily specials you could die for. The sommelier—provost?—looks like Orson Welles. Then there's Kenyon, the second-best Italian restaurant in town, easy to get into, almost never wait in line for a table, go for a carafe of the house red, and the food's damn good, really, not that they're breaking any new culinary ground out back, but they're serving recognizable grub in family-size portions, and the waiters—some of these guys have been around for ages!—don't glare if you ask for a doggie bag. All of this was on my mind still when Will Scott, a history professor, sat down in my office for a morning meeting of Bullshit 101. Scott seems pretty happy here. He's skeptical of colleagues who chafe at

Kenyon and blame its teaching emphasis for the decline of their scholarly ambitions. "People's creative lives die, and they blame Kenyon," he says. "But careers die because we let them die. The best novels have been written with far less opportunity than we have here."

Granted, Scott has his share of beefs. But he hasn't lost sight of the fact that Kenyon is a good place to be. "My relatives can't believe I make the salary I do," he tells me. I don't know what Scott makes, but some old-timers are up over $60,000, and newcomers with Ph.D.s get $33,000 or so. "They can't believe I have a guaranteed annual raise. They can't believe I can't get fired. They can't believe my medical coverage. They can't believe my kids can go to college for almost nothing. They can't believe I only work eight months a year. They almost want to write their congressman."

If Kenyon's a good place for a professor to be, it's just as good for students, Scott thinks, quirkier and less stressful than higher ranked places. Like Shutt, he mentions Williams, and in no time I'm thinking Italian restaurant again. It's a warm and seductive image: picture not just student or faculty but a whole institution settling for a B/B plus. All at once our strengths are vindicated, our weaknesses excused.

"It's easier to have illusions in Williamstown," Scott suggests. "Being second-rate allows us to relax, relieves us of pretentiousness and self-consciousness. Our kids don't come here as 'the best and the brightest.' There's less strutting around here, more openness to unconventional paths. We don't have fast-track access to Harvard Medical School. We still have freshmen coming here wanting to be poets—how unconventional—not because we have great poets on the faculty—we have none—but because we think that being a poet is an appropriate ambition. That's special. We're rural, isolated, liberal arts, and a fee-paying institution. We have to be elitist, so, if you're going to be elitist, then it's better to be second-rate: we take in more interesting people. Unpredictable. Half the class, when they graduate, have no idea where they're going to be in ten years. Williams has a high rate of predictable success. We have a high rate of *un*predictable success.

"We have to be what we are," Scott continues.

The second-best Italian restaurant in town . . . I'd be happy to leave it at that, I really would, to say that's what we are. There'd still be plenty to celebrate and love and defend. I can't refute what Shutt and Scott have told me. I don't even want to. But there are problems I can't shake. No one advertises being second-best. No one dreams of growing up to become a career minor leaguer. People have ambitions, so do institutions, they have aspirations, or they ought to, laughable and long-shot as their hopes may be. This college—maybe all colleges, but this college more than most—is like a car I once had. The needle in the fuel gauge swung wildly from side to side as I drove on curving roads. Sometimes it showed nearly full, nothing to worry about for miles and miles. A minute later it touched the red zone and we were running on empty, out of gas. Kenyon is like that to me, and I suspect its president agrees.

"Kenyon has been defined by its ambition to enter the ranks of the first-rate schools," he says, "and its inability to get there." So I guess there'll be tension in Gambier for a long time. Something inconsolable. A gap between image and reality, between public face and private self, a gap that leaves us open to hope and vulnerable to doubt, to vast swings of mood and mixtures of emotion that I felt thirty years ago and feel now. If my emotions were not mixed, I sometimes think, they wouldn't have lasted so long.

🌿

A RETURN TO GAMBIER after March vacation. Cold winds, blasted flowers. Mike Stone is having a hard time, I hear. The tumor has gotten into his throat and they performed a tracheotomy. The Kenyon baseball team opened its season with five games in Florida, and they won one, the first. Dan, who lives down the hall, broke up a double play. More news: save your old menus. The second-best Italian restaurant in town just hiked its prices 9 percent.

"I am pleased to send you the Kenyon College Fees and Fact Sheet for 1992–1993," Phil Jordan's letter to Kenyon parents and guardians begins. Next year's tab will be $21,180. Amy, junior class president, isn't pleased. Her dad is an insurance agent, not apt to qualify for scholarship aid but able to feel the pinch of a 9 percent increase.

"I got annoyed," Amy tells me. She's a lively, likable woman, skeptical of officials and official explanations. She put together a letter of protest against the 9 percent raise, claiming that the administration's explanations were insufficient. The actual rise in scholarship aid generated by the price hike would be insignificant, she contended, and the higher cost would make the college less appealing to the diverse student body it wants to attract. What's more—here's the part I liked—she questioned whether Kenyon needed to raise faculty salaries. "Why are we competing, via wages, with schools on the east coast?" the letter asked. "Also, in a recession, it seems unnecessary to raise wages in order to attract and maintain high quality professors, as any job should be highly valued at this time. In addition, given Kenyon's unique atmosphere, any professor who is attracted to this college merely because of the salary would not tend to stay for any significant duration."

Camping out in front of Peirce and Gund Commons, Amy and friends amassed 560 signatures in three hours. She's met with the college's business vice president, Joe Nelson, and with Phil Jordan—"he dodged almost every question I asked him," she contends. She attended a trustees' luncheon: some trustees attempted to defend the raise, while others, she says, gave her the oh-you-cute-little-student pat on the head and sent her on her way. The board chairman, Burnell Roberts, wrote a polite letter of explanation. That'll be the end of Amy's campaign for now. She's a realist. Not all the students who signed the petition even bothered to read it, she concedes, and only 20 of the 560 bothered coming to a follow-up meeting that was called.

It's a year of petitions, that's for sure. We had English majors petitioning for a more closely knit and communicative department. Not much has come of that, so far. We formed a committee. We have Amy battling against higher fees. And, just a few weeks ago, a senior named Charles presented a petition that opposed the administration's plan to reduce faculty teaching loads. For years, Kenyon faculty taught three classes per semester, year in year out, with a sabbatical for tenured professors every seventh year. The current policy is to move to a 3–3, 3–2 scheme that would give professors one course less to worry about for one semester, every other year. It's a small reduction, implemented by some departments already, exceeded by others, but students are sensitive to any withdrawal of services.

"I'd heard a lot of people complaining," Charles told me. A lanky West Virginian who's a religion major, he dropped by the other night, accompanied by his roommate, John. "I'd heard a lot of people complaining they were screwed over on class sizes."

Granted, many Kenyon classes are small. Some, though, have gotten huge. Combine that with all the lobbying and pleading that surrounds registration, the difficulty of getting into popular classes, the fact that students who come to Kenyon wishing to take writing courses can get shut out, year after year, and you can understand why students get testy when they hear about reduced teaching loads.

"Some professors here at Kenyon put teaching first," Charles says. "They are the ones I respect greatly. Others see teaching and everything associated with it as something they don't mind doing, but it's more like ditch-digging labor. Kenyon's trying to be like Swarthmore or Williams. I don't think we need to worry about that. We need to do what we've been doing well for a long time."

"I was one of the ones complaining," John volunteers. He's the guy from my writing class who wrote the intriguing story about a marriage falling apart in Malawi, a betrayed woman transfused with AIDS-infected blood, beckoning her husband to reconcile and make love. Now he's writing his senior comps essay—the paper senior English majors write if they decide not to take a final exam—under my supervision, on Updike's *Rabbit* novels. "The teachers who are the good teachers, who like to do it, they're the ones who have to deal with classes of forty and fifty, and that's ridiculous. Seventy persons in a class is stunning. And, meanwhile, seminars get cancelled. A lot of people know you can't be a non-English major and take an upper-level English class. That just doesn't happen. And, for twenty-one k a year, that's ridiculous."

"Let's just look at this place and make sure we're not turning into something we don't want to be," Charles says. He presents his petition—two hundred students signed it—to the campus senate. The administration turns out in force to meet him: President Jordan, Provost Browning, Registrar Switzer. It's as though Charles were striking matches in a dry field and, suddenly, three fire trucks come racing to the scene, sirens on, hoses out. Phil Jordan heads the defense, pointing out that the college's current enrollment of 1,486 is down, by almost one hundred students, from its peak of four years ago. The student-teacher ratio is 11 to 1. "Pretty good numbers," Jordan says. "There's no ghastly decline." And, if it's true that some courses are large, it's also true that others are small. "Does anybody ever complain about a course being too *small?*" Jordan asks.

Provost Browning argues that research invigorates teaching, that Kenyon competes with other colleges for "people who are interested in greatness." This means, he says, that in "purchasing talent," Kenyon competes with the very best places, from Maine to California. Registrar Switzer allows that, balancing large classes against small, nothing much has changed.

It's an inconclusive meeting. Student petitions don't get very far. Anger fades, people lose energy and interest, get tied up in courses, comps, finals. They graduate and move on. What's left behind is hard to measure. One day's weather doesn't change a climate, but you sense something happening nonetheless: a heightened consumerism among students, a skeptical concern, a worry that they get what they pay for and now they're paying more.

A WINTER DAY, a winter night. I awaken automatically at quarter of seven, get up and turn off the fan that's been running all night, as usual, to screen out the noise. No need for it now: the freshmen sleep late, and when they get up, they get up sluggish, groggy, monosyllabic. I go back to bed and stay there for a while. Mornings are when I miss my dog the most, Max stirring and stretching, pushing me to get the day started. Now I linger in bed, thinking of him. I keep waiting for my grieving to end, the way it's supposed to end, so I can romp in the land of happy memories that I've heard about. But when I picture him I still see him on Dr. Purdy's table. I can't get past that. People call my attention to every canine pregnancy in the village, but I don't want another dog. I want Max back.

I walk down the hall, greet the maids, who are smoking cigarettes and having coffee, and head into the village toward the bookstore. It's just a couple hundred yards, but enough for me to check the sunrise, sniff the air, greet the morning dog walkers, the president and the provost among them. Why is it that academics' dogs are so untrained, untamed, so nearly feral, so long on appetite and low on affect? Permissiveness at home? Secret wild streaks in their owners?

The bookstore opens at precisely 7:30. This I know. A few times, when it was raining, I tried to get someone to slip a *New York Times* out the door a couple minutes early. This led to a complaint that made its way up the great chain of being all the way to the provost, who called me aside one morning and conveyed that I was terrifying the people at the bookstore. It's easy, too easy, to get a reputation around here. I've never felt so *watched* as in Gambier. So I wait these days, till 7:30, for my newspaper.

Peirce Hall, the college commons, is gloriously empty when I enter. I'm almost always the first customer for breakfast. Only a handful of students show up before I'm done. I like kidding with the kitchen crew—Rose, Betty Lou, Mary Jo, Delbert. Then I settle in with the weekly summary of student comments on food. The comments are written on cards, posted on a bulletin board, then xeroxed and distributed. It's the liveliest publication in town.

"Thank you for the brussels sprouts. I, for one, like them."

"Stop the killing. No more flesh meals."

"How can I tell the Bleu Cheese from the Ranch dressing without tasting it? People give me a dirty look when I dip my finger in the dressing containers."

"Great clam sauce Saturday night."

Okay. I plead guilty in advance. We all have bad days and this next one was from one of mine:

"It is 8 A.M. Tuesday morning. Do you know where your breakfast potatoes are? Swimming in an inch-deep artery clogging pool of grease. I've pointed this out to several of your staffers and they agree: it's disgusting. Go back to the drawing board on potatoes."

After breakfast, I head over to the History Department and, weather permitting, pull a chair out onto the front steps and smoke a cigar while finishing the paper. There's no smoking in college classrooms or offices these days: the pipe-smoking professors you remember are displaced persons now, furtive sneaks. Sitting outside, I watch the college awaken. Ted Mason drives by in a red pickup truck, dropping his kids at school down the street. Patti Rossman walks to the Admissions Department, Doug Campbell marches uphill to the Alumni Office. I toss my cigar down onto the grass, which is starting to resemble a Central Park dog run, carpeted in cigar turds, and step inside to check in with Scott and Rutkoff. We ought to be hearing how the vote went on the faculty tenure and promotion committee. Rutkoff sounds as though he's already resigned himself to defeat. "I think, as a collectivity, we've proven ourselves so notoriously chickenshit," he says, "that it won't make much difference."

Around ten o'clock I head for the English Department and my third cup of coffee. The mail arrives around then, and I usually volunteer to sort it, mainly so I can see who Ron Sharp is in correspondence with and accuse him of trawling for a position in the big time. Then I walk with Lentz to English 1–2, where he's teaching *The Tempest*.

"What kind of an island would you say Shakespeare's created?" he prods the class. "A fair place? A good place? A very good place? A great place?"

After priming the pump, he launches into a solo flight on slavery and freedom, varieties of both, and strikes up a paean to life. "What is life itself except a kind of miraculous island we find ourselves on? The earth is an island, this little island that gives us everything we need. We go to sleep at night and awake each morning refreshed, and who's capable of appreciating this? Only those who are truly free."

When Lentz is done, I head across Middle Path to the Biology auditorium, where Ryn Edwards glances at a clock that's five minutes slow, spreads out her notes, takes a deep breath. "Okay," she begins. The class looks up, puts away some just-arrived J. Crew catalogs, and pays heed. "Okay. The amazing story of how a foreign cell gets into a woman's body and fuses and forms a fetus. We're going to do it in the next hour."

The race against time begins. Three hundred million sperm in an ejaculation. Several hundred of those moving in the right direction through the endocervical canal. Two hundred sperm reaching an egg. One sperm fusing with the egg membrane and—why ask why?—I'm suddenly reminded that I'm due at an Admissions Department meeting this afternoon.

I skip lunch—the first meal of the day for most students—and retire to the dormitory for a half-hour nap. I begin the second half of the day at the bookstore. Like everyone else in Gambier, I'm in the bookstore two or three times a day. It's student union, salon, general store, gossip central. Except for a depressing remainder table, the books are full price. So is everything else: I could buy a tuxedo with the money they charge for a hooded Kenyon College sweatshirt. But the coffee's pretty good, the chairs are comfortable, you can read magazines for nothing, and, if you wait long enough, everyone on campus shows up. On slow afternoons, I rummage through a catchall folder that holds the papers that people have left behind in the xerox machine. I've found class quizzes: "Discuss how socialism and feminism can be taken too far, destroying good things in the name of individual freedom and equality." I've found a love letter: "I feel like shit because I missed your call on Friday." Why make a copy? I've found rough draft poems:

She sleeps above me
beside the teddy bears
on their backs
without their pants

And I've found a fraternity's scrawled instruction about a pledge's induction: "Then there will be bananas in the first floor bathroom and shaving cream him up. He will then have to proceed to the third floor bathroom where he will chug an egg yolk and drink or wear a beer."

Next, the admissions meeting. John Anderson has been remarkably open about letting me into his operation. I sat through the first early decisions meeting. I've dropped in on regular admissions meetings from time to time. A couple weeks ago, I sat in on an odd, schizophrenic session, half of it dealing with rich, troubled, shaky kids who have connections to the college, the other half with black and Hispanic applicants, kids with heart-wrenching stories, strong aspiration, sometimes appalling test scores.

That was a tough meeting, but today's session is worse. "The second thoughts meeting," Anderson calls it. He begins by reviewing the numbers: Kenyon seeks an entering class of around 420. Of 2,130 applicants, Kenyon has so far admitted 1,389, and of those more than half have indicated they'll be applying for scholarship aid. Subtract the ones who are just trying to get lucky and you have an estimated 450 "hardcore" aid applicants. And that, says Anderson, is a disaster. It's time, he says, for some "gut wrenchers." The point of today's session is to take a hard look at the "C" list of scholarship applicants. They've already been preliminarily admitted, though they don't know it. Now, given the limited amount of scholarship money, their tentative admissions must be reconsidered. Partly, this is for the applicants' own good: admitting someone who requires aid that isn't available is needless cruelty. Cruel to the student and cruel to the college's yield figures: when those students go elsewhere, they're added to the list of students who turn the college down for other reasons. "This is tough," warns Anderson. "It is not fun. But it is irresponsible to blithely admit students without regard to the impact of the decision."

I can feel the mood around the table darkening. Some of the other meetings have been fun—hectic, thoughtful, hardworking, but fun. Not this. This puts the admissions people up against the wall. These are people who've visited high schools, solicited applications, talked to parents. Now they're looking over a bunch of kids who've basically been admitted, and they've got to select some of them out, the ones least likely to receive the money they need. It's euthanasia time in Ransom Hall. "There are wonderful kids who aren't going to come to Kenyon," Anderson says. "And, yes, I'm worried about our yield. It's what killed us last year. We send out 1,400 admits and that makes us look bad."

Everyone grants the need for this conversation, but the consent is grudging. Opening wide to swallow suspect applicants is one thing.

Spitting out good ones is another. "If we have a hard job to do, I can do it," one admissions officer protests, "but we haven't let kids just slip in." "I just want us to realize the implications," counters Anderson. "I've got some ethical worries," a third voice offers. One counselor says they might as well get on with it: "I would prefer, if you axe them, you axe them with us." But another disagrees: "If they're going to be destroyed, why watch it happen?" "Six weeks on the road, talking about what this college is, and encouraging applications," someone says with a sigh. But Anderson persists. "We don't like calls coming in, asking why we accepted them and then they didn't get any money."

So they start in on the C list. The first student has slight need. A keeper. The next student, needing $19,000, goes from admitted to wait-list. "I don't want him to read a letter and say, 'Wow, I got admitted to Kenyon,' and then read that we're not going to give him any aid." They keep the third and fourth, move the fifth and sixth, keep the seventh, wait-list the eighth and ninth. A special plea saves the tenth. "He's one of my most favorite kids in this pool," Patti Rossman says, "and one of my favorites in that school, and I just got off the phone with his father. He's a wonderful kid. Of all of mine, he's the one I want the most."

While they've been cutting down the C list, odd things have been going on outside, a freezing rain, turning to ice. No running today. When it's over—the C list cut in half, twenty-seven to fourteen—there's ice all over. I spot John Macionis driving by. He stops, rolls down his window. "We won," he says, beaming. The tenure and promotion committee failed. More than half the faculty voted for it, but less than the required two-thirds. I stop by Peirce Hall on my way home, find Harry Clor looking over some of the 250 applications for permanent directorship of IPHS. One of them belongs to Harry Brod, his third—and last—chance for a permanent berth at Kenyon. I spot Brod at the bookstore, browsing around the magazine rack, looking like a man who's seeing the worst possible scenario play out and who can't quite believe it's happening to him.

I have supper by myself in Lewis Hall: beans, greens, smoked ham hock, cheap wine. Sometimes I go out in Gambier, but how much pizza can you eat? Pizza and short stories are two things Gambier has wrecked my taste for. I make coffee, eat a Fig Newton, settle in with part of the pile of papers that comes at us this time of year: contenders for the Muriel Bradbrook Fiction Writing Prize, which Patsy Vigderman, another professor, and I have been asked to judge. She warned me only one was prize-worthy, but she didn't say which one. I read a movie-influenced mafia story. I turn to an allegory involving a guy who gets hit by a truck while ogling a woman in a black dress. She revives him, somehow, and takes him to a bar where everyone—customers and bartender—addresses her as "Death." It goes on from there. Another allegory involving a character known as "The Master" and another known as "The Traveler." Then, there's a *Thelma and Louise*-ish female revenge fantasy. Two accounts of molestation. One of them—restrained, oddly funny and winning—is my favorite. I recognize the style: one of last semester's writing students. This pleases me. Last are several tales of international romance, clearly derived from junior years in Europe and thus another on the list of arguments against this distracting, revenue-diverting, curriculum-busting fad.

The phone rings several times while I'm reading. I'm mentoring four comps essays, all of which are due tomorrow. Every one of my students contacts me tonight, seeking a last-minute consultation, a little assurance, an implicit sharing of credit, or blame. They'll be up all night, I guess. Not me. I turn off the lights, put on a cassette—Roy Orbison tonight—sit in a chair, and look out across the grass toward Norton Hall, the same lawn I walked across when I was eighteen. Odd, how music follows you around. I listened to Orbison when I was a student here, staying up late working on the college newspaper. We'd drop the *Collegian* off at the printer's in Mount Vernon and go out for beer, and "Only the Lonely" and "Crying" were on the jukebox. We sang along. Now I'm back here. Orbison is dead a couple years already. Still, he reaches me and that connection—just that—is what I used to hope for my own work, not that it would last forever but maybe outlive me by a couple years. That's all. It's not the Hall of Fame I'm wanting. I'd just like to be an "Oldie but Goodie!"—to have just a bit of an echo, an extra skip of a stone across a pond, before it sinks.

These are the thoughts that come to me here, where the lawn, the trees, the path, the hill seem to go on forever. You recognize them in pictures that are more than a century old, college pictures with students in the foreground, every one of them dead now, but there's that line of trees, that graveled path, that curve of hills, outlasting every class of freshmen, outlasting the nineteenth-century fraternity boys, the 1930s polo players, the 1940s poets, and well on their way to outlasting a middle-aged member of the class of '64, fifty years old now, not in bad shape, but his teeth are mostly crowns, his hair's turning gray, he's pissing a lot more at night, and he's about 30 percent as famous as he wanted to be when he was a student, walking out there on that grass, thirty years ago. And Roy Orbison reproaches him. "Only the Lonely."

I go to sleep. But not for long. That icy rain that came down all afternoon, that rare combination of rain and temperature and wind, results in something that doesn't happen every winter, a full-force ice storm. At 1:15 A.M., the lights all over campus suddenly go dim. Computers with students who are just hitting their stride on essays due tomorrow winkle into obscurity. All of a sudden comes the most amazing sound. I swear you can hear it from every building on campus, a collective scream of rage and joy that I remember from the old prison movies, when there's a jailbreak, a cry of freedom, a call of the wild, hoots and howls and the sound of stampeding students, up and down the hall. Instant Walpurgisnacht. We gather at windows and look out at a sky filled with bolts of lightning, with blasts of orange, pink, and yellow, the death throes of a transformer, flowering gorgeously in freezing rain. *This* is a gift from above! As of 1:20 A.M., it is impossible to study at Kenyon College. Got that, dude? Even if you wanted to, you couldn't. The place is dark. The computers are out. No studying. No sleeping either. Packs of students forage up and down the hall, in search of food and drink. One brave pack heads for the college cemetery, whether to drink or desecrate, it's not clear.

In the morning, we awaken to a college transformed, heart-stoppingly beautiful, all silver, every branch, stem, and petal, a college gilded and merciful; comps deadlines are extended by a day. Any way you look at it—the wonderland outside or the day's extension—it's an act of God, the sort of beneficence I'd expect Lentz to do a riff on in English 1–2, though it might be a stretch, working an ice storm into a discussion of *The Tempest*. I love this place this morning. I inhale it. I walk in wonder.

Life is good.

🌿

"WE OVERPAY all the time around here," a student tells me. "So I steal. I know it takes away from the scholarship fund, but I don't care. I get nothing from the scholarship fund, and anyone who pays full fare is not going to be impressed by talk of scholarships. So I'll eat a candy bar in the backroom of the bookstore, and I'll heat up a bagel I don't pay for. I might as well, if they're going to overcharge for everything else."

The college generates scholarship money from the profits of the bookstore. But one of the things I've discovered this year is that scholarships aren't sacred. Partly this is because the college's tuition dependency is no secret. This year's full-pay students realize that they are paying for this year's scholarship winners. But something else has happened, too: a change in the way scholarships are awarded and administered.

Once, scholarships went to smart kids from poor backgrounds. That's the kind of scholarship that got me to Kenyon instead of Rutgers. Being a scholarship kid carried some risk of alienation, from either the world you were entering or the one you left behind, but—whatever the personal angst—scholarships had a crucial connection to the quality and integrity of the college. They still do: if a liberal arts college is ever going to shake off the aura of a country club, scholarships are vital. But it's not that simple.

About twenty years ago, Kenyon shifted to need-based scholarships, giving aid to students who qualified for admission, period. The change made sense: it had to do with diversity, with opening up the college. This didn't mean that Kenyon could take any otherwise acceptable applicant who was poor. The college had less scholarship money than its competitors. It had to pick its shots. It sorted its need-based applicants into A, B, and C lists. And then—as I saw in that depressing admissions meeting—it had to cull the C list, deleting the less attractive applicants. Still, they were need-based scholarships. They went to students who were able, not necessarily extraordinary. "Not prizewinners," an admissions counselor says, "but people we'd like to have on campus."

The need-based system didn't last, though. Some colleges started giving out merit scholarships, buying talent in the same way that deep-pocketed baseball owners try to purchase a World Series on the free-agent market. "The other schools started a bidding war," Dean of Students Craig Bradley says. "Denison is a classic case. They offered a free ride to high school valedictorians in the state of Ohio. Kids who historically went to Kenyon went to Denison. That dragged us into the war—reluctantly. We were losing some really talented kids."

While retaining need-based scholarships, Kenyon began offering a handful of merit scholarships to the best and brightest. These were *need-blind* scholarships. These scholarships were costly—especially when you realized half the recipients could afford to pay their own way—but the college had no choice. It regretted being pulled into a bidding war, and it also regretted that, compared to other places, it could bid so little. "Merit scholarships are where we take a hosing," Craig Daugherty, the scholarship director, tells me. "Other colleges have more merit money."

The old linkage between bright students and poor backgrounds had snapped. Most scholarships were need-based; others were need-blind.

But more changes were coming. A couple years ago, the merit scholarship recipients complained about being required to maintain a 3.5 grade point average. "Students said, 'We feel a lot of pressure,'" John Anderson recalls. "They said, 'We're tempted to choose courses so as not to risk our scholarships.'" The college checked around, says Anderson, and found out that, yes, its requirements were "by far the highest." Result: Kenyon lowered its standards for merit scholars from 3.5 to 3.0.

Now another reduction is coming. This time, complaints arose from students with need-based scholarships, who'd been asked to keep a 2.67 GPA, significantly higher than the 2.0 (C) it takes to stay in school and graduate. Why, they wondered, should they be held to a higher standard than the full-pay, i.e., richer, students? That's not fair, they charged, and their charge picked up added force when it was realized that almost all of Kenyon's hard-sought minority students received need-based scholarships. Surely it was not Kenyon's intention to discriminate against the poor, the black, the Hispanic, by holding them to a higher standard than everyone else? No, no, the college responded, no double standard here. So the required GPA drops from 2.67 down to the ubiquitous 2.0. "The college," says one official, "has to stay competitive."

A funny competition, no, that goes lower rather than higher? Mulling it over, I find myself in the position of a driver who has followed directions to the letter, making all the designated turns en route to a worthy destination, only to arrive in an unmarked cul-de-sac, littered with beer cans, junked vehicles, and burned mattresses. I can understand every left and right that was made, admire and defend need-based scholarships, the imperative for merit scholarships, the lowering of standards for those with merit scholarships, the next lowering for need-based students. But I can also understand why full-pay students with parents scraping to make escalating payments regard scholarships skeptically, and why they have doubts about a system that gives need-based scholarships to students who aren't especially scholarly and merit-based scholarships to students who aren't necessarily poor. And I guess I can understand why a student goes into the bookstore and eats a bagel for nothing.

❧

THURSDAY NIGHT, a column of women—and some men—marched through the campus to protest sexual harassment. "Take Back the Night" was the slogan of the evening. They proceeded through college dormitories—Lewis Hall included—and marched through the village, through fraternity divisions at the south end of campus, chanting slogans, sometimes ripping *Playboy*-type posters off of dormitory doors. Whenever they passed a spot where an incident had occurred—a gesture, a remark, whatever—they chalked body outlines on the ground: one of them right outside the English Department. The march ended outside of Old Kenyon. On a vile, wet night, speaker after speaker rose to give accounts of bad things that had happened to them. It must have been a powerful occasion; even its organizers seem to be surprised by its success.

"It was very scary," says one woman who'd initially been skeptical. "A woman I know from class, intelligent, mature, assertive, forthright, came forward and said she'd been raped at five in the morning. She cut her hair because a guy climaxed in it, trying to get her to go down on him. Later she got called a dyke, a lesbian, a pro-activist. When she finished talking there was a stunned silence." Says another woman: "You looked around the crowd and everyone was crying."

I missed the march: flu's been keeping me home. But the following night I was invited to speak at a senior class beer party in the basement of Peirce Hall. What I said was harmless enough—my usual blend of affection and criticism—but I noticed extraordinary tension in the room. So did my wife, here on her fourth visit of the year. Women kept coming up to her to tell her how upset they were, how badly treated they felt, women who were down on men or down on Kenyon. After we left, I hear, there was shouting and shoving, accusations of date rape.

Saturday night was worse. To get away from the dorm, Pamela and I stayed off campus, at a friend's house on the Kokosing River, near little Millwood. In my valise, I had an invitation to a party we decided not to attend: these student parties don't get going till past ten o'clock. The Delta Kappa Epsilon—Deke—fraternity was giving its annual caveman party. The invitation showed a grinning, club-wielding ape man hovering over a prostrate, curvaceous woman. That was the party theme. Buy a plastic club and a carpet remnant, to use as a loincloth, one of the Dekes advised me.

The party started slowly, I hear, guys in carpets with clubs, AC/DC and Guns and Roses playing, beer drinking, and a sense that maybe people were staying away this year. A little before ten, the protesters showed up outside. Mostly women but some guys, my friend Charles among them. "There was a great deal of anger about that invitation," he says. "It was meant as a joke, but it got taken seriously. There was a lot of tension."

The protesters marched up to the steps leading into the caveman party, carrying signs that read, "You're Smarter Than This," and, "Sexism Sucks." The Deke president came out, talked to the marchers, apologized for sending out such an invitation at such a time. The marchers weren't mollified: that kind of invitation would be bad at any time, they insisted. Other party-goers came out, too. "Drunks talking to sober people," one guy says.

Arriving late, a student of mine named John found forty or fifty people outside the Deke division in Old Kenyon. "Some Deke came out and shouted, 'You guys, you liberals, you don't know me, I'm not sexist,'" he says. John attempted to talk to him, to calm him down, but his peacemaking got mixed reviews from the marchers. "Some thought it was good I talked to him. They encouraged me to do it. Others thought it was male bonding. I was usurping their role."

Inside Old Kenyon—starting to feel like a Bastille—one party-goer slipped off his trousers and mooned the crowd. "Free Mike Tyson!" shouted another.

Now the *Kenyon Collegian* is full of letters from both sides, protesters pressing their points, fraternity guys feeling harassed and violated themselves. And, every day, the tables in Peirce Hall are covered with xeroxed, numbered, anonymous testimonies of sexist victimization: child molestation, harassment, date rape. There's some consolation, I guess, in seeing that most of the offenses occurred away from Kenyon, on summer vacations, or back during high school—even grammar school—years. Still, there's a lot of anger here right now, and a lot of people who think of themselves as victims.

"Alcohol has a lot to do with the incidents that have happened here," Dean of Students Bradley says. Like me, he's noticed that most testimonies of abuse derived from experience elsewhere. And he's detected a fairly standard pattern in Kenyon incidents: *I got drunk at a party, and this guy I know in class said he'd take me home, and the next thing . . .* "If we were totally dry," says Bradley, "there'd be a lot less of this going on. But would we still be in business? I'm not sure."

It's not just drinking, though. That's only a catalyst. The deeper problem—Bradley doesn't put it this bluntly—is that, although 70 percent of students who show up here are sexually active, though the college health center has a candy bowl full of free condoms, though the days when women had to be out of men's rooms by midnight are history, men and women have a hard time talking to each other: they screw more readily than they talk.

"I don't think men and women have learned to communicate about sex," says Bradley. "Including when they're in bed. How far to go? What are the limitations? You couple that with being drunk and you've got a big problem. The students know about racism, and they talk about sexism, and—though they're still sorting things out—they're aware of homophobia. Those things are fine. But that still doesn't help them. They still haven't learned to communicate about sex."

Women have been here at Kenyon for twenty years, and, by most measures, they do better than men. Check out the Phi Beta Kappa membership, the students sitting onstage at Honors Day, the people running student government: women are doing fine. But when it gets dark, when weekends roll around, it's another story. Lots of stories. Some women love parties, fraternity parties, even Deke parties. Especially Deke parties. But others, often seniors, have had it up to here with a small rural college that still relies on men's clubs to furnish its social life.

"I've never been assaulted on this campus, raped on this campus, sexually harassed on this campus," says one woman I know. "I stay away from parties where it might happen. But I remember this one party . . . a dress-up party. 'Come have a nice time,' the invitation said. But I got there and it was a circus. People were throwing up on the floor, tripping over each other in tuxedos. Velvet gowns were doused in beer, and women were hanging on guys saying, 'Isn't this great?!'"

For every woman who walks around angry, there's another who's mostly happy, I suspect. And another—or maybe a couple more—who are bored. "You can hear anger from the radical feminists," says a female junior. "But the rest of us are just bored and semi-pissed off. Kenyon men are jerks. The maturity level isn't there. In high school, guys are immature. You say, 'In college they'll catch up.' But it doesn't happen. They drink beer, they drive Isuzu Troopers, they play rugby. You can party with them, but you can't have a serious relationship."

※

STEPPING INTO THE HISTORY DEPARTMENT this morning, I spotted a long list of names posted on the front door: the results of the History Department's comprehensive exams. Thirty-three people chose to write essays, and—I couldn't wait to find Rutkoff and kid him—every one of the thirty-three had passed, eleven of them obtaining distinction in the process. Every kid a winner! I chortled. Or—how did Phil Jordan put it in his convocation address last fall?—"very little risk of disappointment."

My glee is premature, on several counts. Faculty members are deeply divided about these outside-of-class senior-year papers that students may choose to write instead of facing final departmental exams. Some people feel that the comps essay is a crucial, independent intellectual enterprise that's the capstone of the student's experience here. Others maintain that the comps essay is a pain in the ass that distracts second-semester seniors—who are easily enough distracted—from their remaining course work.

"I'll do anything to subvert comps," one history professor tells me. "I'll always vote against them." There's no sign of regulation or standardization: department requirements vary wildly. If this were show-and-tell, you'd say some departments want students to produce eggs, while others will settle for them bringing in a bird's nest. History permits students to submit three previously written essays—one of them rewritten—and a fourth essay on the practice of history. So when I kid Rutkoff about a 100 percent success rate that would be the envy of your average driver education school, he gives me a look that makes me feel I've been living in a cave. "You're faulting us for not playing by the rules of a game that we're not playing," he admonishes.

The English Department still requires a major essay. Each essay is read by two professors. If one professor fails the essay and another passes it, the essay passes. If both fail the essay, it goes to the department chair for a third opinion. "The idea," a colleague instructs me before I sit down to read my share, "is everybody passes."

Then, this afternoon, we have a department meeting to discuss performances of students who, instead of writing essays, elected to take departmental exams. Bill Klein heads the committee that went through the blue examination books. Now he goes down the list of student names, and the results are pretty much the same. Every kid a winner, lots of distinctions awarded. Sometimes, when we know that someone suspect is getting through, Klein grins impishly and just whispers the name while others wince and groan. "Thank you, Jesus," someone says after hearing one student pass. "Good," says another after a student gets distinction. "At least you won't have to deal with her father on the phone!"

❧

THE STUDENTS in "American Literature since 1945" can read. I know that. And—thanks to my increasingly unpopular pop quizzes—they are reading: Kerouac, Banks, Mukherjee, Roth, and Bradley, so far.

I work hard on my lectures and in class, and I know they listen: no one falls asleep. Whatever they think of me, and of the stuff I make them read, some sort of connection is happening. They don't talk as much as I'd like in class, and they almost never drop by my office unless they're asked to, but meetings in bar and bookstore encourage me to hope that things are going well.

Then come their first papers—four-pagers, their choice of subject, anything that caught their interest in the first five books we've covered. Don't give me back my lectures and your notes, I had begged them: this isn't stenography. Better to argue with me, take issue, find an angle, a disjuncture, a loophole. Show me up, prove me wrong: this isn't true-and-false. I care about how you write as much as about what you say. I want clean copy, well-organized arguments. So give yourself time to do a first draft, to let it sit, to return and revise. And—please—don't turn me into a copy editor. Proofread your stuff. If you make annoying, trivial little errors how can anybody trust you not to make large ones? Remember: neatness counts.

The papers are bad. The deadline was too close to the deadline for comps essays, someone tells me. It was an inconvenient time for them. Going through these papers is agony. It's like taking out my eyeballs and rolling them in a plate of breadcrumbs. I have a hard time connecting this seemingly sophisticated, bright-looking, attentive class of English majors with the pile of slapdash, half-assed, dead-on-arrival prose in front of me.

The first paper ducks right into the passive voice, into detached, disembodied, pseudo-scientific jargon. "This," I later tell the class, "is the language of urinalysis." Example: "In each of the two books the reader is introduced to a non-married couple faced with the task of overcoming their contrasting personal and cultural experience to create an emotional bond." "The reader is faced with . . ." "It may seem natural for one to associate with their heritage." The second paper, though it's lively, gives me misspellings like *frusteration, visciously, consiously;* like many other students, the writer doesn't seem sure about when to put an apostrophe between the second and third letter of *its*. The third paper—on *Continental Drift*—is all jargon, referring to "an entrapped state in which the socio economic forces have stagnated and continue to stagnate Bob's life." Paper five: *premiss.* (I sense a thesis on the impact of spell-checkers on American thought.) Paper six: "To assume that Bradley wrote *The Chaneysville Incident* to provoke the collective guilty conscious of white Americans is unlikely." Paper seven:

another English major wrestling with the word *its,* while number eight gives me the word *acedemic.* Papers eleven and twelve are passive and flat, while paper thirteen says that Bharati Mukherjee gives the reader "a picture of America through the impersonal and removed eyes of Jasmine." Paper fourteen: "Having been ten years in the making, we can be assured that Bradley has presented us with what he considers to be a finished product." Paper seventeen: "*On The Road* was a fascinating novel. Kerouac was able to reach me." It goes on that way, paper after paper, and it's not as though stylistic awkwardness and grammatical errors were mere blemishes on otherwise good jobs. These are cranked-out, warmed-up notes coming back at me, lectures half-digested and vomited back out. How could I have been so foolish! I thought that the students' goals in writing were the same as mine when I get down to work. I was taught to be concise. That was the lesson of Kenyon, the lesson of every newspaper and magazine I worked on. Write tight, save space, save paper. Students write to kill time, fill space, waste paper. And I thought we were on the same team! Paper twenty-two: "In this paper, however I shall study the gender roles of this society, 'the beat generation,' and conclude with the verdict: is Kerouac's *On The Road* a great American novel!?" Paper 27: *surviver, lessoned, Haitan.*

I'm disappointed. I'd hoped for more. I flash back to a dinner with one of the Philosophy candidates, a stiff, awkward repast in a windowless locker in the basement of Gund Commons. "How does it feel," the candidate asked during a lull in conversation, "to be a member of the famous Kenyon English Department?" Right now, it doesn't feel so hot. I feel like a shyster. I seek consolation.

"My worst nightmare as a teacher," says Peter Rutkoff, after hearing my misery, "is how this whole place goofs off for ten weeks and goes bananas for four. Every semester. The first ten weeks, they're attending but not working, the last four weeks, they're working but not attentive. And the worst of all are second-semester seniors."

Across campus, Ron Sharp takes a longer view of things. It's as if he knew I'd be coming to him, eventually, feeling like this. "What one expects has changed in fundamental ways," he says. "A lot of it has to do with familiarity with literature. They don't write as if they've read a lot, or have read criticism, or have a common language. You don't have a feeling they're writing about stuff they're passionately engaged with, committed to, serious about . . . I don't have any idea what the numbers are, but I think we get a certain percentage of students who love literature and really want to study it and chose Kenyon for that reason. Some of them are good, some not so good. Another group we get by default. They kind of like to read, they want to get by, so why not be an English major?"

Next, I recall a session with one of Kenyon's most highly regarded professors. Everything was off the record, so I call this professor Hesh II. "One of the things I've learned since I came here," Hesh II said, "is . . . well . . . I think of the students as not quite knowing what they're doing. I see them as caught in a larger cultural failure, a failure of the imagination, of other ways to grow up and be middle-class. If you graduate from high school you go to college. The average student here seems to be going through the paces." Hesh II pauses. We were sitting at a table in Peirce Hall, late one afternoon, tea for Hesh, coffee—some kind of brown, warmed-up liquid purporting to be coffee—for me. "I think of these kids as coming from privileged families, having no particular pressing needs. Out of every fifteen, three or four are quite remarkable. But it's not a student body you'd die for. What's missing? *Urgency*."

I never thought I'd feel quite this shitty. So I take my misery-loves-company tour of Gambier to Lentz's home. I sensed he'd have something to say. In 1977, I remembered, he shared a plane ride with a *N.Y. Times* writer. Soon after they talked, he found himself appearing in the lead paragraph of a *Times* article on shrinking reading requirements in college courses. Lentz said that Denham Sutcliffe, our teacher, had assigned more reading in the early sixties than he—Lentz—was assigning fifteen years later. "In two and a half weeks spent on Hawthorne, he would assign seventeen stories and two full novels. I regularly assign eight stories and *The Scarlet Letter* itself." Well, that was fifteen years ago, and some people say that the caliber of students has come up since then. But not, alas, when it comes to what you can count on them to have read, or to read.

"Henry James, for God's sake!" Lentz exclaims. "For Sutcliffe, we'd read both *Portrait of a Lady* and *The Ambassadors*. It's like watching water run out of a bathtub. I assigned *The American* and *The Ambassadors*, then just *The Ambassadors*. Now I don't even do *The Ambassadors* anymore. That's part of it. Volume. The other part is, I spend a lot more time on texts. With Sutcliffe we studied literature. Now we study how to study literature. They're just not as well read as we were. Period. They haven't read as much as we had, and it's just more difficult for them. I assigned *The French Lieutenant's Woman* last semester. And someone said, 'Three hundred and sixty pages . . . that's a lot to ask in a week and a half before Christmas!'"

Writing skills have headed south as well. They write lively petitions, Lentz knows. When it's a plea for the department to waive a requirement, student writing is passionate and calculating. But they're not comfortable critics of literature, not at ease in essays. "They don't conceive of essays as something they can control, to infuriate or persuade or convince," Lentz says. "They're helpless before the form they are trying to use. Crafting or controlling one's own writing is something our students just don't have."

This, I guess, is the nadir of the year. This is the moment when I plead for something to rescue me. I picture the class as it sits in front of me, two days a week. It's easy to do: I urged them to sit in the same seats every time—you learn names faster that way. In front, on one side, a bunch of fraternity guys, game and good-natured, who enjoy the kidding and banter and mostly like the reading. Next to them, several women, smiling but anxious, and a couple of them who may be getting tired of the white males in the books they read—Rabbit and Portnoy, et al.—and tired, also, of the white male who's been lecturing them. Up front, too, is a kid who loves books, loves talking about them, is always the first to raise his hand and thus risks the genial, laid-back contempt of the others. In the middle rows are some women who enjoy the class, regard it as unkempt relief from the stuff they've been getting elsewhere. There are some good writers in there, I know, not that I can prove it now. Some hard workers, too. A scholarly kid who wants to be a writer, a couple women interested in journalism, people I can sense lighting up when they come across these books and discover that American literature is still happening. The back of the class hasn't changed since high school: the shy, the intimidated, the quietly pissed off, and two students so lacking in affect that I don't know what to make of them.

That's the class, and if Hesh II got it right—"it's not a student body to die for"—I nonetheless believe there's some gameness and intelligence in the room. That makes it harder to connect those people with these papers, so formal in tone, so sloppy in execution, so lacking in critical confidence. Rescue me. I didn't come here to brutalize students, to strut the old days, to celebrate decline. Rescue me. An alumnus who brags how students used to write is uncomfortably like an alumnus who brags about the way they used to drink. Nostalgia is corrosive. Rescue me. If they are bad, we are bad. We're in it together. We can't go around for long claiming all our virtues are local, all our failures started someplace else. Rescue me. From double elitism, from the elitism of class and race that brings our students here, the pathetic counterelitism that leads us to live for the handful, the one or two or three pet students who make us feel less guilty about it all. Rescue me. Rescue me from the intimation that our students come here less prepared than before, that they do less while they are here, that they are judged less strictly on what they do. Rescue me. There's a problem with writing around here. In introductory courses we span genres, centuries, cultures, continents. In upper-class courses we teach lots of interesting things: black literature, women's literature, plague literature. Literature and landscape, literature and friendship. We teach various authors, we teach some theories. Hell of a menu at this Italian restaurant. Only—rescue me!—WE FORGOT THE KNIVES AND FORKS! WE DIDN'T SET THE TABLE! SOME OF OUR STUDENTS ARE EATING THESE FINE MEALS WE COOK ... WITH THEIR FINGERS! THE FOOD IS GOING DOWN THEIR THROATS AND UP THEIR NOSES AND IN THEIR EYES! We need to diagram sentences in public. Rescue me. We need composition, rhetoric, grammar, a grunt course that's exciting and as cutting-edge as a blackboard. We need spelling bees, for Christ's sake. Rescue me. Who'd want to teach that kind of course? Then again, who ever said college had to be fun? Rescue me. Rescue me from being a cranky Mr. Memory. Am I asking for the moon? I just want to be able to give an A—well, maybe an A minus—without hating myself in the morning.

ONE BY ONE, the big issues I forecast dribble away. This afternoon, the discussion of residentiality came and went. I continue to think this is crucial: whether Kenyon will defend its identity, possibly integrity, by insisting that people who work here be here more than a couple days a week. Not that there aren't potent arguments the other way, about freedom, professionalism, marriage. Sometimes, it sounds like a discussion about parenting: is it the quantity or quality of the time we spend with our babies? After hours of preliminary talk, the faculty affairs committee decided to bring the matter before the whole faculty, which would be asked to choose between three options. Option one is to tighten up requirements, specifying a certain number of hours per day, and days per week, faculty should be on campus. The second is a general statement that would just remind folks of our identity as a small residential school: toothless, unenforceable boilerplate. Option three is to do nothing: "drop the subject."

They didn't even get started on it before 5:50 P.M., when the auditorium was already emptying. After a little light sparring, they took a vote at 6:10. Thirty-four people voted for the general statement. Seventeen went for the stricter requirements. And—the only surprise—one person votes to "drop the subject." That was Lentz.

"We have regulations in place," he tells me afterwards. At first, his vote seemed to contradict his loyalty to Kenyon, his commitment to living and working in this small place. Now he makes it sound as though the battle I'd been looking forward to has already been fought—and lost. "The fact is the administration won't level sanctions against senior faculty who don't appear at faculty meetings for twenty years, or against junior faculty who divide their office 'hours' into four fifteen-minute segments per week."

Unless the faculty declares itself in favor of such administrative discipline, there's no point in talking, Lentz thinks. Especially when the talk doesn't start until a little before six o'clock in a meeting that had only half the faculty there to start with. The whole thing felt askew to him, talking about professional responsibility in the absence of the very people who need to hear it. "It's like coaches who, when a team is doing badly on the field, turn and scream at the substitutes sitting on the bench."

Drop the subject.

❦

I WAS HOPING for rescue, rescue from sourness and anger, and rescue comes. In front of the bookstore the other day, catching some sun, a student tells me about a reading group that gets together every week to work over a chunk of *Finnegans Wake*. Responding to my complaints about Ohio coffee, two separate groups of students invite me to come over to their rooms for espresso, anytime. And, unexpectedly, a senior English major comes by to tell me what it feels like, some nights, studying late in Ascension Hall, and she reminds me of my own all-nighters, years ago, when the whole world circled around this Ohio hill. "There's something that makes you feel really intellectual if you're in there studying hard, and guilty and stupid if you're not," she says. "And walking home under that night sky, under a sheet of stars . . . walking in brisk cold air—I said to myself, *I'm here for knowledge.* I had a sense of communion with other scholars. And right then, Kant started making sense."

Rescue comes from a student in Lewis Hall, whom I ask about his first year. It turns out he's liking it here, it turns out that Lewis Hall works for him, so does Kenyon. "I don't mean to kiss your ass," this guy begins, "but living down the hall from a writer is a gift. Walking around a beautiful campus is a gift, and getting to know people, and having access to teachers. Being able to talk in class and not just taking notes. Twenty k is a lot of cabbage, but you can make it worth it."

This student was one of a group that gave a party for me a couple weeks ago. It was an idea I'd resisted. I was sure there'd be beer, and, though I wouldn't be buying it or serving it, I still feared a hassle with the campus cops. I know how word travels around Gambier. "You hear about Professor Kluge? Caught him in Lewis, getting shit-faced with a bunch of freshmen!" But we got away with it. Printed invitations, coat and tie required. They showed me the beer bong, the shotgun, the upside-down shotgun, swallowing brew as easily as a 200,000-mile clunker inhales a can of Quaker State.

"The ice storm!" the freshman resumes. "The way the campus looked after the ice storm—or the way it looks in the morning, in the mists: that's worth twenty k maybe. Ascension Hall! The church! Studying in amazing rooms. Walking freely, in safety. And Middle Path is the coolest thing, it's such a bring-back, it's like the college was designed by people on acid: one line you walk along and you see everybody. It's so strange, so dippy, but it works. And Old Kenyon! What a name, with all those ghosts and great stories. And the bookstore—magazines you can read without buying them, everything on the planet, and you can just walk around and sit in great chairs. We don't have all these big classrooms. We have classrooms in houses. You take class in a house instead of some gray, boring monster. And Gambier is a place with one of everything: one market, one bar, one bookstore, just one. And Peirce Hall! You look up and it's fantastic, it's beautiful, all those authors in stained glass. Remember the freshman sing? On the steps of Rosse Hall? The freshmen singing college songs in front of seniors? I thought it was bullshit till I told my brother about it. Then I got chills, thinking about how we'd be standing there four years from now. All these things you think are bullshit . . ."

It's an astonishing riff. With students, it's easy to convince yourself that what matters to you doesn't matter to them. You worry about the distances. Those written assignments that make the distance infinite.

Now, thank God, I sense some connection. I'm all right again. Some of them will remember this season, remember when they come back for their fiftieth reunion, I'll be dead then. I'll have been dead a while. But I'll be part of what they remember. That's not bad. It's not like I'd gotten a call from the Library of America that they were reprinting my novels, it's not like that. It's not like being Roy Orbison. But I'll take it.

❧ *April*

L IKE A STUDENT threatened with a grade of "incomplete," winter throws a little late work at us, light snows and chilling rains, all scattered and disorganized. Then spring comes rolling into Gambier, warm and green. Students take long walks on country roads, play lacrosse and frisbee on the Lewis Hall lawn, sunbathe in front of the bookstore. Moods lifting, we laugh good-naturedly at things that last month made us wince. Ted Mason tells me about a student who wrote on William Conrad's *Heart of Darkness*. Ron Sharp remembers a paper that referred, a dozen times, to Wordsworth's "Imitations of Immortality."

Work keeps piling up, deadlines left and right, but there's a springlike mood of silliness that you can feel all over. The silly season. Students play "the Killer Game," stalking each other with water guns, ambushing each other, one by one. Silliness: on her way to the laundromat, Marilyn Hacker, editor of the *Kenyon Review,* stops by a Harcourt Parish rummage sale. She deposits her knapsack at the door and starts browsing, returns to find her knapsack's been mistaken for a donation, her dirty laundry's about to go on sale. Silly season: in Peirce Hall, diners come across a letter, purportedly from Delta Kappa Epsilon, apologizing for that sexist, tactless invitation to the caveman party. "April Fools, motherfuckers," it concludes. Silly season: a colleague moves her Lowell-Bishop seminar out onto the second-story porch of Sunset Cottage. Suddenly, from down below, out on the road that passes in front, the class hears a protracted fart. As one, they rush to the railing to see who the culprit is. Down below, walking one of his dogs, is Kenyon's president. The class dissolves in laughter. Order is restored, sort of. "Maybe it was the dog," someone suggests, and the session falls apart again. Silly season: the beautiful college throws a weekend for prospective students and their parents; many of the students have been admitted but have not yet agreed to come. I sit in the bookstore and listen to some parents chuckling about Phil Jordan's speech to them. "You said yes, we said maybe," Jordan told the parents. "Now, we've said yes, and you say maybe." Out in front of Mather Hall, maintenance guys are raking and currying the grass where graduates will sit, just six weeks from now.

THE SILLY SEASON is baseball season, too. They're connected. The college swim team is legendary—thirteen straight national titles for the men, nine for the women. Tennis, soccer, and golf teams are competitive, too: we do well at leisure-class sports. But when it comes to baseball, basketball, football, the blue-collar sports, "small but slow" is the order of the day. "The only thing Kenyon students do fast is swim," says Bob Bunnell, athletic director.

Losing a lot is no reason not to play, but it can test your love of the game. The college baseball team, the Kenyon Lords, has had eight winning seasons in eighty-three years. "It may be the worst record in collegiate history," Bunnell speculates. He coaches baseball. He asked to do it. It has its rewards: the things you remember.

"We were playing our last four games last season against Case Western Reserve up in Cleveland," he recalls. Bunnell savors the story. He came here from Philadelphia, where he coached in winning programs at Temple and Philadelphia Textile. Living in a small place appealed to him, even though he now suspects that the much-advertised sense of community here is false: "There is no sense of community. It's all visuals." Still, he loves coaching, and talking, baseball.

"The kid pitching was a little left-hander from Chicago, Bill Lockwood. He was the team wit. Still writes me once a month. It's the second or third inning. Kenyon's ahead by a run, and the next batter, right-handed, is leading the conference at .421, though he'd fouled out on a bad pitch in his first at bat. I go out to the mound to talk strategy. 'You can walk him,' I say, 'or you can see if he'll fish at some bad pitches. What do you want to do?' He backs off and crosses his hands. 'Coach,' he says, 'I'm indifferent on this one.' 'What?!' 'I'm indifferent. I could go either way.' The umpire comes walking out to the mound. 'What's going on?' he asks. 'The pitcher's indifferent,' I say."

Then there was that famous dugout conference in Florida, where Kenyon begins its season during March break. Kenyon had left the bases loaded in the first three innings, scoring only a run or two. "I don't want to be a hardass," Bunnell remembers. "I needed to talk to them in a manner they'd understand. 'Gentlemen,' I say, 'I'm rather discomfited at this juncture, for we have squandered myriad opportunities to register tallies in these initial three frames.' There was quiet for maybe a two-count. One thousand and one, one thousand and two. Then someone says, 'Coach . . . I think *myriad* is a noun.' I went, '*What?*!' 'I think *myriad* is a noun. You used it as an adjective.' 'It can be used as a noun *or* an adjective,' I say. This goes on for thirty seconds. The team is clearly divided. The umpire comes over. 'What the hell is going on?' he asks. 'I'll find out tonight,' I say. 'I'll let you know.' So we finish the game. We lose. Nothing new. I call up my fiancée, ask her to look up *myriad*. It's a noun or an adjective, she tells me. 'Great,' I say, 'that's what I want to know.' The next day I say to the team that I've got great news, I was correct, *myriad* is a noun or adjective. Either way."

Bunnell pauses in his story. He's pronounced *either* so that the *e* rhymes with *tee*.

Another silence follows his announcement about *myriad*. Then: "Coach?"

"Yes."

"That's *eye*-ther," the player says.

This year, Kenyon won its first game in Florida, a come-from-behind victory against Shenandoah. The team felt good about itself, living up to Bunnell's slogan, "a whole new ballgame." During the winter months they'd had to practice indoors at Kenyon, and that's not fun. "We were indoors for an eternity," one of Bunnell's players tells me. "It's terrible, it sucks, it's death. Bad hops, no fly balls, no throws longer than 150 feet."

In Florida, though, it seemed that the dreary practices were paying off. They were undefeated! Players dared to hope that they could win twenty of their thirty-five games. Bunnell was only a little more cautious: fifteen wins sounded reasonable. But after that first victory, the team fell apart, exhausted. "It was like that one win was enough," Bunnell says. "We could have packed our bags and gone home." Four losses followed before the team returned north, practicing lethargically in cold, drizzly weather. Two wins and seventeen losses are its record now.

"Offensively, we're not a bad team," Bunnell says. "We're an average, mediocre Division III team. We don't strike out much, we put balls in play, get walks, and at this level of baseball, you can go out there without a bat and score five runs. You have to fuck up to make an out, the defense is so bad, and the pitchers don't throw strikes."

Defense: that's the problem. Kenyon scores 4.3 runs per game . . . but it yields 11. This year, Kenyon's catchers threw out just three of seventy base stealers. "A walk is a double," one player laments. The team's biggest single weakness is its inability to throw. "We catch the ball okay," Bunnell says, "but we can't throw for shit. We've watched videotapes, we've made videotapes, but they just don't throw enough. I'm forty-one, and I might be the best pitcher on the team. They've never learned to throw. A lot of them come from prep schools where the head baseball coach was the nice-guy math teacher who could drive a van. They hate to throw. Their mechanics are wrong. It's like breathing. How do you teach someone to breathe?"

The field where Kenyon plays is a dandelion-spotted pasture on the edge of campus, across the highway from the Kokosing River. It's a tenuous-feeling place compared to the world-class sports palace where Kenyon swim meets take place, a baseball field that might go back to pasture any minute. Kenyon's field of nightmares this weekend: consecutive doubleheaders with Allegheny College, losses of 11–7, 7–1, 10–0, 15–2.

"I stand there in the coaching box," Bunnell tells me afterwards. "I love the kids, I really do, but you want to win, and I stand there at third base and wonder what I'll say to them after the game. Blast them? No. You make a commotion. We're losing 15 to 2, but I'm clapping my hands, saying, 'Start us with two.'"

It's been a much worse season than anyone could have guessed, and the opposition hasn't made things easier. "Allegheny had a guy stealing when they were eight runs up. I'd have put the next pitch between the batter's ears, if I had anybody who could throw hard enough."

✻

"THIS IS YOUR ONE SHOT. You guys have been bitching for years that the trustees won't listen. This is your chance to get it together. The trustees are you, only fatter and older. They're no smarter. They've gone through a lot of things, but they think like you do."

Back on campus, Bob Price sits in the Alpha Delta Phi Lounge in Old Kenyon, talking to representatives of eight fraternities. They'll be meeting with trustees later this month, and Price has come to help them organize their arguments. Sophomore members not entitled to live in fraternity divisions, loss of lounges—it's a litany by now—but some new arguments emerge. Increased vandalism in lounges ever since they were taken from fraternity control. Not a bad argument, Price thinks: "Everywhere in the world except American college campuses and Cuba, people realize that something that belongs to everybody belongs to nobody. That's socialism, and it doesn't work." Other arguments: sniping, captious noise complaints from women residents. "We got the shit harassed out of us during 'Take Back the Night,'" someone says. Losing control of dormitory lounges, fraternities have been using lodges to give parties, though not all of them have lodges. "If we retreat off campus, who is going to give the parties for the nonfraternity people?" Price asks, shaping the argument and turning it against the administration. "They don't want you here, they're doing everything possible to make your life miserable. And they haven't thought through what they've done. You leave, and the lounges get trashed. You go to the lodges for parties, and the campus goes dead."

Price helps parcel out the various complaints, arranging who will make what point to the trustees. He makes it sound as though the future of the college will be on the line a few weeks from now. And he's convinced that what's at stake is more than housing.

"It's political correctness and Ryn Edwards and the whole fucking thing," Price says. "Why do they want you out? That's easy. You're not politically correct."

❧

"GIVEN THAT WE ALL SUFFER and that we will die, and given that we cannot accept traditional religious or philosophical consolation, why live? This is where Keats begins."

Ron Sharp on John Keats, just yesterday. I'm sitting toward the back of the room, against the wall, behaving myself, taking notes like any other student, while Sharp sets up the conventional wisdom on Keats: that he was a tenderhearted idealist who had turned into a tough-minded, sharp-edged realist by the time he died at twenty-five. Then Sharp gives the class his own take: that the thoughtful, skeptical Keats was there from the start, along with the romantic visionary.

Listening to Sharp warm up to a topic he loves—"deep beauty in the core of suffering and death"—I glance at the students, the way I wish I could look at my own class sometimes. They seem evenly divided between stenographers—scribbling away—and starers, the ones who might be getting all or nothing. A hard group to read.

"What if you went to a doctor's appointment after class and found out you were going to die?" Sharp asks. It's funny. I'm sitting quietly, poker-faced and polite, but Sharp can't seem to meet my eyes. Every time he looks my way, the John Crowe Ransom Professor of English starts to grin and turns away instantly. "I don't mean this as a cheap teaching technique, to get the tears flowing. How would it change your view of life? Of friends? Of Middle Path? Would you walk in gloom and darkness? Or in beauty? This is the stuff of tearjerkers and newspapers, but there's a real issue here, and it's at the heart of Keats's sense of things."

Rhetorical question, the class realizes, with a sense of relief: no answer called for, thank God! The stenographers keep jotting, the starers—contemplating death or summer jobs—keep staring.

Death is what gives Keats's work a heightened poignancy, Sharp says, imparting beauty to the natural world and . . . and . . . and all of a sudden he looks my way one time too often and he loses it. What the John Crowe Ransom Professor of English is feeling now is that terrible feeling travelers have when they awaken in motel rooms and nothing tells them where they are. He flushes and gropes a bit; a couple stenographers prompt him. He laughs about it, glances at his notes: Keats's use of religious symbolism, oh yeah, and proceeds. Later, he tells me that he's come close to the edge in the past, gone over it a couple times.

"I've had to cancel a couple times over the years," he says. "One time, I was teaching 'The Rime of the Ancient Mariner.' Only I misspoke, I said 'Ancient *Marinater.*' I laughed, and I corrected myself. But I kept doing it! Seven or eight times! And before long, I couldn't go on, I was laughing so hard. Another time, I'm teaching a seminar on critical theory. It's a three-hour, nighttime seminar, right before the spring break, and the students are kind of punchy. One of the students, a girl, is giggling a lot. I tried to be sympathetic. 'I understand,' I said. 'I'm a giggler myself.' 'What do you mean?' she asked, and I told her about the 'Ancient Marinater.' And the next thing I knew, I was giggling all over again."

This time, Sharp recovers and resumes his somber, bracing, bittersweet lecture, contrasting Wordsworth with Keats. "For Wordsworth, flowers are a symbol of something, a symbol of nature, of participation in the grand harmony of nature, and nature is a colossal abstraction. Keats wants to see that flower down there, in all of its timebound specificity, locality, concreteness. He saw everything through the lens of someone who was going to die."

🌿

WE'RE ALL GOING TO DIE. Mike Stone did that just today, owing me one paper. He'll come back next week to be buried here, where he'll remain a local hero for as long as people remember him. I think of him on Honors Day, when we recognize professors and bright students with an array of prizes that goes on a little longer than the country music awards. It was a nice-feeling ceremony, though not without a few small flaps. A worried administrator fretted about Jewish professors marching in behind college flags with Christian symbols, and this sensitivity was rewarded, by one grousing colleague, as reminiscent of the heavy-handed liberality of a grade school teacher who pointedly remarks that Jewish kids aren't obliged to sing Christmas carols in class. Two of the honorary degree recipients were recent female graduates, pleased as punch to be recognized, some thought prematurely, but the college is eager to celebrate its women. The other awardee, a graduate of the Kenyon of forty years ago, made some faculty wince when he referred, in a kind of ponderous gallantry, to women as "the fair sex." Silly stuff again. Along with a music professor, Ben Locke, Lentz received a teaching award from the trustees, an award many think long overdue. "Perry may or may not be the best professor here," Will Scott remarked, "but everybody *thinks* he is, and if he didn't get that award we might as well have all packed our bags and gone home."

A few days later, I thought of Stone again. Robert Mezey, a poet who was a Kenyon student in the fifties, came back to give a reading, which I almost skipped. You get your fill of circuit-riding poets and writers. But Mezey, coming back here for the first time, was a treat, full of memories of the place, of all the old magic. John Crowe Ransom in a classroom. E. L. Doctorow a fellow student. And James Wright walking along Middle Path. "So you think you're a poet, kid?" Wright asked Mezey. And then proceeded to recite a long Thomas Hardy poem from memory. Mezey then quoted part of an unpublished poem of Robert Frost's, a bad poem on the whole, he says, but with four lines that might have been written for him, and for me, and for Mike Stone, and maybe for this college in this season.

It shall be no trespassing
If I come again some spring

In the grey disguise of years
Seeking ache of memory here

❦

MAJOR LEAGUE BASEBALL SEASON comes again, and two Kenyon freshmen welcome it. I hear them chatting on the lawn outside my window.

"What ever happened to Cincinnati having the opening game of the season?" one asks.

"Toronto got into the act," the other replies.

"Yeah. Canadians ruin everything."

"Baseball."

"Hockey."

"Acid rain."

"Acid rain?"

"Yeah. Never would have heard about acid rain if it weren't for their whining butts."

❦

CALL IT SILLY SEASON, spring fever, spring cleaning, but some extraordinary things have been going on in classes lately. Sharp's memory lapse was just the start. April has gotten to Lentz and Edwards, too.

First, Lentz. He was teaching a quiet, measured class on *Paradise Lost,* introducing the class to its themes, Christian virtues opposed by Satan's classical—and dramatically appealing—strengths. Christian themes figure heavily in Lentz's teaching: one student referred to the class as "the Lentz conversion experience." His response is that he goes with the vision of the authors he teaches, whether John Fowles or John Milton. Still, Christian themes prevail, and whenever Lentz starts working on the blackboard, illustrating a plot or a philosophical scheme, it's better than even money that before he's done you'll see some arrows pointing upwards, to heaven.

"My own Christianity," he suddenly remarks, "is so weak and faltering, I don't think it could be a model for anyone. I really do hope there's no one here after eight months who believes they have to agree with me to make a good grade."

It starts as a word of caution, a midcourse correction, a spot of assurance, a promise of open-mindedness, and, when he stops, I guess that this comment—which might have been as much for me as for his students—is over and we'll be back to Milton. But then his apology, or disclaimer, turns into a credo.

"In college today," he says, "atheistic thinking tends to be instilled, and the fashion is not to believe. Well, Christianity has committed some unspeakable outrages. In the seventeenth century, half of Europe was depopulated in wars between Catholics and Protestants. But I'm not convinced that, in their essential materials, atheist religions bring clean hands to this argument. Nazism, Communism. My grandfather was Jewish, and I'd rather he be a prisoner of the Austro-Hungarian empire, which was Catholic, than a prisoner of the Nazis."

I'm still mulling all this over as I head toward the Biology auditorium and settle in for a session of Ryn Edwards's course in female sexuality, which, like Lentz's course, I've been trying to attend two meetings out of three. Not a great attendance record, I grant: in a whimsical mood, Edwards filed a deficiency report on me with the dean of students. But I'm there often enough to see that the class has settled into a pattern. Mondays and Wednesdays are lectures, packed and intricate. You want biology, they seem to say, you get biology, glands, hormones, chemical reactions, and all. She works hard on, and in, these classes, but there's a problem. At the start of the course, Ryn Edwards told the class that she was uncomfortable with traditional academic grading. That's a defensible position, I guess, and not a bad strategy for enlisting student rapport, but the down side is that I see her killing herself at the blackboard while many students stop taking notes, merely listen, doodle, stare. "There's no way I'm going to have to know that stuff," one of them tells me.

Friday sessions are wildly different. These are discussion periods. Ryn Edwards takes a seat among the students, and a group of them, half a dozen or so—and sometimes two groups in one period—march to the front to lead discussions that sometimes bristle with conviction, sometimes feel forced and dutiful. After a while, discussion is thrown open, as in open season, open mike, open-ended. Last Friday it opened a little wider than ever before.

The topic of the day was the health problems of black women, an above-average incidence of high blood pressure among them. And then it was something about American Indians, how they'd been treated and portrayed in the media. And something else about how Alcoholics Anonymous aims to get rid of people's anger, which might or might not be a good thing because anger, when channeled, can lead to important social change. But all of a sudden—it was like spontaneous combustion—a Native American student, an African-American, and an Asian-American—all women—raised their hands and expressed discomfort about the way their people are discussed and, sometimes, not discussed in classes here and their resulting ambivalence about their situation, about being used—or maybe, not being used—as specimens, examples, quasi-ambassadors. Suddenly, the mood in the Bio auditorium turned angry and wounded. The discussion must have preyed on Ryn Edwards over the weekend, because today, Monday, she said she'd been thinking about what was said on Friday, minority students saying "hard things," and majority white students sitting there, feeling attacked.

"It is true that we have no control over who we are or where we are born," Edwards said. "If God said, 'Ring up who you want to be,' the world would look different. We don't control class or color. But no matter what our class and color, sexuality, et cetera—I'm not saying we're at fault, I'm not talking about faults . . . I'm talking about gaining a realization of color and class and how it impacts on us."

We need to acknowledge who we are, Edwards says, the privileges that define us, and the lack of privilege that oppresses others. That's her first point. We also have to acknowledge that our privileges are conditional and temporary. "You can be upper-class, ruling class, top 10 percent, and if you lose in the stock market the upper class doesn't give a shit. They don't care if you fall. It's only making it in the upper class that counts. Economics and ableness . . . are all temporary."

She pleads for students to be attentive to differences, aware of privileges, to listen to others, to consider carefully the choices they make in life. "You might decide that white is best and might is right," she grants, "but there are a lot of people out there, networking, and you might wind up in the ditch."

She continues in this vein, criticizing media. "How come we don't hear about candidates like Leonora Fulani?" She attacks our violence-oriented culture. As she speaks, I glance around the room. This, I think, is what many of the students came for: this kind of declaration, this tension, this vulnerability.

"I didn't mean to lecture," Edwards says, "but I get so disheartened. This course is hard. It's hard for me. It's hard for all of you . . ." She stops. She's crying. "It's not perfect. We're all trying. Just don't stop trying. We have to look at what's hard to look at, have to look at ourselves in order to become people again. If we don't, I honestly believe, as a biologist, we'll go extinct."

Again she pauses, but the class is still riveted. I can't say whether we have wandered off the track of this course in female sexuality, or whether this is where we were headed all along. The skeptic in me, and I'm not the only skeptic in the room, complains that this is sensitivity therapy, an Oprah program on a good day, classroom become clubhouse. But, in this spring season, when so many of us are dealing in credos, in declarations of faith and hope, I cannot begrudge Edwards this moment, any more than I begrudge Lentz's moment on Christianity, or Sharp's on Keats and death.

"Anybody want to say anything?" Edwards asks. No one takes her up, not right away.

"Yesterday was beautiful," Ryn Edwards says. "All the flowers came out."

🌿

ALONG WITH THE FLOWERS came the college's announcement that every one of its professors who were up for tenure—"appointment without limit"—received it. This generates an interesting chain of reactions. Within departments, among friends, there are congratulations, sighs of relief, assurances that the issue was never in doubt. "You don't mean to say you were actually worried?" That comes first. Then there's a harsher consideration of promotions in other departments. "I can't believe he got it. If the administration were ever going to get tough, they should have gotten tough with him." Then, a third reaction: if that other department's weakest member got through, our weakest should have nothing to worry about, when the time comes.

So it goes. This year, in the English Department, our two candidates were shoo-ins. Tim Shutt got tenure at a place he dearly loves. Now maybe he'll feel less embattled in his conservatism, his support of fraternities. Amen. It would have taken a felony conviction to disqualify him. Maybe not even that. I hope he sticks around forever. And—another amen—Ted Mason became Kenyon's first black tenured professor, a position he'll take and, if I've learned anything on our many runs this year, handle in his own way.

I was around when Ted Mason showed up for job interviews a couple years ago. Two earlier English Department hires of black professors hadn't worked out, I knew: one professor suffered what appeared to be a nervous breakdown, another charged job discrimination when her contract wasn't renewed. Controlled and poised, Mason struck me as someone who'd do well at Kenyon. Granted, there was some inane talk that he might not be "black enough." Maybe they were picturing some-one black and bald, like Isaac Hayes, glowering and angry like Sonny Liston. Mason resembled Bryant Gumbel. He'd lived in Europe, was married to a white woman, knew his way around a wine list, and wasn't going to play the role, white or black, that others might cast him in. Since then, he has turned out to be a personable colleague, a busy writer. He's acquired a reputation for tough grading that somehow hasn't cost him student friendship or respect. And one of the things they've respected is that though he's a black man teaching—among other things—black texts, he doesn't turn those texts, and his classes, into Afro-American show-and-tell periods.

"My basic rap in teaching Afro-American literature is, look, that you're black doesn't necessarily advantage you, and that you're white doesn't disqualify you," he says. "Criticizing Alice Walker—her meta-phors, her moves toward closure—isn't criticizing her blackness. Don't imagine that this class is about you. It's about how Toni Morrison writes—and not all black writers are doing the same thing. Yes, it's hard in some ways to be black and to be a woman, but these texts are not compilations of everyone's misery. This course is about the way people put literary texts together. Some have to do with misery, some don't. We don't need to view African-American life through one lens. The basic thing is, *this is not therapy.* I'm not good at it. My degree's not in it. And group therapy for thirty isn't particularly effective."

Mason feels good about being tenured at Kenyon College. I'm sure of that. And I'm sure of something else besides. I can see in him the same mixture of emotions I saw around campus when tenure decisions were announced, pride and pleasure compromised by intimations that the system isn't working as it should. And that's one of the things we've been talking about all year, up and down the Kokosing River running trail: what would it take to make a good college great?

"Kenyon has worked itself into a position where it can't get rid of anyone," he says. "There are no standards, judging the system by its results." Kenyon's rate of tenure and promotion approval is up above 90 percent. Every kid a winner. To be tenured or promoted, faculty must demonstrate excellent teaching, lively research, and service to the community. But—says Mason—almost everyone gets good teaching grades from their departmental colleagues. Scholarship requirements are generously defined and gingerly applied. And service to the community doesn't amount to more than being a good scout.

"I can't imagine the argument you could make against someone,"

Mason says, "without making a historical rupture with the notion of tenure and full professorship as entitlements. You'd have to bang an undergraduate not to get it, have to commit a clear moral, ethical transgression. And it flies in the face of logic to imagine that everyone we've hired, except those who fall off a truck, that all those who come up for tenure are deserving of it. It doesn't make any sense."

It must feel odd, having been awarded lifetime membership in a club that has lost its ability to discriminate, to say no, to punish or to reward, a club where equity is the ruling standard. What this leads to, Mason fears, is a kind of resignation that permits the interests of the community, warm and supportive, friendly and forgiving, to override the harsher and more abstract interests of the college.

"To change things, we would have to change ourselves in many ways that are uncomfortable," Mason says. "This is one of the most comfortable places I've ever been at. That's the good news. And the bad news."

❧

A SIGN in Peirce Hall, at breakfast time.

Keep Harry Brod
Don't Let Kenyon Loose Him
Sign the Petition Now

❧

A FEW NIGHTS before the spring trustees' meeting, much of Kenyon's senior class dresses up for a sit-down formal dinner with the manners maven Letitia Baldridge, a member of Kenyon's board of trustees. Like many Kenyon occasions, the Baldridge dinner has a wishful air of let's pretend. At Philander's Phling, students strolled a casino with endless wads of counterfeit money. Earlier this month, they hunted each other with water pistols in the Killer Game. Tonight the pretense is subtler—I wonder what Thorstein Veblen would make of it—and it amounts to this: let's pretend we are all accomplished and deserving, that we're at this important dinner, and while one difficult-to-eat course follows another, Ms. Baldridge—sitting at the head table behind a microphone—counsels us on how not to embarrass ourselves with shrimp cocktails or with those slippery cherry tomatoes that are too big to swallow, too hard to cut, and that spritz juice and pits when stabbed with a fork. All this dining advice comes with other tips on office etiquette, on being a

good weekend guest, plus anecdotes from Ms. Baldridge's time in Camelot as Jacqueline Kennedy's social secretary. The entrée, well in keeping
with the hard-to-eat theme, is Cornish hen, a dish more suited to a bio
lab than a dinner table. My advice, always, would be go for the duck.
I'm not Letitia Baldridge. She tells us it's okay to pick up one of those
dead midgets to get at the meat, what little meat there is. "This is so
good," you should announce to your hostess, "that I'm going to take it
in my hands."

🌱

I'M STANDING OUTSIDE the History Department on a gray, mean
morning, taking a break from grading papers, when I see them walking
toward me, Bob Price and Ray Grebey and some others, fresh from their
appearance in front of the board of trustees, and something in the way
they move tells me that the session has not gone well. I usher them into
the History Department conference room so they can conduct their
postmortem.

"The board's conception of itself is as a fund-raiser," Ray Grebey
declares, holding an unlit cigar. "Their primary responsibility is governance, and they don't want to touch governance, they just want to touch
money. Not governance. It's a giant fiscal committee. Kenyon's feeling
and culture—they don't give one hoot in hell about that. That's for
Jordan to take care of."

"Ray was superb," one of the others says.

"Hey, we didn't get a sale," Grebey counters, unconsoled. "No
close."

They complain they got cold-shouldered, that Jordan pointedly
glanced at his watch while Grebey spoke, that some trustees announced
they had a plane to catch, all this while Grebey was speaking about "a
rape of trust and confidence." He had a bomb to drop, too, a report
that changes in the college's treatment of fraternities have induced one
potential donor, an eightyish widow, to cut a million-dollar donation to
Kenyon out of her will. That got some attention, they feel, but on the
whole the meeting flopped.

"I want to sue," Bob Price declares. "I'm gonna sue Phil, the college,
and some, maybe not all, of the trustees."

"Phil has these guys hoodwinked," another alumnus complains.

Later, other accounts of the trustees' meeting come to me. The vice
president for development, Doug Givens, garrulous and argumentative,

tells me that Grebey demanded a podium, that Grebey wielded his unlit cigar like a cannon. And when I catch up with him, Phil Jordan is unequivocal about what happened. "He blew it," Jordan says, "he totally blew it. Rhetorical posturings at the beginning took an inordinate amount of time. There were no particulars until the end. And he closed with threats: we'll sue you, we'll withhold hundreds of thousands. And they didn't tell us anything we didn't know already. What the board heard, they had known."

❦

NOW WE LURCH from euphoria to exhaustion, like runners at the end of a marathon. Sometimes we sprint—we dance—and suddenly, like that woman in the Los Angeles Olympics, we double over in pain, walk crabwise, falling and crawling toward the finish line. At the deli, I lunch with a disconsolate Peter Rutkoff. He's depressed by a college that he thinks is dropping the initiatives he values—diversity, variety, outreach—and is now "hunkering down and looking inward." The only answer seems to be for him to hunker down as well, though it's not a posture that appeals to him. "Next year I'll be on sabbatical," he says with a sigh. "After that I'll be History chairman for one more year. And after that, I'll just teach."

I've enjoyed my office in the History Department this year, enjoyed schmoozing with Rutkoff and Scott, our Bullshit 101 meetings. So I try to cheer him up and needle him a little, too. He got paid this year, right? And next year—when he's on sabbatical—and all the tenured years to come, no? And his kids go to college at a discount, no, and his heart attack was covered by the college medical program? And his TIAA-CREF retirement plan that the college contributes to, that must be growing apace. And summer's coming, too. That's not bad, I say, compared to a lot of other jobs. But what I've been reminding him about isn't exactly what's getting him down. I might as well have remarked, Ryn Edwards style, that the sun was shining and the flowers came out. I've spent a lot of time here now, heard complaints, shared some pain, learned a little. But one question persists. I can't answer it. Why aren't people happier here?

❦

I'VE GOT TWENTY-EIGHT 10–15-page papers in front of me, and one large suspenseful question: will I be able to give an A in English 68, section 2, "American Literature since 1945"? I've gone through them once, preliminary reconnaissance, best at one end of the row, worst at the other. Now I'll go through again, making comments. It's a heap of work: I've been popping vitamin B like candy lately. But when I've gotten through this bunch, it's spring, it's summer, and I am free.

The assignment was to take any novel written since 1945 and ask an interesting question about it and answer it. I set aside a whole class to discuss proposals—everything from *In Cold Blood* to *Fried Green Tomatoes*—and it was one of the best classes we've had, like going shopping together in the bookstores I hope they'll be patronizing for the rest of their lives.

There is some good news, definitely. I can tell they've read the books, engaged with them, often thoughtfully, and written about them at length. A lot of the sloppiness that marked that first wretched pile of papers is gone: fewer errors, tense confusions, misplaced modifiers. They cleaned up their act somewhat. The bad news is that, when you solve small problems you discover larger ones, like clearing out a yard full of weeds and underbrush, only to discover an abandoned septic tank. This time I notice confusion of the author's point of view with that of the author's characters, i.e., mixing ventriloquist and dummy. I notice references to events happening "in the course of the book" and "during the novel." When the hell else? And, finally, that Bermuda Triangle of undergraduate writing, the passive voice, continues to exert its irresistible magnetic pull, betraying an underlying lack of critical confidence, revealing shaky writers removing themselves from the scene of the crime, effacing themselves, as though writing traffic tickets—"the book is seen," "the character can be likened," "one could characterize," "the fact is illustrated," "it is also evident,"—instead of literary criticism. There's a gap between the way they think and the stuff they put in papers they turn in to the English Department. I don't know where it started, whether it's the result of something we taught or failed to teach, but somewhere along the line our students got convinced that this denatured, disembodied, pseudoclinical jargon is the mode of critical discourse. Maybe it's our fault—I hope it's not—but it seems to me that we're going to have to develop not just a basic grammar course, sentence diagramming and all, but a second course in composition: clean writing, plain style, lively critical faculty. Our students are promising, but their writing is scared and tentative.

I go to the paper at the top of the pile. After receiving a not-great grade on her first effort, the woman stopped by my office to talk. In itself, that's not important. In fact, it's suspect. Students assume that simply dropping by to express concern, in itself, ought to be worth about half a grade, the way a visit to an elderly relative in a nursing home ought to count for points when the will gets read. *Kiss butt for half a grade.* This student was better than that. She planned to write about gender roles in Russell Banks's *Affliction.* She'd read it once already and had roughed out some arguments she wanted to try out on me, and she'd found textual evidence to back up her points. Now, I see, she's accomplished what she set out to do, and, what's more, she's moved from "liking" and "not liking" a book—what Lentz calls "ejaculations"—to contending with it on its own terms. It's a very good job. Is it an A, though? What about that sentence that proclaims: "This scene renders Wade impotent." Or: "Wade looks like a cretin to everyone in and out of the text." Oh, shit. She was close. She worked hard. She was one proofreading away.

A minus.

I move further into the pile, check out the next bunch of contenders. A slickly written piece on Tom Wolfe and Jack Kerouac. Gender roles in *The Women of Brewster Place.* Water imagery in *Seize the Day.* And here's one I had hopes for, the role of that long Cass Mastern section in *All the King's Men:* is it a wordy digression or does it connect importantly with the novel's major themes? Interesting question that I don't have the answer to. The paper's long, too, I see. The guy really got into it, I guess. Starts kind of slowly. I keep going, into the second paragraph: "While the above list may be far from exhaustive it does help illustrate the epic size and reach of Warren's weighty tome. It is an obvious conclusion, therefore, that the salient scope of his work renders inadequate any brief study that attempts to analyze it in its entirety."

Oh, gosh. Too bad. We're in the land of B plus, and—I glance at the two dozen papers that remain—we're headed south. Outside the dorm, I hear Aaron Neville's voice keening "Everybody Plays the Fool." The night air smells of freshly plowed fields. And a dog is barking someplace. Other places, dogs bark when they hear something stirring in the dark. Out here, I suspect, they bark from loneliness, hearing nothing.

❧ *May*

"**A**FTER SEVENTEEN TO NINETEEN written themes, twenty-two quizzes, seventy-five classes, I have enough information to justify giving you any grade I want," Lentz tells his last class, before describing a final exam that will give them a chance to lift their grades. Then, after some talk of deep patterns in *Paradise Lost, The Tempest, Walden,* and *The French Lieutenant's Woman,* class is over. "Well, thank you," Lentz says. Black suit, black tie. "I've enjoyed this class very much."

Ryn Edwards opens her last class with an announcement about how to get to a Rodney King protest in Antioch, Ohio. Then, after finishing up an earlier discussion about what women should want from a health care system, she reaches into a box she's carried into the Biology auditorium, pulls out and puts on a jacket covered with buttons from dozens of meetings, marches, protests—gay rights, no nukes, lick Bush, freedom of choice. "This is what it means to be an activist," she says.

She passes around a project made by one of the students, a wood-and-cloth model of female genitalia, as seen from the inside out. While that moves up and down the rows, Edwards reads a half-dozen poems by female poets. I sit there, trying to decide what I think, my internal needle bouncing from "corny" to "touching." Someone hands me the genitalia model. A lot of work went into it, I see: it looks kind of like a birdhouse, the glued-down pubic hair like a thatch of twigs.

Edwards tells the class that she hopes what they've gone through has made them stronger in love, stronger in making love, in making choices. She thanks them for caring, urges them to keep on caring, keep up the struggle, to "go forth and not be silent." Then, for a closing, she reads everyone's name and, as their names are called, the class stands up, one by one. She applauds them, they applaud her: double standing ovation.

By comparison, my last meeting of English 68 is nondescript. Though there are some things I believe, my convictions don't buttress my course in the way that Lentz's beliefs inform his. And, though I've got my share of working-class anger, sometimes pointed toward Kenyon, this doesn't impart the sense of mission that propels Ryn Edwards. I taught a variety of books—not as great a variety as some students would have liked, it turns out—and these were books that worked, and sometimes didn't work, in a variety of ways. They suggested—only suggested—a variety of things about America: the restlessness in Kerouac, Banks, Exley, and Nunn, the yearn to move, even as returns diminish; the binding ambivalence of minority life—Mukherjee, Roth, Bradley; the search for purpose in work—Banks, Updike, Exley; the search for magic, often in ordinary places, Hoffman and Updike; the failure of country, faith, work to define and redeem us, and the consequent preoccupation with sex, romance, and marriage, which often fail us; the need, which one senses in all these novels, to belong to something larger, without knowing what that something should be. One other thing: the ability of literature to realize life, to capture, criticize, and, on good days, transcend.

It wasn't important that the class like the books. Still, I wonder, so I ask for a show of hands. Which books should remain in the lineup? Which should be moved to the bullpen? Or out of the game? The only shoo-in is David Bradley's *The Chaneysville Incident*: its vigor and ambition earned respect, and the fact that it is by a black writer doesn't hurt either. Bradley gets away with things that would have drawn protests in white male writers. And, boy, have they had enough of white males: Updike, Banks, Exley, and Roth tested the patience of some female students. I've resisted teaching Toni Morrison, who is taught in other courses; I've been suspicious of her instant canonization and wanted to wait a few years, but I sense pressure building, especially from women. Students get proprietary when you teach contemporary literature, as though it's a jukebox that I've been hogging, playing only *my* favorite records. Odd, though. After Bradley, the class divides evenly on all the other books, with one exception: the female writer Bharati Mukherjee. What I see in *Jasmine* as clear, bitter vision, they find cold and heartless. So it's not just women authors, it's certain kinds of women authors.

Well, they didn't have to like the books. They didn't have to like me. But, again, I wonder. Colleagues warned me against asking for course evaluations. They'll bum you out, I was told. Even if most students liked the course, you'll be wounded by the ones who hated you. But I decide to take my chances. I ask for an unsigned letter in a sealed envelope—hit me with your best shot—and collect them as class ends.

The next part is tricky. I'd told myself that I'd wait for weeks to read the letters, wait until I was well away from Gambier. But I don't even get back to Lewis Hall; only as far as the bookstore, where I dump myself into a chair near the magazine rack and tear into the first envelope, hands trembling. The first letter is great, thank God. "I have enjoyed our class. I have looked forward to each class meeting with both nervousness and exhaustion. When I leave each Tuesday and Thursday, my head is always tired from the amount of information packed into it. I have learned more in the class than I bargained for. I like how you go over what seem to be tiny details in the book and show how they are integral to what the author meant to say. I like your choice of books. Most of all, I like the way eloquent metaphors roll off your tongue. It is truly a pleasure to listen to you describe a piece of text." Yes! I love it. Next envelope, please. Oh shit! Compliments me on being dynamic—"I never felt once like falling asleep"—but has huge problems with the reading list. "We read a lot of novels about shitty lives and I thought a lot of them were boring. . . . Did we ever read one book where a woman wasn't raped or abused? I can't think of any. It's not that I want to read about happy couples and feminism all the time, but give me a break. I started wondering why you chose those books to teach. This is 'Contemporary Literature,' not 'Contemporary Misogynists.'" Not so hot, that one. Do not try guessing who wrote that letter, do not try matching the style and the typeface with other papers, I warn myself. That's not the point. Next envelope: mixed review of "Kluge's Twisted Fiction 101." Hated the pop quizzes, not wild about the reading, felt that I rushed along too much. Next: "It was a fun class despite the fact that you could get called on even if you didn't raise your hand. There were lots of books in the syllabus I might not have been exposed to otherwise. The fifteen page paper was a pain in the ass though." What you win in Boston, I guess, you lose in Chicago. But this is the best writing I've gotten, the most direct and vivid and committed, the most in-your-face. In my face. Next, a thumbs-up: "one of the funniest and most dynamic teachers I've had." Liked the reading, didn't like the hurry and the time spent on plot summary. "While my friends labor over neuropsych and books entitled *The Bible of the Oppressed* at hard desks, I sit in comfy chairs and chuckle over sex-crazed Jewish men." And this: "I think it was pretty interesting having both you and Perry

Lentz simultaneously, he being of the Dead White Male camp and you being of the Confused Live Male and Occasional Female." The next letter is an outright slam: hated the quizzes, loathed my up-close-and-personal style, accuses me of "unprofessional conduct." This is getting to be a roller coaster ride. No wonder people don't ask for evaluations. Next envelope: mixed. Thought I was remote and impersonal but found the class interesting. The next evaluation is offbeat, cast in the form of a long vignette set in a bar, students talking about the course over beer. I come off as a daunting figure, bristling with opinions, the kind of guy you either love or hate. "If students are aware of the high intelligence of a professor, it either forces them to respect him or resent him and in our class there are some with the respect and others who possess the resentment philosophy." But, the letter goes on, "I have never felt like falling asleep in Kluge's class so he must be doing something right." The next letter brings a sickening plunge: poorly chosen books and hurried plot summaries make this the writer's least favorite course in four years at Kenyon. Now I've hit bottom, I guess. Next envelope: mixed but upbeat review. Complaints about the amount of reading. I thought nine novels in thirteen weeks was fair. Maybe not. Still: "I enjoyed the reading in this class very much, probably more than in any other class at Kenyon. I was psyched to read. (Though I didn't always)." Next envelope: more women authors please, but liked the class on the whole and recommended it to friends. Next, a rave: "Entertaining and interesting. Thanks for a very good class. . . . You even talk like a writer. Everything is a quick note or a sketch ostensibly to be transcribed later and elaborated in full. Whatever. I found it a fascinating and credible alternative to 'non-writerly' English courses. I really believe I now have a better sense of how many different Americas there are. I credit your class for this new understanding. Thanks again." Okay. That's more like it. And the next envelope puts me on a roll. "As this senior completed the final college semester, she realized that yes, in fact, she was even learning something." Good. But I want this to be over now. I'm exhausted. A complaint begins the next letter: "The Great American Male Pity Party . . . almost two thousand pages of stupid women, pathetic families, terrible jobs and bad sex." But then it changes, offering some good-natured advice. "I can't really suggest which books to get rid of. But it has to be done because students are going to want some female authors. Take Back The Night was big here in Gambier, as was the DEKE party sit in, etc. Many students, especially women students, are ready to pounce. This is just a neighborly warning." Jesus, a neighborly warning. I get shaky all over again: it feels like *Treasure Island* and I've just been handed a black spot. Or *The Godfather* and I get a tuna in the mail: *Jack Kerouac sleeps with the fishes.* Eleven more letters to go. Next: "Your rapport with the students is exceptional. It's rare to find a professor that is overtly sensitive to, and interested in, life on campus and the lives of individual students and, moreover, seems to willingly inundate himself in the themes, gossip and chaos that travels around town. . . . All in all, I enjoyed the course and enjoyed you as a character on campus." A character on campus, yet: it's time to leave for sure. Next: "Great class. The first class I have experienced at Kenyon College which did not include an extensive feminist reading selection. Last semester, I was in an English class in which one of the students was visibly angered that Tennyson did not include Penelope in his 'Ulysses' poem. That upset me for days. Though I am a woman, I am greatly aggravated by the urgent necessity for feminist literature in English classes at Kenyon. . . . Thank you for not overdosing on that sort of material." My class is starting to sound like *Rashomon.* Am I the woman, the samurai, the woodcutter, or what? The next note is friendly, though it claims my commanding presence stifled class discussion. The next two are thumbs-up reviews, and after that a rave. The fourth-to-last—I'm anxious to be done and let the healing process begin—compares me to other members of the department. Lentz, this student says, is "brilliant, witty, intimidating and insane." I am "hard-nosed yet not intimidating, not insane (yet)." The third-to-last is a rave, the next-to-last is friendly, and now I face the last, praying that it won't be a bummer. "The best thing about your class is that it is unlike any other English course that I have ever taken at Kenyon. I get the sense that each novel you teach is included because you really enjoyed reading it and that you realize that your commentary on the novels is based on personal opinion rather than some kind of sacred truth." He or she got that right. I read on. "I have spoken to some people in the class who think that your point of view is too masculine (you aren't p.c. enough for their taste). You have also gotten the reputation on campus (from many women) that you are not interested in our issues." Wait a minute! I feel myself getting mad. Suddenly, Gambier is feeling small, not as in small-precious, the way I usually manage to think of it, but small-petty. I read on, and it turns out that, if I've been attacked, I've also been defended. "While I do agree that what we have read this semester has centered around the male perspective, I do not think that the reading list is problematic; you teach what you know and anyone who enrolls in your class looking for feminist interpretations of contemporary literature is probably barking up the wrong tree." Thanks, I guess. She continues, suggesting some novels by women I might want to consider for next year: works by Ellen Gilchrist, Susan Shreve, Robb Forman Dew. And then, this final paragraph. "I am glad that I am ending my English career at Kenyon with your course because I really needed something to restore my faith in my major. I will never again be able to write a paper (like I did in my glory days of high school and lower level college course) with titles like Symbolism in *The Scarlet Letter* or Kate's Revenge in *The Taming of The Shrew*. I am too disillusioned (and unwilling to shovel that kind of shit anymore) to play that game; thanks for not forcing that upon us. Being in your class has reminded me why I became an English major in the first place; I love to read."

They're done. I put them all back in an envelope and sit there for a while, trying to recover my balance. The news was mostly good. If it were an election, I'd have won. But, ah, how those negative comments haunt me. Granted, some students damned me for the same qualities others praised. What came off as vitality and humor to one student was cocky, sarcastic swagger to another; one student's "personal touch" was another's "unprofessional conduct." Still, there were definitely some lessons for me. To go more slowly, I guess, to never rush. To announce large, open-ended questions at the start of a book, and—what I didn't always do—return to those questions at the end. To keep an eye out for the larger themes that connect these books with each other and with underlying issues. What else? Well, on the way out of the bookstore, I grab a copy of Sylvia Plath's *The Bell Jar*. How about pairing it with *On the Road?* The works of two short-lived iconic figures. Jack and Sylvia, the blind date from hell.

❦

LAST NIGHT IT was sad, seeing Lewis Hall get dismantled, packing boxes in rooms, books in piles, posters peeling off of walls; gone, Elle McPherson, gone, the Budweiser women, gone, the Swedish bikini team. Sure, the students will be back next year, but by then the college will have sorted them into new patterns, sorted them by major, by fraternity, by sports and drama and leisure-time activity. This year's freshman camaraderie will not happen again.

This morning, there are cars all over the lawn around the dorm, crowding the grass, like turtles come ashore to spawn, the parents claiming their quarter-educated offspring for the summer. It is more than I can stand to watch. Avoiding the corridor, I leave through my apartment's outside door and walk to the Kenyon Inn, where Bruce Haywood, the former professor and provost at Kenyon, now president of Monmouth College, joins me for breakfast. Haywood is passing through town quietly, seeing a few old friends. He's enjoying his return too much for me to ask him to replay the events that led to his leaving. After breakfast we sit together on Middle Path, on a bench under the maples, surrounded by tulips, watching traffic. The town is filling; every parking place is crowded, and the cops are out. I wonder, when someone chooses a career in law enforcement, do they picture themselves walking around the backs of cars and putting chalk marks on the left rear tire? Is that something they dream of doing when they grow up? Haywood would have sat with me all day, checking the comings and goings out of the bookstore, the Peoples Bank, and the post office, the daily stirrings in a place he used to love. And still does. That's the peculiar thing about Gambier. Conventional wisdom is that when you leave a place, leave with mixed emotions, you move on, forgive and forget. But Kenyon isn't about forgiving, not if it requires forgetting. Memories are what make this place, especially in springtime when the thin thread of present tense that carried us through winter is now woven into other chords and tenses, past, present, and future.

"I had a dream about you the other night," a student says to me as I sit on my bench. Haywood's gone. "I dreamed that I was pushing you across a parking lot with two friends. You were in a shopping cart, and we were pushing you. And the cart banged hard against the curb. You went flying out of the shopping cart, and you landed between two cars. But you weren't hurt. You got up, and you came back to us, cheerful, and you said, 'That's all right, I'm okay.'"

I assure her that I am okay, and she moves on, cheerful. It's funny how students treat you after a class is over. Some go out of their way to talk, tease, banter, as if to demonstrate that they meant it when they laughed and smiled in class; it wasn't just an act they went into for a grade. Others turn away when they see me coming, their faces go blank, as if the last place we'd seen each other was in the waiting room of a VD clinic.

What a morning! Dog walkers. *New York Times* buyers. Jim Hayes, grocer-banker, steps out of the brick house next to the bookstore and steps over to the Peoples Bank. He's just up from Florida, in Florida togs: yellow sweater and plaid pants. Next to the bookstore, a book buyer sets up a table, ready to pay hard cash for used textbooks. "Get Those Books Off Your Back!" his sign urges.

In the early afternoon, still avoiding the emptying out of the dormitory, I take my chance on Kenyon baseball. The Kenyon Lords are finishing their unfortunate season with a doubleheader against Case Western Reserve. There are maybe thirty people in the stands when I arrive, a friendly and forgiving group, sitting out on a windy day. The score is 2 to 1 Case Western Reserve when I arrive in the second inning of the first game. It's 9 to 1 by the time the inning ends. I aim a sympathetic wave at Bob Bunnell and leave.

Back in Lewis Hall, a few students are sitting in a stairwell, and one of the guys is telling about an evening's adventure in Columbus, a party of five with free tickets to a World Football League game, the Ohio Glory against the Frankfurt Galaxy. After the game, the Kenyon group went drinking on High Street, where they fell into conversation with someone who told them JFK was the Antichrist. A car chase rounded out the evening, the Gambier contingent pursued by a truckload of "guys with long hair and no teeth." I go into Mount Vernon for dinner, to check out the Saturday night scene. The downtown is dark at night, but convoys of kids cruise Main Street and circle the square with the Civil War monument, a ceremony right out of *American Graffiti*, though time has turned yesterday's rite of passage into something quaint, and quaintly stupid. Three circuits around the square are all the law allows: the cops have drawn the line. Back at Lewis Hall, I learn that Kenyon won the second game of its doubleheader against Case Western Reserve, closing the season with three wins and twenty-two losses.

❦

"I'VE GOTTEN KISSED a couple times," Phil Jordan tells me. "And I said, 'Thank you.' I've been given things. Raunchy paperback novels, letters stolen from the entrance sign to the college. Unpaid parking tickets. A mask from a Molière play, a beaked mask. And money. Coins. I keep a collection plate right at my side."

I'm talking with Kenyon's president about commencement ceremonies, the things that happen when students cross the stage to shake his hand. I'd lost touch with Phil Jordan in recent months, ever since our December foray on the alumni trail. I guessed that was inevitable. It was never in the cards that we'd be intimate; he's not that kind of man. The more I've been here, the more I understand the distance he keeps, not just from me.

Phil Jordan is past sixty. This is his seventeenth year as president: an extraordinary run. He could step down tomorrow—or it could be several years. No one knows. And twilight is an unequivocal, unkind time. "He's a better president than we deserve to have," says someone on the Kenyon payroll. "He is moral and honest and straight as an arrow. He's revised everybody's level of expectations. But he's overstayed. You come to a point where you're staying for your own reasons. You think you're helping, but you've already made your contribution."

"Phil Jordan may be the greatest president in the history of Kenyon College," says another professor. "He's been here longer than almost any college president in America. But he's not demarcating bold new directions." What Kenyon needs, this professor indicates, is a new, aggressive president, a tough-minded liberal who'll push scholarships, open up the faculty, shake up the curriculum some more. Another Kenyon person tells me what Kenyon needs is a consolidating, conservative president, someone to impose standards, get control of the faculty, cut spending, and kick ass.

Looking at him now, I realize that all year long I've been trying to hit upon an image that would capture his role here. Father and children? No, too much of his work is elsewhere, away, out of the house; this place is small, not intimate. Family metaphors won't work. Corporation head? No, business won't fit either. There's no clear sense of product, no bottom-line way of measuring success, no stock, no market. General and army? Forget it. No one can agree what we're fighting for, or about, no one could recognize victory or defeat, even if it came to that. Coach and team? Baseball manager? Baseball owner? Nothing works. Captain and ship? No, we mostly sail in circles. Chef and waiters? Shepherd and flock? Landlord and tenant? Hold it! That's worth exploring. Jordan's the guy who owns a building. He presides over rents and leases. He stays close enough to worry about the roof and the boilers, to monitor changes in the neighborhood, but not so close he gets drawn into tenant quarrels, noise complaints, not enough hot water, the elevator doesn't work. Not bad, but I still haven't nailed it: that combination of presence and absence, of power and laissez-faire, of caring and indifference, that hand that can make a fist, offer a handshake, pat a back, reach into a pocket, stifle a yawn, wave farewell.

Today, in our final interview, Jordan tells me that the college has had a pretty good year. He takes a long, philosophical view of the faculty's decision against a tenure and promotion committee. It failed, he thinks, because professors saw that there was a daunting amount of work involved and—second reason—they doubted that having a group of colleagues read their letters of assessment would add much to the tenure and promotion process. Sure, he wanted a tenure and promotion committee. "Its absence makes us increasingly odd," he declares; this continued avoidance of "the central task of self-government" reflects "a failure of nerve." But it can also be read, he says, as a sign of confidence in the administration.

Those hiring searches in Women's and Gender Studies and the Integrated Program in Human Studies were touchy, he grants, but the touchiness was confined to small areas—"cockpits of conflict"—and didn't spill over to infect the campus as a whole. As for residentiality—the drift of professors off campus—he decided, he says, not to push things hard, to take gentle, nudging measures. "I didn't come at it," he says, "in terms of, 'You have to be here, God damn it, most of the time.'"

My list of hard questions has evaporated, and, once again, I sense a disjuncture between Jordan's view of the college and almost everybody else's. He's a vigorous, optimistic man, and sometimes he makes me feel disloyal, asking him hard questions, though those questions don't start and end with me. He wonders, I suspect, why I'd want to be here at all, why anybody would, and he has a point. He reminds me that not many places are as good as Kenyon. But we're not as good as we could be, perhaps not as good as Jordan thinks we are, and if you spend a lot of time on the inside, you walk around exasperated. And you risk rankling a president who has all he can do defending an already vulnerable institution from outside attack. A difference of perspective, I guess. Winding down, I ask the standard catchall question: low and high points of the year. The lows involved worrying about money in a worsening financial climate. And, he admits, "the deep emotion and combativeness" about fraternities bothered him. That issue remains unsettled. A few days ago, the college and trustees issued a carefully worded statement that, one source tells me, went through fifteen drafts. Jordan says it was more like four. It said that the trustees talked things over, that the administration runs the college, including the housing, and that fraternities have a place at Kenyon. And it allowed that, wellll, yessss, housing policy might be subject to review, but that would be when the administration decides to review it, on its own schedule, and not to meet any alumni-imposed deadline. So this long-running melodrama will continue. Sometimes it has seemed to be about housing, sometimes about fraternities, sometimes about politics, about who runs the college, about power and about ego, about claiming victory and acknowledging defeat.

"The highs of the year," Phil Jordan continues, "are simple moments. Honors Day. A student recital. Talking with a student about a problem. We can get so preoccupied by conflict and querulousness that we lose sight of these other things. This is an absolutely wonderful college. We do what we do wonderfully well."

WALKING TOWARD SUNSET COTTAGE, I see two people sitting in the college cemetery, on the grass next to Mike Stone's grave: his mother and Tracy Schermer, the college physician. I wave and walk over, hoping I'm not interrupting a private moment. The two—make that three— of them went through a lot together. They've been talking about Mike, I guess, and Schermer has put together a framed collage of pictures that I glance at. But then I notice that there's something on Mike's tombstone, a stuffed animal, a cougar that his mother says is called "Cougsey." She's placed it right on top of the tombstone, and it's as if the toy creature had flung himself there in mourning, or was taking a nap, or maybe conducting a conversation down through the stone. "I asked him if he wanted Cougsey buried with him," Hays Stone remarks. "'No,' he said. 'He has years of life left in him. Bury him with you.'"

THE FIRST TIME I dropped by Provost Reed Browning's office, he was kidding with his secretaries and I asked what they were laughing about. It turned out that once, long ago, he played the part of the White Rabbit in a production of *Alice in Wonderland*.

"*I'm late, I'm late, I'm late, for a very important date,*" Kenyon's provost sang out. A light moment, but he got into it, and it felt as though that role had prepared him for what's clearly the most harassed and unpopular job in town, straw boss and faculty wrangler, a position that a predecessor, Bruce Haywood, called that of "the Abominable No Man." "*I'm late, I'm late, I'm late.*"

A day late and a dollar short defines this thankless position. If ears burn when people talk, Browning's ears should be charcoal. He contends with departmental staffing—which bailiwick gets to add a hiring line. He deals with candidates and searches, with tenure and promotion, with merit increases, and—though rarely—with burnout and indiscipline, with a bewildering array of committees and an unending stream of complaints. Positioned between a venerable and elusive president and a restless, divided faculty, Browning takes the blame for everyone's unhappiness. Whatever he does is scrutinized by a hundred and a half smart, prickly people, quick to charge him with dithering and delay, with favoritism, expedience, inconsistency. His two predecessors stood for something, it's said, though what they stood for is variously construed, right versus left, tradition versus change, old versus new. Browning lacks that clarity of presence and cannot be relied upon as enemy or friend, cannot be relied upon period. Whatever you get from him, people warned, get it in writing. No wonder Reed suggested we meet at lunch, away from the campus.

Ten miles from Gambier, at the crossing of Routes 36 and 62, there sits the little town of Millwood, a time-warped collection of houses and dead storefronts whose only sign of life is a BP gas station on one corner and the restaurant inside, where folks in flannel shirts, Big Yank slacks, and John Deere caps start with thick soups, chew artery-clogging fried entrées, and remember to leave room for the pie. We've come here a half dozen times this year. At our first lunch, I remember, I asked him why on earth he wanted to be provost. He'd been a respected history professor and History Department chair. Was there something about Kenyon's departments that reminded him of his academic specialty, the ever-popular, always-on-the-critical-list Hapsburg empire? He told me he liked what he'd been doing, but, as time passed, he wanted to do more. Someday, he thought, he'd like to be a college president. The job of provost was a step in that direction. The next step has eluded him so far, though he made the next-to-last cut at Wabash College three years ago. Now, he indicates, he'll give the provost office a couple more years and, if nothing turns up, go back to being a history professor at Kenyon College.

I've come to enjoy these Millwood lunches, even though the notes I come back with are on the skimpy side. A loose tongue and a temper are luxuries Browning cannot afford. His comments—though often helpful—are careful. He tells me what he thinks he can. Sometimes, I sense, he'd like to tell me more. If there were a way of getting sodium pentathol into coconut cream pie, I'd try it on Browning. Meanwhile, I get what I can from him.

That welcome-to-the-finest-liberal-arts-college-in-America line he delivered last August was partly cheerleading, he indicates, but he does believe that Kenyon's professors are good and getting better. "The younger faculty, on the whole, with exceptions, are stronger than the older faculty," he says. He thinks searches have gone well, the college often getting its first or second choice, and that a lively and varied gang of professors has turned up here, even though their commitment is more to the trade that they practice than to the institution that employs them. This last morning, I find him reeling from faculty reaction to some letters of evaluation he'd sent out. This year, it seems, Browning has added something new to his assessments: letter grades. After commenting on performances in each of the college's important categories— teaching, scholarship, service to the community—he awarded three grades, just like the As and Bs we give our students, and this has resulted in howls of outrage. How dare he do this, one professor wondered, showing me his letter. "Only *I* can judge my teaching," said another.

"They think it's demeaning," Browning says with a sigh. "They grade students all the time, but a lot of people aren't prepared to be graded themselves. A grade of B to a faculty member is awful. We have a lot of room to create our own worlds here, and anything that jolts us makes it hard to sustain."

Today, I press him about Kenyon's every-kid-a-winner tenure and promotion system. Going for broke, I leaf through my notes, read him some of the funnier and more pungent denunciations I've come across, people speculating comically about what it would take—just what kind of crime, committed in what kind of place, in front of what kind of an audience—for some tenure-track professor to get the boot. Browning laughs at some of the stuff I read, laughs and winces, looks down a moment, and, when our eyes meet again, I think: NOW! But he shakes his head, catches himself, says he can't respond fully. He'd like to, but he can't.

"Departments like the people who work in them," he says after a while. "They never criticize the people they bring forward. It's always the other department. And if the faculty wants to change that, at the level of my office, it will take instructions from the faculty."

We leave it at that, drive shortcuts and backroads to Gambier. Ohio in springtime, we agree, is New England without a case of the cutes. Reed Browning's job is impossible, I've decided. If I ever set a murder novel on a college campus I'll make the provost the victim. Or, more plausibly, the killer. Later that day, I encounter Susan Browning—Reed's wife—at a college function, and she confirms my hunch that Browning was right on the edge of confiding in me. "He really wanted to speak to you today," she says.

🌿

OUTSIDE, WE HAVE the smell of lilac, we have whole hillsides full of dogwood, pink and white, we have phlox and trillium blooming along the road, violets and dandelions dappling the lawns, skunk cabbage and May apple along the Kokosing River. Inside, though, Lewis Hall is desolate. I walk the hall, poking into one vacant room after another. It's as though there'd been a jailbreak, and everybody was in on it but me. The freshmen leave behind clothing, soft drinks, sneakers, and tumble-weed-sized dust balls. You could write a long novel with the pens and pencils they've left behind, and fill a cart at Kroger spending the loose change they didn't bother to pick up. The maids cleaning the rooms carry purses. "Those pennies add up," one of them tells me. I feel foolish, pacing halls that were so full, so noisy, in the end, so wonder-fully accommodating. As usual with me, I realize too late that I've been happy. Now my guys are gone. But, it later turns out, I hear from them. Out of the blue, Mark, the master procrastinator, writes a kind of thank-you note to me: thanks for sharing his freshman year. A while later, Matt checks in. What we had in Lewis Hall last year, he tells me, was true fraternity, no dues, no pledging, no hell week, just random, unforced friendship. Next comes an envelope from George, stuffed with eight pages of reflection on Lewis Hall. He asks me to be kind, in my memories of the place. "Do you recall stopping in my room the last night," he asks. "I was packing. I was a little drunk. The words that passed between us were very strange. (I think you knew I was tweaked.) That night I noticed something. P. F. Kluge is not good at saying good-bye. What a fumbler."

Late one May morning, while sitting in Adirondack chairs on the lawn between Lewis and Norton, Kevin and I have the talk we've been meaning to have for months. Kevin was the head resident adviser in Lewis, a soccer and basketball player, a shrewd, personable campus character. That was enough, but there was more. Kevin is black. His parents, rural Jamaicans, moved to England, where his father worked in a steel mill, his mother was a nurse. Somehow, he wound up here, and it looked like he liked it. Frankly, I've been wondering whether I could find someone who could challenge the notion that all black students who come here are destined to be miserable.

"I love Kenyon to death," Kevin tells me. He'd been flirting with a pro soccer career in England, was spotted by a coach from the University of Tennessee, applied to Sewanee and Kenyon, got a little money from Kenyon, worked through a tangle of red tape about his visa, arrived late to start his freshman year, got a D on his first English paper, and has prospered ever since, majoring in economics and passing his comps exam with distinction.

Soon after arriving here, Kevin attended a meeting of the Black Student Union. "My first BSU meeting, a lot was being said that was different from my issues. 'Watch out for white people,' and, 'We have to stick together'—it's the only way to get through,' and, 'Everyone out there is working against you.' That was the tone of the whole thing—to be suspicious of whites."

Kevin didn't agree. "My neighborhood in England, we were the only black people for miles. The people closest to me were white. And the people who'd been nice to me here were white. They were the ones I was supposed to be cautious of."

Kevin went his own way at Kenyon, and it wasn't necessarily the easy way. There were some affronts, some blunders. Someone called him "Sambo." One night, when firecrackers went off at 5:00 A.M., Kevin called security and identified the culprits. The next night, he found "nigger" written on his door. His roommates cut the sign down. "Hey, brother, how you doin'?" someone else said, and Kevin wondered how to take it, till he realized the guy spoke that way to everyone.

"A black who comes here should be someone that's tolerant," says Kevin. "You have to give a lot, initially. A lot of people say things they don't mean. Something offensive is said, and there are two ways to react. You can explain why it's offensive, or you can scream and shout and turn that person against you."

Kevin prospered on this small, overwhelmingly white campus, but his relations with some of Kenyon's handful of black students remained strained, especially after he found a white girlfriend, even more so after he met and liked her parents, who liked him back. "I understand," Kevin says. "I sympathize. I try to talk. I just wish they'd give me an opportunity."

After four years, Kevin thinks he knows what kind of black will do well at Kenyon, and it's not necessarily the ones the college is desperately recruiting. Kevin thinks Kenyon needs blacks who can contend not only with the differences of race but with the differences of class as well. "I don't think you can bring an inner-city kid, black or white, to Kenyon. Kenyon is conservative. There's no way to escape the evidence of money. And that's what they react to. They'll never have it. It's been kept from them. It's important to get students who can survive academically *and* socially. And socially is more important. If you can't survive socially, you'll never get your academics done. The ones who survive are the ones who blend in. Kenyon should get three or four who can survive and cope instead of flooding the place with black students who have no hope of surviving. I can look and tell you the ones who will make it here and those who won't."

Bringing blacks to Kenyon—and keeping them there—is tricky. I don't think Kevin has all the answers. No one does. What he's suggesting is interesting, though: that the college find a handful of solid, durable winners rather than decorate itself with students who—temporarily, unhappily—feel that they're being used to make the college look like what it isn't.

"'You know what it's like when you come,'" Kevin imagines himself saying to other black students, especially the ones who don't talk much to him. "'You knew what it was like *before* you came here. And you still decided to come. So you should work with the system and help it to change.' Too many people come here and say, 'Hey, it's the worst place ever.' And my response is, 'Why are you here?'"

🌿

THIS WEEK BEFORE graduation—"senior week"—the graduating class has the campus to itself, just as it did when it arrived for freshman orientation four years ago. The circle closes. There are parties and picnics.

This is the week of a beer truck—"the fucking beer truck," Peter Rutkoff calls it—all the brews you want, all over the place. Such sanctioned drinking added a querulous note to the last faculty meeting of the year. In recent years, there's been a problem with drinking during commencement ceremonies. The marching-in graduates hid champagne bottles under their robes. Corks started popping and flying as soon as they sat down. Some just missed the commencement speaker. It got embarrassing, having the first few rows of graduates sloshed and raucous. This weighed on Phil Jordan's mind when he asked the faculty for their unanimous support in requesting that seniors behave themselves this year. It's not like we can strip-search our prides and joys before marching them into the future, but at least we can ask them to behave. That seemed reasonable. But not to everyone. "Given how much this college encourages students to drink," said Robert Hinton, a history professor, "it would be hypocritical to ban drinking on this one occasion."

I thought Hinton was being captious, but late last night, around 1:00 A.M., I guessed he had a point. The evening started with a party at a farm owned by Jeff and Annie Robinson, a Kenyon alumnus and his wife. It's a nice occasion, beer truck on hand. I left early, returned to Lewis Hall, watched television in the lounge. A couple seniors came by, lugging a case of Old Milwaukee, and, I learned, the whole senior class was invited to return to the freshman dorms, back to where it all began for them. Closing the circle. The idea was, they'd have an ice cream party. The food service was just setting it up when I went to bed, an ice cream buffet, all sorts of flavors and toppings, all you could eat.

Or throw. I was asleep when all hell broke out: screams and shouts, alarms, doors slamming. Slipping into my bathrobe, I stepped out into a hall that was one long puddle. They got to the fire extinguishers. Water and beer cans everywhere: the smell of a flooded brewery. Around the corner, where a security guard was talking into a crackling radio, another smell assaulted me, that of ice cream, melting into the lounge carpet and starting to stink. Later, it's discovered, someone went into the toilets and kicked a urinal to pieces.

❦

PHIL JORDAN WHIPS OFF his tie, unbuttons his shirt. The president of Kenyon College is wearing gold chains. He reaches around back, pulls a bandanna out of his pocket, ties it around his forehead. He stares out at the seniors, who are sitting in Peirce Hall under the dour, dark portraits of Jordan's predecessors. Dean of Admissions John Anderson and Dean of Students Craig Bradley join Jordan onstage. The three men start drumming. Jordan chants.

They call me Iron Phil
Wild Man of the Hill
I live with Steel Sheila
Bard of the Monongahela
Yo, Steel Sheila!

He started the year doing the Charleston at the faculty banquet. Now he's onstage at the senior class banquet, enacting an *Iron John* parody written by Wendy MacLeod, Kenyon's playwright in residence.

> Every day when work is done
> I go off to pound my drum
> With Iron Craig and Iron John
> We drum and drum and then we bond.
> Yo, Iron Craig! Yo, Iron John!

Seventeen years is a long run. One of the reasons he stays on, I guess, is that he likes the job. He's on his third provost, his sixth chairman of the board of trustees. He must like it. In a way, though, I hope he leaves soon. The sooner he leaves, the sooner they will start to miss him. If I were Jordan, I'd enjoy a few years of that.

> We sing to Philander Chase,
> A wild man with a scary face,
> Who founded Kenyon on this Hill,
> An iron man with an iron will.
> Yo, Iron Philander!

Philander Chase rode off into exile, five years after he came to Gambier, the first of a long line to leave town, feeling ill used. But his name still is called. The past sticks around. That stream of time that Thoreau went fishing in, it flows right through here.

> Oh, Iron Jacks and Jills
> As you prepare to leave the Hill,
> Pound your drums and grow your hair,
> You might as well—
> There're no jobs out there!
> Yo, jobs!

Earlier this week, the same day the senior class spent at Cedar Point Amusement Park near Cleveland, the *New York Times* announced that the job market for college graduates, especially in the liberal arts, is as bad as anyone can remember. The next day, the seniors drank champagne and ate strawberries, listened to bagpipe music, and danced around a maypole in the president's backyard.

> Yo, Class of '92,
> We drum twice as hard for you.
> Yo, Class of '92.
> Here's a toast to you.
> Yo, seniors!!!

Yo! Grievance complaint. I told Harry Brod that I would under-stand if he didn't want to talk with me. Things haven't gone well for him here. Several weeks ago a woman, Laurie Finke, was chosen to head Women's and Gender Studies. And last week he got bad news about his application to head IPHS. The committee deadlocked and obliged the administration to choose between Brod and another candidate, Michael Brint. The administration picked Brint. So, counting his application to the Philosophy Department a couple years ago, Brod has gotten close three times . . . and lost out. One search was aborted, one extended, one deadlocked.

Measured, soft-spoken, Brod slips me a lengthy document. It's a copy of a grievance complaint he's filing. He makes numerous charges about his trouble as acting head of Women's and Gender Studies—"unceasing intense attack . . . blocked and thwarted . . . consistently sabotaged"— and about his fate in three searches that he found "unprofessional, unethical and discriminatory." Then he lowers the boom. He says that his experience, combined with that of two other people who lost or left their jobs here lately, suggests that Kenyon College is guilty of anti-Semi-tism.

"We are New York intellectuals," Brod declares. "We do not fit the profile of the Kenyon 'type' at a campus marked by deeply entrenched traditions of conservative WASP gentility. By Kenyon standards, we appear loud and abrasive, overly eager to bring innovative change to a staid environment. The College's strategy seems to have been to re-move the ostensible thorn. Within the College's faculty Jewish commu-nity, we talk openly to each other about strategies for surviving the pogrom."

Oh no, not this, I think. This year we've had a threatened lawsuit from the right about fraternities. I've heard—and, in small ways, been accused of—sexism. I've heard charges of rampant political correctness. We've had tension between rich and poor—reflected in attitudes toward tuition and scholarships—as well as between black and white.

There's an old guard in town, Brod tells me, a genteel network that scrutinizes outsiders, judges them, decides who can stay and who can't. "There are networks that go back a long way," he remarks. "I'm not saying there's a conspiracy. But there's an ethos, tone, atmosphere, climate . . ."

Brod's grievance will first be informally investigated by Provost Reed Browning. If that doesn't lead to a settlement, next fall it'll get shipped to a faculty grievance committee headed by Bill Klein. After that, there could be a lawsuit.

There's no way I can tell whether, or how, Harry Brod got stiffed here. But his obvious pain breaks the springtime mood of celebration and congratulation. And he's not the only bitter note. I sat with a minority professor who doesn't want his name used—he'll be looking for work—who alleged that Kenyon *students* are racist, not faculty or administration, *students*. They reacted with "contemptuous, aggressive behavior" to his presence in class, he charges. "It was a shifting of the burden of proof," this professor says. "They didn't have to prove they were good students. I had to prove I was a good professor. There was a general presumption that I can't be as qualified to teach white literature as a white scholar would be, as if it came in our genes. A hostile, quizzical attitude."

I've got my doubts. The same dinner Jordan performed his Iron John chant, Ted Mason walked off with an award as the teacher who'd meant most to the senior class. The person who got hired for IPHS instead of Harry Brod is Jewish, though possibly not the kind of abrasive East Coast intellectual Brod says Kenyon cannot abide. Anyway, in this time of champagne and strawberries, Brod puts his house on the market, plans a return to California, and mulls over an article about his sojourn in Gambier: "The New Anti-Semitism, the New Mc-Carthyism."

❧

TED MASON'S BEEN tapped to chair the English Department next year. Already, he's taking on chores. As usual, we brought in some outside examiners—from Ohio State, this year—to examine English majors who were candidates for honors. They could be awarded highest honors, high honors, honors, and—I'm not sure this has ever happened—a plain "pass" if they crashed and burned. Well, the results came out, and the same grade inflation that's infected every other aspect of college life, from grading freshman papers to awarding lifetime employment contracts, infects our cream of the crop as well. Honors—mere honors—was taken as insult. So now Mason's drafting a statement, reminding folks that honors, per se, is just fine, and sometimes, in a special case, we might swing for high honors, and then again, once in a long while, highest honors might be appropriate. Be still, my heart! Could the tide be turning?

❧ *Commencement*

NOW WE ARE CLOSE, we are very close. Seniors' parents start coming to town, arriving in a leisurely and celebratory mood. I spot some artsy-looking New Yorkers, some East Coast ethnics, a handful of blacks, but mostly I see people who wouldn't be out of place at the Greenbrier or the Homestead, comfortable people who walk the campus with an air of friendly proprietorship. Drop $80,000 in a place and you get attached.

For students, the bluff is called. No more kneeless jeans, unlaced sneakers, farmer hats, no more laid-back, hangdog, show-me manner. They're scrubbed and dressed for success in the land of suits. The college preens as well: gardeners and guides are everywhere, and the campus cops have been warned to go easy on the tickets. An Amish wagon, full of pies long on cornstarch and low on berries, clomps into town, parks near the post office. Rows of folding chairs sit in front of Mather Hall, empty now, awaiting tomorrow's execution.

Maya Angelou charges $10,000 for a commencement address, the *New York Times* reports. Caged bird sings *expensively*. The college has had some star speakers—Richard Dreyfuss, for instance—and some star bloopers. "It's very nice to be here at Wellesley," Shirley Chisholm told a Kenyon audience. Our best results have come from local heroes, Kenyon graduates summoned home, like the Pulitzer Prize–winning political cartoonist Jim Borgman and another cartoonist, Bill Watterson, proprietor of "Calvin and Hobbes." This year the call goes out to another local hero, a onetime circus clown, actor, playwright, wise-cracker, and vaudevillian who—talk about unpredictable success—now serves as cultural program director for National Public Radio, Murray Horwitz, class of '70.

"I was a candidate for asshole of the year," he reflected when I dropped in on him in Washington last summer. A Jewish kid from

Dayton, Ohio, Horwitz led protests, founded an improv troupe, hanged the president in effigy, and successfully petitioned to spend five weeks of his senior year at a circus clown school in Florida. Later, he worked three years as a circus clown.

"The place had a shambling informality, a genteel poverty, a certain shabbiness," he recalls of the 1960s Kenyon, "like an English peer who had to sell off his paintings after the war. At Kenyon, I had to grow, had to learn how to make friends out of people who had no respect for me, had to assert and define myself. At Ohio State, say, I would have lost myself, would have hung out with a few people who didn't challenge me."

Horwitz kept in touch with Kenyon, served a few years on the alumni council, watched the place grow, mutate, gentrify, become more attractive to what he calls "the pink and green club, white WASP kids from Grosse Point Farms or whatever." What struck him about Gambier, then and now, was its intensity, the highly charged tone that ideological battles take on when fought at close quarters.

"If you're living in New York, or Indianapolis," he said, "the ebb and flow of life tempers ideas. They change in the marketplace. In Gambier, they stay as they were when they arrived—hothouse flowers. There's not enough commerce with the outside world, not enough coming and going. Elsewhere, you grow a professional hide. But they don't do that in Gambier. They're nice folks, but if you get into a dispute, it gets taken personally."

Last night I sat with Horwitz at a dinner for the commencement honorees. After coffee, moving from table to table, Phil Jordan delivered a tribute to Horwitz and the other guests, the sociologist Digby Baltzell, the set designer Ming Cho Lee, the outgoing chair of the board of trustees, Burnell Roberts, Anne Wilson Schaef, a writer and philosopher, Clifton Wharton, the head of the TIAA-CREF pension fund, and two retiring Kenyon professors, Robert Burns and Robert Goodhand. It was an elegant, impromptu speech, Jordan at his finest. Sitting there, I thought of a line Horwitz quoted to me last summer, something from *Portnoy's Complaint* that has often occurred to me since then, something like: "That WASP thing, doctor, when it's impressive, it can be very, very impressive."

❧

THE TIME HAS COME. Dressed in caps and gowns, aligned in a rough order of seniority, we assemble just inside the gates of the south campus.

Beyond, in the middle of the village, the graduating class assembles and begins to march toward us, while college bells begin pealing. Through us they pass, two by two, some stiff and formal, others beaming, one or two already starting to cry. Some nod at me as they pass, a couple reach out for a quick handshake. And then, as they have passed through us, we pass through them—so much a part of each other, so tied and tangled are we—on our way up to the stage, where we take our seats.

I counted nine different speakers, short and long, musical interludes, and, I'd been warned, it takes time moving four hundred students across a stage. I start on a Sunday *New York Times* crossword puzzle during the honorary degrees, but I put it away when Murray Horwitz arises to speak. He's funny, brisk, pungent, he counsels, challenges, needles. When he finishes, there's a haunting moment: the chapel bells ringing "Kokosing Farewell."

Old Kenyon, we are like Kokosing
Obedient to some strange spell
Which urges us from all reposing
Farewell, Old Kenyon, fare thee well.

And now it begins, the parade across the stage to where Jordan sits waiting with diplomas. The faculty secretary, Joe Klesner, reads the names in English, degrees and honors, if any, in Latin, which results in some long and problematic mouthfuls. His Latin rendering of "international studies" would lead a Roman to believe we'd given a degree in "far-off things." Some of the faculty complain about this ceremonial use of Latin, dead white men, dead white language, pomp turning into pompous, a charade for upper middle–class white customers. They'd rewrite commencement the way they rewrite wedding ceremonies, but not here, not yet. And, though it is long, it is moving, every minute of it.

Alphabetical order, Adler to Zuliani, a last glance at the students I know—a minority of the four hundred who are graduating—and, for the first and last time, put face and name together in students I'd only heard about. *Aguilar.* Quiet, smooth, wants to test his fate in Hollywood. *Bartlett.* One of the women who didn't hate my class. Wants to be a journalist. *Beardsley.* Took me out for pizza after class was over. *Becker.* Resident adviser in Gund, regaled me with tales of freshman grotesquerie. *Bergman.* Wanted to convince me that you could be bright, suave, sensitive, and yet belong to Delta Kappa Epsilon. *Busby.* That's a life I might have changed. She caught fire as a writer, was writing all the time, a couple stories simultaneously, all sorts of stuff, and won a college writing prize. No knowing where that will lead. *Cope.* Did a Kluge imitation for the senior class, swaggered onstage saying, "Okay, *I* wrote *Eddie and the Cruisers* and *you* didn't!" *Douglass.* Found an old yearbook picture of Lentz and me, copied it, plastered it all over town, like a wanted poster. *Haid.* Told me what it felt like walking home under a cold winter sky, after a night of studying. *Hallenback.* Nonchalant, chunky, talented, and smart, a bookstore lay-about. Off to try the music scene in Minneapolis. His father was a classmate of mine here. *Harris.* Wants to be a journalist or a singer. *Hartman.* Maybe a photographer. *Jarrett, Jones, Keightley.* More students. *Kracklauer.* Her senior essay—on Marlene Dietrich, among others—drew enthusiastic reviews from the English Department. It's funny, what you remember. Sophomore year, Kracklauer showed up in my writing class, a sophomore among seniors, quiet and tentative, but she wrote about a woman who, having just delivered, contemplated her body, all stretched and adipose, "like claymation gone wrong." *Lehmann-Haupt.* We were supposed to get together and drink tequila before graduation: a friendly salute. Too late now. But it was champagne and strawberries outside Sunset Cottage yesterday afternoon, all our seniors and their parents, the same ones who are sitting out there now. There's Rachel's father, leaning against a tree and aiming a camera as she passes in front. The first champagne cork arched through the air as soon as Jordan launched into his welcome, and I could see him stop in midsentence, wondering whether to admonish the graduates and risk making things worse, or soldier on. He proceeded, and it hasn't been bad at all. *Melville.* He came into class one day with an answer written down for a pop quiz I decided not to give. *Mills.* Students get applauded as they walk across the stage, some with rousing ovations, others with meager pit-pats: that's four years of cohabitation, measured in a minute. *Nowell. Opdahl!* My buddy, a legend in his own time, Deke pledgemaster this year, and, in keeping with tradition, got kidnapped by his pledges. A scary tradition. Guys get dumped, sometimes without clothes, several hundred miles away, right in the heart of *Deliverance* country. Someplace in the middle of Kentucky, he hitched a ride with a drunk, an out-of-work guy he paid $50 to drive him to Cincinnati, then another $50 to chauffeur him the rest of the way to Gambier. *Pfriem.* I don't know him, but I know his sore arm contributed to the baseball team's godawful season, and I know that on the last day of the season, figuring his arm had the rest of his life to feel better, he went out and pitched Kenyon to its third victory of a twenty-five-game season. *Reibel.*

Riegler. Senior. Dropped by my office, toting a twenty-dollar water rifle—this was during the Killer Game—and talked about being one of Kenyon's handful of math majors. "I've had three classes in which I've been the only person," he said. *Sheffel, Stamper, Straus, Tino.* Another student who discovered writing. His parents seemed delighted. *Ursu. Voth.* We shared a ride back from a John Macionis party a couple nights ago, and, as we got to the top of the hill, I asked the guy who was driving to slow down and switch off his headlights, and there was the college hill, all covered with moonlight, so bright you could see the steeples, the bark on the birch trees, the moon's reflection in the slow-moving river. I told Voth he would miss all this, and soon. Months from now, I get a postcard saying I was right. *Wallison.* I meant to get to know him, damn it! He came into the English Department one morning, preoccupied and harassed, obviously a student ready to make a plea. "Could I borrow a piece of paper?" he asked the secretary. "How big a piece do you need?" Barb asked. "Big enough to kiss butt with," he rejoindered, and I told him, then and there, he was in the book. *Zuliani* steps across the stage, and, like that, it is over. Like me, they are of the past.

🌿

AFTER THAT, it falls apart quickly. There's an hour of milling around on the grass, a picnic lunch that not everyone has time for, and people start piling into their cars. Afternoon brings a thunderstorm, and the emptying quickens. When I get up on Monday morning, only a handful of stragglers remain. Then they're gone. Summer comes.

I'm toast myself. I'll stick around through next weekend, reunion weekend, when the alumni roll in to stake their claim. I'm here! they say to the campus. So am I, the place responds. It's a dialogue in which Gambier always has the last word. Ron Sharp will lecture on friendship and inscribe copies of the *Norton Anthology of Friendship* he edited. Phil Jordan will speak of Kenyon's beauty and its need of tradition and change. Dressed in topcoat and tails, Tim Shutt will lead a ghost tour of campus, its haunted places, ending in the cemetery where Mike Stone rests.

I came here to live, not to judge, to listen, keep my eyes open, react and remember, and, in a place where everybody has their own vision of things and their own version of events, to give mine. Yet judgments come. They are forced upon you. They are extracted from you. Well, okay. I think a lot of people are getting away with a lot. I think our students—often not as deserving or hungry or curious as one would like—can get through here without being particularly challenged or, come right down to it, honestly graded. It is possible to get a wonderful education in Gambier, but it is not required. We encourage them to get to know professors outside of class. We do not press them to get to know books outside of class. Then there's the faculty, who seem more self-interested, more distracted, more divided than the professors I remember. Not less talented, but less committed to the college. And the administration, the people who run a pretty good college sometimes, seems to lack, not just the money, but the heart to risk unpopularity, to set prudence aside and gamble on greatness, to swing for the fences. What it all comes down to is niceness: community prevailing over college, collegiality over competence, well-roundedness over jagged excellence. Niceness creeping over Kenyon like kudzu over a southern forest. I may be wrong.

Those aren't my last words, though. When all my complaints are registered—there's more. Despite its failures—some imported, some homegrown—and its limits, Kenyon College remains a good place to live, to teach, to learn. Every time I come back here I'm more convinced of a truth I used to doubt when I was younger: the idea of a small college in a small place, a college community, a place where you're all in it together, an island. The college needn't apologize for its size or location or history. Those are strengths. Philander Chase was right: you can have a wonderful college on a hill in the middle of nowhere—if you can get the right people to come. Some of that is happening now. Always has. That a small place survives is something; that it grows is remarkable. But whenever I'm here, I can't stop imagining how much better we could be if we asked more of ourselves. It's like looking at a picture out of focus, outlines blurred, people soft around the sides, a genial vagueness in the very air, like gel wiped over a camera to spare an aging movie actress. But, oh, the possibilities, the potential, the chance of magic, if only we could sharpen the edges, be less perceptive, more visionary. I may be wrong. I picture a college more diverse *and* more intense, a college students of all races and backgrounds can flunk out of, a more daunting college, a place that graduates remember not only with affection but with awe. I may be wrong. I picture an administration that makes—and accepts—no excuses. I picture a faculty that engages openly in disagreement but feels a larger commitment to this place and realizes that being here, every day, is a gorgeous blessing. I may be wrong.

There's more. A few nights ago, when the village was filling up with parents, I was walking in front of the post office and saw something that stopped me in my tracks and kept me standing there a minute or two, right in the middle of a busy, laughing evening. I saw my parents as they had come to pick me up at my own graduation, thirty Mays ago, Mom and Pop, housewife and machinist, Stuttgart and Hamburg and Ellis Island, who told me to "sit on the table" and "to eat my plate." I saw them clearly, which you don't always do when people have been dead so long, but I really saw them well this time. I noticed the slightly cocky, pleased-as-punch look on my old man's face and something deeper, shyer, prouder in my mother. What I remember of that weekend is that we attended a reception at the English Department, where much was made of them. Then, though I wasn't a member, there was a party at the Psi U lodge. Those days, reunion weekend happened at the same time as graduation, not a week later as it now does, so that afternoon, in addition to students and parents, there were fraternity alumni around. One of them, drink in hand, came over to my father, this beaming, bowlegged machinist, and asked, "Are you Psi U?" I only heard about it later, when the story started making the rounds. Pop didn't understand the question, I'm sure, or the implication. "I'm Freddy's father," he replied.

That happened here, and that's what I love about a pretty good college in a small place, the way life enlarges, the way it involves everyone who's here, or ever was, the kid of eighteen that I was, the man of fifty now, and my parents and my classmates of thirty years ago. I know the guys in the dorm, and I know the people in the graveyard. I claim the benches, the trestle over the river, certain hills and paths out east of here, and I not only accept but welcome my own aging, seasons into years, years into life, for life is fuller and more resonant here, like an echo that hangs in the air a little longer, like a stone that goes skimming, four or five hops across a pond.

All year, I've been wondering what we are loyal to when we say we are loyal to a college, and whether we are kidding ourselves, or letting ourselves be kidded. I say *we* because I brought the question to Lentz the other evening. What do we mean when we talk about a college? Surely not the president, not the trustees. And not our colleagues of the moment, or the students who come and go each year. Are we loyal to the books we teach? But you could take those books and teach them anywhere. Is the college this landscape, this hill with a river running around the front? But who builds a life around some scenery? Is it that we were students once, where we are teachers now? What nonsense that would be, what narcissism and nostalgia.

"There's loyalty to all sorts of things," Lentz said after a while. "I don't know if I'd be so quick to characterize the past as past. The past is dead in some ways. But memory isn't." It comes back to memories, a past that lives, a connection—here, in this small place—between then and now, yesterday, today, and tomorrow, all coming together on this island. Memories of good and bad, memories of promises kept and promises broken and promises still open, memory holding onto love and keeping anger young. I pack up and drive off, and I am looking forward to all sorts of things. The tiny village slips away: a single turn erases it, and the empty campus, too. For a while, the river stays beside me, then turns lazily away. The hill itself becomes a wrinkle in the cornfields, a dot on the map, and I wonder how long it will take before I start to miss it.